# Looking at *Ajax*

Also available from Bloomsbury:

*Looking at* Antigone, edited by David Stuttard
*Looking at* Bacchae, edited by David Stuttard
*Looking at* Lysistrata, edited by David Stuttard
*Looking at* Medea, edited by David Stuttard

# Looking at *Ajax*

Edited by David Stuttard

BLOOMSBURY ACADEMIC
LONDON • NEW YORK • OXFORD • NEW DELHI • SYDNEY

Bloomsbury Academic
Bloomsbury Publishing Plc
50 Bedford Square, London, WC1B 3DP, UK
1385 Broadway New York, NY 10018, USA

BLOOMSBURY, BLOOMSBURY ACADEMIC and the Diana logo
are trademarks of Bloomsbury Publishing Plc

First published in Great Britain 2019
Paperback edition published 2021

Copyright © David Stuttard, 2019

David Stuttard has asserted his right under the Copyright, Designs and Patents Act, 1988, to be identified as Editor of this work.

For legal purposes the Preface and Acknowledgements on p. ix constitute an extension of this copyright page.

Cover design: Terry Woodley
Cover image © Attributed to Brygos Painter (Greek (Attic), active about 490 – 470 B.C.)
*Attic Red-Figured Kylix*, 490 – 480 B.C., Terracotta 11.2 × 39.1 × 31.4 cm
(4 7/16 × 15 3/8 × 12 3/8 in.)
The J. Paul Getty Museum, Los Angeles

All rights reserved. No part of this publication may be reproduced or transmitted in any form or by any means, electronic or mechanical, including photocopying, recording, or any information storage or retrieval system, without prior permission in writing from the publishers.

Bloomsbury Publishing Plc does not have any control over, or responsibility for, any third-party websites referred to or in this book. All internet addresses given in this book were correct at the time of going to press. The author and publisher regret any inconvenience caused if addresses have changed or sites have ceased to exist, but can accept no responsibility for any such changes.

A catalogue record for this book is available from the British Library.

Library of Congress Cataloging-in-Publication Data
Names: Stuttard, David, editor. | Sophocles. Ajax. English. 2019.
Title: Looking at Ajax / edited by David Stuttard.
Description: London : Bloomsbury Academic, 2019. | Includes an English translation of Sophocles' Ajax. | Includes bibliographical references and index.
Identifiers: LCCN 2018048927 (print) | LCCN 2018052254 (ebook) |
ISBN 9781350072329 (epub) | ISBN 9781350072312 (epdf) | ISBN 9781350072305 (hb)
Subjects: LCSH: Sophocles. Ajax. | Ajax (Greek mythological figure—In literature.
Classification: LCC PA4413.A5 (ebook) | LCC PA4413.A5 L66 2019 (print) |
DDC 882/.01—dc23
LC record available at https://lccn.loc.gov/2018048927

ISBN: HB: 978-1-3500-7230-5
PB: 978-1-3501-9061-0
ePDF: 978-1-3500-7231-2
eBook: 978-1-3500-7232-9

Typeset by RefineCatch Limited, Bungay, Suffolk

To find out more about our authors and books visit www.bloomsbury.com and sign up for our newsletters.

*To Tom Davidson, an outstanding Teucer*

# Contents

| | |
|---|---|
| List of Contributors | viii |
| Preface and Acknowledgements | ix |
| Introduction: Ajax, Bulwark of the Greeks  *David Stuttard* | 1 |
| 1  Some Visual Influences on Sophocles' *Ajax*?  *David Stuttard* | 15 |
| 2  Ajax the Hero  *Laura Swift* | 29 |
| 3  'Shield of the Achaeans'  *Sophie Mills* | 43 |
| 4  The Power of Ajax's Sword  *Rosie Wyles* | 55 |
| 5  The Sounds of Ajax's Grief  *Alyson Melzer* | 67 |
| 6  Ajax's Suicide  *Robert Garland* | 77 |
| 7  Looking at the Isolation of Ajax  *Richard Seaford* | 89 |
| 8  Tecmessa  *Hanna M. Roisman* | 97 |
| 9  A Grief Observed: Tecmessa and Her Sadness-Work in Sophocles' *Ajax*  *Stephen Esposito* | 117 |
| 10  Heroic Values and Lesser Mortals  *Carmel McCallum-Barry* | 131 |
| 11  Odysseus and Empathy  *Brad Levett* | 141 |
| 12  Post-Traumatic Stress Disorder and the Performance Reception of Sophocles' *Ajax*  *Emma Cole* | 151 |
| Sophocles' *Ajax*  translated by *David Stuttard* | 161 |
| Bibliography | 219 |
| Index | 227 |

# Contributors

**Emma Cole** is Lecturer in Liberal Arts & Classics at the Department of Classics and Ancient History, University of Bristol.

**Stephen Esposito** is Associate Professor of Classical Studies at Boston University, USA.

**Robert Garland** is Roy D. and Margaret B. Wooster Professor of the Classics at Colgate University, New York, USA.

**Brad Levett** is Associate Professor of Classics at Memorial University, St. Johns, Newfoundland, Canada.

**Carmel McCallum-Barry** is Lecturer in Classics at University College, Cork.

**Alyson Melzer** is a PhD candidate in Classics at Stanford University in California

**Sophie Mills** is Professor of Classics at the University of North Carolina at Asheville, USA

**Hanna M. Roisman** is Professor of Classics, Arnold Bernhard Professor in Arts and Humanities at Colby College, Maine, USA.

**Richard Seaford** is Emeritus Professor of Ancient Greek at the University of Exeter.

**David Stuttard** is a freelance writer, historian and founder of the theatre company, Actors of Dionysus.

**Laura Swift** is Senior Lecturer in Classical Studies at the Open University.

**Rosie Wyles** is Lecturer in Classical History and Literature at the University of Kent.

# Preface and Acknowledgements

Most modern theatre goers will be unfamiliar with Sophocles' *Ajax*. The Archive of Performances of Greek and Roman Drama (APGRD) lists only three productions of the play in the ten years between 2008 and 2018 (two in the UK and one in Italy), along with another three adaptations of Sophocles' original (Ellen McLaughlin's *Ajax in Iraq* performed in New York; Timberlake Wertenbaker's *Our Ajax* in London; and Homayun Ghanizadeh's *Ajax and the Report of a Suicide* in Tehran), with material from *Ajax* being used in Jeroen Olyslaegers' epic 24-hour-long *Mount Olympus: to Glorify the Cult of Tragedy* which toured European cities. However, while productions may have been few and far between, interest in the play has been sparked by its use in treating suffers from PTSD (Post-Traumatic Stress Disorder) in both the USA and UK.

My own involvement with *Ajax* began over twenty years ago in 1997, when I translated and directed it for a production by Actors of Dionysus, which toured the UK from early September to Mid-November. While that experience brought me face-to-face with issues of staging and characterization, it has been a hugely exciting and revelatory experience to revisit the play while working on this book.

Like other volumes in this series, it contains chapters by international experts. While their opinions may not always coincide, this is no bad thing: Greek tragedies were written to provoke debate, and that they still do is evidence of their ongoing validity. Inevitably, there is the occasional small overlap between some essays, with which I have not interfered, and, while I suggested that authors use the forms 'BC' and 'AD', I have respected the wishes of those for whom it was important to use 'BCE' and 'CE'. Nor have I interfered too prescriptively in their choices of forms of transliteration from the Greek.

For the first time in this series I have included an essay of my own, in part standing in (albeit inadequately) for James Morwood, whose sad death occurred while the book was being compiled, and whose kindness, urbanity and scholarship are already sorely missed.

While some contributors have quoted from translations of their own choice, others use my own translation (a heavily revised version of my 1997 version), which is printed at the end of the book. Readers wishing to use it for productions of their own can contact me through my website, www.davidstuttard.com, where applications for performance should be made before the commencement of any rehearsals.

Finally, I would like to thank all those who have been involved in the production of this book, especially the contributors, who have so generously given of their time, and with whom it has been such a pleasure to work. At Bloomsbury, my thanks go to Alice Wright, who commissioned the book, her editorial assistants, Emma Payne and Lily Mac Mahon, Rachel Singleton from Bloomsbury and Merv Honeywood from RefineCatch, who coordinated the proofing process, copy editor, Paul King, and Terry Woodley, who designed the splendid cover. Especial thanks are due, too, to Chrys Chatzopolou of the Martin von Wagner Museum in Würzburg, who went more than the extra mile to ensure that I received the correct version of the Kleophrades Painter's amphora, which I discuss in Chapter 1.

But my biggest personal thank you goes to my wife Emily Jane, whose belief and support sustain me, and who puts up with my disappearances into the classical world with near saintly equanimity – as well as to the home team, our cats Stanley and Oliver, who, meandering across the keyboard or roosting on top of crucial books, have been faithfully present, despite their disapproval of Ajax's treatment of their fellow animals.

David Stuttard<br>
Brighton, 2018

# Introduction: Ajax, Bulwark of the Greeks

## David Stuttard

Since the first decade of the twenty-first century, *Ajax*, one of Sophocles' earliest surviving tragedies, has been experiencing something of a renaissance. A searing exploration of how the pressures of prolonged warfare lead to a noble combatant's mental breakdown, it has become (as Emma Cole discusses in her chapter for this book) the go-to play for those wishing to use Greek drama as an aid for helping sufferers from Post-Traumatic Stress Disorder (PTSD), be they military veterans or civilians. However, while this is an undoubtedly valuable response, there is more to the play than the plight of the living Ajax. Of equal importance is the question of how to treat the corpse of a fallen adversary, not to mention the vexed issue of how to define friendship and enmity, problems that Sophocles explored in another of his tragedies, *Antigone*.

And, while *Ajax* has much to say to us today, to understand it fully, we must try as far as possible to understand both what Sophocles may have intended it to convey and how its first audience may have been expected to respond to it. This is the subject of most of the chapters in this collection. But before we come to them, it might be useful to consider briefly a few issues surrounding the context of its first production – what the audience might have known of Ajax, including from myth and literature; who Sophocles was; his take on Greek religion and morality; and the nature of an Athenian theatrical performance – as well as the processes (and pitfalls) of translating the ancient Greek text into modern English. We shall begin by looking at Ajax.

## The myth of Ajax

The framework of the story was as follows. Ajax was born of heroic forebears, all of whom had connections with Troy. His grandfather, Aeacus, king of Aegina (an island just south of Athens), had helped the gods Apollo and Poseidon to build

Troy's walls (though his handiwork was less strong than that of his colleagues) and in death he was honoured as one of the three judges in the underworld. Aeacus had three sons: Telamon (Ajax's father), Peleus (father of Achilles) and their half-brother, Phocus. But Telamon and Peleus were jealous of Phocus and killed him, for which they were exiled, which was how Telamon came to the nearby island of Salamis, where he married its princess, fathered Ajax, and in due course took the throne. A man with a finger in almost every myth set in that period, Telamon's career embraced not only the fabulous Calydonian boar-hunt and Heracles' expedition against the Amazons, but a successful assault on Troy (also in the company of Heracles), for his part in which he received as his reward the princess Hesione, by whom he fathered Teucer.

When Agamemnon launched his attack on Troy, Ajax and his cousin Achilles were acknowledged to be the bravest Greek fighters, each stationing himself on opposite wings of the encampment so that together they might protect their fellows. Screened by his huge shield made from seven layers of ox-hide faced with bronze, and accompanied by his half-brother, the archer Teucer, Ajax, never wounded, cut down swathes of Trojan enemy, and was not afraid to face Hector, the most dangerous of them all. In one encounter, when Hector led an attack on the Greek ships, Ajax boldly fought him off, leaping from deck to deck wielding a long spear. After another, the two even exchanged gifts, Hector receiving Ajax's battle belt, Ajax Hector's sword. Always Ajax fought for the good of the Greeks. When Achilles withdrew from battle, piqued because Agamemnon had stolen his slave-girl, Ajax was chosen to try to change his mind – along with Achilles' tutor Phoenix and the persuasive Odysseus; and, when Achilles was killed in battle, it was Ajax and Odysseus who retrieved his corpse – Odysseus fighting off the Trojans; Ajax carrying the body to safety, slung over his shoulder.

But it was now that disaster struck. Which of the Greeks should inherit Achilles' armour? Ajax believed there was no question: it should be him. But Odysseus, too, staked his claim, and in the end he was successful. Quite how he managed is unclear. Some sources suggest that Greek spies, eavesdropping on the Trojans to discover which of the two the enemy feared most, overheard women proclaiming that, while Ajax did carry Achilles' body from the battlefield, 'even a woman could manage that'; it was manly Odysseus who had protected him. Others describe how, presided over either by Achilles' mother, the sea nymph Thetis, or by the goddess Athene, the army (or perhaps just its commanders or even 'the sons of Trojans', see below) voted to award Odysseus the armour. Still others suggest the vote was rigged.

The humiliation was too much for Ajax to bear. Maddened with anger he set out on a killing spree, intent on murdering the Greek commanders, whom he blamed for slighting him. But Athene protected them, and instead Ajax turned his sword on sheep and cattle kept by the army not just for food but to offer in sacrifices to the gods.¹ (It is in the immediate aftermath of this rampage that our play begins.)

Coming to his senses, Ajax, now faced with total ruin, committed suicide by falling on his sword (or, rather, the sword he had been given by the Trojan, Hector). But the Greek generals, targets of Ajax's unsuccessful attack, were loath to honour his body, and according to one tradition insisted that it should be buried instead of being accorded the usual heroic cremation.² In classical times Ajax's grave mound was shown on the southwest shores of the Hellespont (Dardanelles), where the flowers of purple hyacinths bore (or were imagined to bear) the letters 'AI', suggesting not just the beginning of Ajax's name but the sound of lamentation.

Ajax left behind a son, Eurysaces, fathered by the captive princess Tecmessa (whose city he had sacked and whose father he had killed). When the war was over, Teucer took mother and child back home with him to Salamis, but he received a frosty welcome from the aged Telamon, who blamed Teucer for leaving Ajax's body at Troy, and exiled him. As a result, Teucer took himself off to Cyprus, where he founded a new city, which he called Salamis after his homeland. Meanwhile, back on the island of Salamis, Eurysaces in time succeeded Telamon as king.

As for Ajax, even in death his status was ambiguous. While to some he was a protecting hero, the *Odyssey* presents a very different picture. Wishing to find out the future, Odysseus conjures up the spirits of the dead. Among them is Ajax. Odysseus himself narrates their encounter, which (given that it is the earliest account of events that dominate our play) is worth quoting in full (*Odyssey*, 11.543–65):

> Only the soul of Ajax, son of Telamon, stood apart, simmering with anger at my victory, when I defeated him beside the ships in the contest for Achilles' armour. His queenly mother [Thetis] set them up as a prize, and the sons of Trojans sat in judgement along with Pallas Athene. I wish I'd never won such a contest! Because of it earth covered Ajax, so noble a man, who in looks and deeds surpassed all other Greeks, second only to incomparable Achilles. I spoke to him with soothing words: 'Ajax, son of noble Telamon, even in death won't you put aside the anger that you nurse against me because of that cursed armour? The gods brought it before us to cause misery to the Greeks, since in you they lost such a tower of strength. We Greeks grieve your death to our very core, just as we grieve Achilles. Zeus is responsible – no-one else – for he hated the Greek army bitterly and settled death on you. But come now, king, listen to my words, my speech. Control your anger and your proud spirit.' So I

spoke, but he made no reply. Rather he turned back to Erebus [i.e. the underworld] to join the other spirits of the dead.

## Ajax in Athens

Undoubtedly Sophocles' audience was considerably more familiar than we are with Ajax. There were many reasons for this. For political (and military) purposes Athenians were divided into ten tribes, one of which boasted Ajax as its special patron, so roughly a tenth of the audience felt a special connection to him. In addition, Ajax enjoyed the status of a hero, which in Greek terms meant a mortal man who, through his exploits in life, had proved himself so exceptional that he was honoured in death as semi-divine, his spirit being believed to live on to protect those who honoured him. Indeed, not only was he worshipped in Athens at the Eurysakeion, a shrine named from his son Eurysaces, he was believed to have lent his martial aid to the Greek fleet when it defeated the Persian navy at the Battle of Salamis (480 BC), in thanks for which the Athenians dedicated a trireme (warship) to him.

In addition, audiences would possess a rich knowledge of the deeds of Ajax not only from stories told to them since childhood, but from works of art, including vase paintings (discussed in my chapter 'Some Visual Influences on Sophocles' *Ajax*?'), and literature. The details each contained would have varied – Greeks possessed no canonical versions of their myths, so creative artists and writers were free to alter or embellish specific episodes at will – but at the core of all of them were the accounts of Ajax's exploits contained in the two great epic poems attributed to Homer, the *Iliad* and *Odyssey*, which formed the basis of an Athenian male's education and (by Sophocles' time) had achieved the status of 'establishment' texts. In addition, Ajax appeared not only in other poems of the so-called epic cycle (that filled in the blanks in the story of Troy before and after the action of the *Iliad* and *Odyssey*), specifically the *Aethiopis* and the *Little Iliad*, which dealt with the period covered in our play, but in poems and songs by other authors, including the Theban praise-singer Pindar. Furthermore, in the very theatre in which they were now sitting, many in the audience would have seen already other plays about Ajax – not least a trilogy by the mighty Aeschylus, and perhaps even other tragedies by Sophocles.[3]

## Sophocles and the life of Athens

Sophocles' life spanned almost the entire fifth century BC. Born in the outskirts of Athens around 496, the son of a wealthy arms manufacturer, by the age of sixteen or seventeen he was already sufficiently prominent to be chosen to lead the chorus that performed the victory hymn after the Battle of Salamis (in which Ajax was believed to have lent his aid). One source (Plutarch) suggests that Sophocles' first dramatic venture came in 468, when he defeated Aeschylus at the City Dionysia under somewhat controversial circumstances – the outcome decided not by the usual jury consisting of one member of each tribe chosen by lot, but by Athens' ten elected generals headed by the pro-Sophoclean Cimon. (For more on Athenian drama festivals, see below, 'Staging *Ajax*'.) Recently doubt has been cast on this anecdote, with 470 suggested as the year of Sophocles' debut. In truth, however, we simply don't know when he first began writing.

Sophocles' earliest extant dramas appear to date from the late 440s or early 430s BC. An ancient biography suggests a link between his *Antigone* and his tenure as general during the revolt of the island of Samos from the Athenian Empire (440–439), though it is more likely that he wrote *Antigone* as a result of his experiences than that he was elected general because of the success of *Antigone*. By now he already had experience of public office, having served for a year (443/2) as one of the board responsible for tribute paid by members of Athens' empire. Indeed, he would play an active part in public affairs throughout the rest of his life, too, perhaps again as general (though given his reportedly less-than-shining record on the Samian campaign this is possibly unlikely), certainly as one of the commissioners appointed to steer the state during a low-point in Athens' war with the Peloponnesians (413–411).

He was actively involved in the state's religion, too. In 420 he participated in the introduction into Athens of the healing god, Asclepius, temporarily lodging his earthly incarnation (a snake) in his house, in recognition of which Sophocles was given the name 'Dexion' ('Receiver') and worshipped posthumously (like Ajax) as a hero. His death came shortly before the defeat of his beloved Athens (406/5), some said from inadvertently inhaling a grape pip, others because he was trying to recite a lengthy speech from *Antigone* without taking breath. While neither version is likely to be true, both just possibly may be – until recently it was not unknown for actors to recite speeches with grapes in their mouth as part of their vocal training.

In fact, Sophocles was known to have a weak voice, and this was partly why he gave up acting in his own plays. In every other respect, however, theatre was in his blood, and he is credited with several dramatic innovations, not least the introduction of painted scenery (whatever that meant in the context of Athenian drama) and increasing the number of speaking (or singing) performers – those in the chorus from twelve to fifteen, actors from two to three. While all this suggests a desire for greater realism, Aristotle records Sophocles' own statement that he represented human beings 'as they ought to be' (while he said his rival, Euripides, presented them 'as they really are').

Sophocles' output was prolific, his success stratospheric. He is said to have won first prize at twenty-four festivals and written a total of 123 plays, though only seven survive complete. While two can be dated fairly certainly, the remainder, including *Ajax*, cannot, though stylistic analysis suggests that our play is among the earliest of Sophocles' dramas to survive. A recent edition (Finglass, 2011) suggests the 440s, while adding 'a date in the early to mid 430s or very late 450s cannot be ruled out'. To me, the prominence of the twin themes of burial and friendship, both of which Sophocles explores with equal zest in *Antigone*, suggests a date shortly after the Samian campaign, at a time when questions of how to treat a traitorous ally exercised the minds of many. Not only that: a fourth-century BC historian (Duris of Samos) recorded that, when he put down the Samian revolt, Athens' general-in-chief, Pericles imposed on its ringleaders the punishment of *apotympanismos*, whereby they were crucified until almost dead, before being taken down and beaten to death, with their bodies subsequently denied burial – something that may well have bothered his pious fellow general, Sophocles.

## Burying enemy dead: Morality and religion in classical Athens

Sophocles' treatment of the two themes, burial and friendship, is rooted in the popular morality of his age. While the living were considered to be under the ultimate jurisdiction of the sky-god, Zeus, the dead were the concern of his brother, Hades, and their souls (*psykhai*) should be allowed to travel freely to his kingdom in the underworld. To permit this travel, Greeks believed that the soul must be freed from the body, a process that could be achieved only through burial (either actual or virtual, as in Antigone's sprinkling of earth over her dead brother) or, when circumstances forbade this, through cremation. To deny burial or cremation, therefore, was to deny the soul access to the underworld, which was arguably an offence against the gods.

In some extreme circumstances, however, it was considered permissible to forbid the burial of certain individuals within a specified area. For example, Athenian law forbade the burial of traitors within Attica (the territory of which Athens was the chief city), and there were (rare) instances in which bodies were even exhumed and their remains deposited unceremoniously across the border, presumably for others to rebury, though this was arguably a purely symbolic act – shutting the stable door after the horse, or soul, had bolted. Completely to forbid or prevent burial was very uncommon indeed. We have already considered the practice in as far as it was part of the punishment of *apotympanismos*. Another instance occurred during Athens' war with the Peloponnesians, when for many days her Theban enemies refused to allow the burial of Athenian dead at Delium (424 BC). But these examples are remarkable simply because they are so unusual.

While by the second half of the fifth century BC the (cremated) remains of war dead were regularly shipped back to Athens to be honoured in an annual public ceremony, in Homeric epic Greek warriors were given funerals at Troy (in occupied, if hostile, territory). It is this that, prescient in the face of death, Ajax fears will be denied him, a fear that Menelaus shows is all too justified (1062–6):

> We're going to throw him out on some toxic bit of sand and leave him for seabirds to peck at. So keep a lid on any anger. We might not have managed to control him while he was alive, but now he's dead, he's in our hands, whether you like it or not. He's completely under our jurisdiction.

Menelaus' words may have set alarm bells ringing in the ears of the first audience: yes, Ajax was wrong to try to kill his commanding officers, but morally Menelaus is more wrong in denying Ajax burial, since this will surely offend the gods, just as Creon's refusal to permit the burial of Polyneices in *Antigone* leads to not only the pollution of the land of Thebes, but the death of most of Creon's family and Creon's personal downfall.

There is no evidence that the denial of burial was an element of the Ajax story prior to our play (though it had powerful parallels in the Iliadic story of Achilles' treatment of Hector's corpse, and his permission for its burial only when confronted with the realities of shared humanity and the grief felt for their sons' deaths by Priam and his own father Peleus). So, while it is wrong to construe absence of evidence as evidence of absence, it may be that Sophocles was the first to introduce the forbidden burial. Whatever the case, he approaches the issue from a different angle to that in *Antigone*. For whereas there he focuses primarily on the repercussions of the edict on the man who made it, in *Ajax* he chooses chiefly to use the scenario to explore (and resolve) fraught questions about the nature of friendship and enmity.

At the heart of Greek popular morality was the notion that one should help friends and harm enemies. This was all very well as long as they knew who their friends and enemies were. But occasionally, as in our play, the boundaries become blurred: what are Greeks to make of a man such as Ajax, who for almost all his life was their champion (Homer calls him their *herkos*, 'bulwark') but whose last act was to launch what might be termed a 'failed terrorist attack' on their generals? Does a moment of madness negate a lifetime of loyalty? Questions such as this would (I believe) have been particularly pertinent at a time when Athenians were having to decide how to treat allies who had tried to revolt from (and attack) their empire.

What makes Ajax's case even more problematic is that he is led astray by the goddess Athene. She, we learn, has long been his enemy – not only since, as he set out for war (767–9), he vowed to win glory without the help of gods, but since (771–7):

> in battle, when Athene was encouraging him to turn and kill the enemy, he talked back to her – quite blasphemous it was, something that he never should have said: 'Lady, go stand with the other Greeks. The line won't break when *I*'m here.' It was words like those that provoked Athene's anger.

Too late Ajax realizes that she, his mortal enemy adhering to the popular moral code of harming enemies, has destroyed him. But (as Brad Levett explores in this collection) there is more to our play than this. For Ajax has another enemy, Odysseus, but in the end it is Odysseus who will have the moral maturity to transcend the popular code and agree to Ajax's burial. While the divine Athene is trapped in the belief that it is 'the loveliest of things to mock our enemies' (79), the mortal Odysseus is more flexible – and pragmatic. Realizing that 'most men can be friends one day and enemies the next' (1359), he prefers to see the wider view, accepting that Ajax 'was my enemy. But more than that, he was a noble man' (1355). Moreover, he shares Ajax's mortality, and one day he too will be in need of burial (1365).

That humans can be more nuanced (or more morally advanced) than gods may come as a surprise to some readers. Most Greeks, however, would have accepted it without a second thought. For them gods were not worshipped because they were any better morally than we are, but because they were more powerful. Nor did most fifth-century BC Greeks have any qualms about imagining scenarios in which gods behaved badly. It was simply the way things were. If gods could get away with such behaviour (and generally they could), then they would. Who wouldn't? So Sophocles' use of Athene as a foil for Odysseus and as a means to move the argument from black and white at the start of the play to nuanced colour at the end would have shocked no-one in the audience. And, after all, this was drama; and in democratic Athens, proud of its right to free speech (*parrhesia*), the stage was somewhere that even the most controversial of ideas might be explored.

## Staging *Ajax*

By the time *Ajax* was first staged (possibly in the early 430s BC), drama festivals had been part of Athenian life for over eighty years. All were sacred to Dionysus, the god of wine, fecundity and transformation, whose major festivals occurred over the winter months. Thus at the time of the winter solstice rural festivals which included drama were held throughout Attica, while within the city itself there were two annual festivals: the Lenaia (which in the early 430s still did not feature tragedy), held in January/February, and attended exclusively by Athenians and Attic residents; and the City (or Great) Dionysia, held near to the spring equinox, when the weather permitted safer travel, attracting audiences from other cities, especially those within Athens' empire. It was probably at this festival that *Ajax* was first performed.

This City Dionysia was part religious, part artistic and part political. It began with a procession through the streets to the Theatre of Dionysus on the south east slope of the Acropolis. At the time of *Ajax*'s first performance this consisted of a slightly raised wooden stage building (the *skene*), probably with one central door. In front of this was the flat circle of the *orchestra* (literally 'dancing floor', an area in which at this time both actors and chorus performed) around which in a narrow horseshoe rows of wooden benches were set out on the curving hillside. Scholars are divided as to the size of the audience (though it was perhaps in the region of 6,000) and also as to whether women could attend. Evidence is contradictory, but my own view is that they could not, since, although girls took part in the preliminary procession, elements of the festival proper – such as the parading through the theatre of tribute from subject states, and the awarding of armour to war orphans, both of which preceded the dramatic presentations, and the meeting of the assembly that concluded them – had political and military connotations, and women were barred from participating in both spheres.

At the heart of the festival (which also included performances of *dithyrambs* or choral hymns to Dionysus, as well as comedies) were three days of drama, on each of which one playwright presented three tragedies followed by a so-called satyr play (a playful parody of tragic themes in which the chorus was dressed as half-man, half-horse satyrs). Greeks were by nature competitive, and the dramatic festivals were no exception. Ten judges (one from each tribe) voted to decide not just the winning playwright but (from 449) the best leading actor.

Each tragedy called for three (male) speaking actors, a (male) chorus of fifteen, (male) musicians and silent (male) supernumeraries (a boy of around six to eight years would probably have played Eurysaces). In *Ajax*, each actor was called on to play several roles, though how these were divided is unknown. One possibility is that the leading actor (the so-called protagonist) may have played Ajax and Teucer, the second actor (deuteragonist) may have played Athene, Tecmessa and Agamemnon, while the third (tritagonist) may have played Odysseus, the Messenger and Menelaus. All wore masks, which, as well as enabling them quickly to change their personas, may have aided their vocal projection (they would certainly have affected it), and which may too have possessed a religious connotation of which we are now unaware.

While actors played defined individuals, the chorus (possibly wearing identical masks and similar costumes) represented a homogenous group, in our case Salaminian sailors, Ajax's loyal troops who sailed with him to Troy from Salamis. Traditionally, choruses (and especially the chorus leader) interacted with actors but seldom intervened actively to influence the action. Additionally, they performed set-piece choreographed songs (called *stasima*, singular *stasimon*, or odes), which acted as bridge passages between scenes (also called *epeisodia* – episodes – literally 'between odes'), and whose subject matter often picked up themes from preceding scene while sometimes preparing audiences for what was to come. Generally these *stasima* were divided into pairs of stanzas called *strophes* and *antistrophes*, each pair of which had identical metres (which in Greek performances were reflected in the accompanying music and dance steps), rounded off with a so-called *epode*. While spoken speeches were written in iambic trimeters, sung *stasima* were written in a variety of metres which matched the emotion of their subject matter. At moments of high emotion, actors, too, would sing, and in my translation these sung passages are usually indicated by a looser typographical layout.

The staging of *Ajax* presents certain difficulties. Despite Aristotle's well-known injunction that tragedy should demonstrate 'unity of place' (in other words no scene-shifts), the first 814 lines clearly take place in front of Ajax's tent (represented by the stage building, or *skene*, a word that coincidentally *means* 'tent'), while the remainder of the action appears to be set in a remote grove near the sea. Whether (or how) this scene shift was shown in the first production we cannot now tell, but Athenian audiences undoubtedly viewed drama less literally than we do, and perhaps they took it in their stride – in much the same way as we do when listening to a radio play.

More difficult to tell is how Ajax's suicide was staged. While stage deaths were not unknown they are rare – in other extant tragedies only Hippolytus must die in plain view. More often they are described by messengers. So, if

Sophocles did mean his actor to be seen falling on his sword, this would have constituted a daring *coup de théâtre*. It would also have set up something of a problem: in the scenes that follow, Ajax's corpse takes centre stage, but three speaking actors are still required, one of whom must formerly have played Ajax. So at some point soon after the suicide – possibly when Tecmessa holds out her cloak in front of Ajax's corpse (see Stephen Esposito's chapter in this book) – a dummy must somehow have been substituted to allow the actor to return as either Teucer or another character. The alternative is that the suicide did not, in fact, take place in front of the audience. Other Greek dramas made use of the *ekkuklema* (the 'roller-out'), a wheeled platform that could be slid into view and back again through the *skene*'s doors, often to show the aftermath of actions supposed to have taken place 'inside'. It is possible that the Ajax actor stood on the *ekkuklema* to give his suicide speech, and that, as he prepared to impale himself upon his sword, the platform disappeared back into the *skene* with him on it, only to reappear shortly afterwards with a dummy substitute.

One scene is easier to imagine. In the last three decades of the fifth century BC, gods regularly appeared as if from heaven, the actors swooping over the stage as they hung by harnesses from a crane (the *mēkhanē*). However, since this device seems to have been introduced only in the late 430s, it is probable that in our prologue the actor playing Athene was rooted firmly on stage, interacting on ground level with both Odysseus and Ajax to the delight of the audience.

## Translating *Ajax*

Poetry, wrote Robert Frost, 'is that which is *lost* out of both prose and verse in translation'. But sometimes meaning – or at least crucial nuance – is lost, too, for words are often slippery protean things, which need context to define their specific sense, and even then might be ambiguous.

To take just a few instances: we have seen the importance in *Ajax* of the theme of friendship and enmity, but the Greek words for 'friend' and 'enemy' mean more than ours do, for *philos* can mean both friend and family member, even member of one's household, whereas *echthros* can mean both enemy and one who is not of the family circle, while, coming somewhere between both, *xenos* (plural, *xenoi*, a word untranslatable in English because we have no equivalent concept) can mean stranger, guest and host, as well as one who is bound to someone else through the exchange of hospitality. To represent any of these words in English, the translator must make decisions that will not only entail compromise but point the reader in one direction, perhaps closing down the fluidity of interpretation contained in the original language, while removing some of the resonances of the original text.

Other words, too, contain a multiplicity of meanings. At the beginning of Ajax's suicide speech I have translated *sphageus* as 'executioner' ('The executioner stands ready, razor-sharp, where it will do most harm') but it could be translated equally well (perhaps better?) as 'slaughterer', or 'slayer', the word Rosie Wyles uses in her chapter, 'The Power of Ajax's Sword'. Still others describe abstract concepts which were part of the Greek psyche but not ours – for example *atē*, defined in Liddel and Scott's lexicon as 'bewilderment, infatuation, caused by blindness or delusion sent by the gods, mostly as the punishment of guilty rashness'; or *mania*, 'madness, enthusiasm, divine frenzy, passion'. Translators must make of these what they will, often rendering one Greek term by a multiplicity of English synonyms, as readers of chapters such as those by Robert Garland ('Ajax's Suicide') or Richard Seaford ('Looking at the Isolation of Ajax') will discover.

Equally problematic can be Sophocles' syntax with its delight in balance, not to mention periphrasis. As I have written in the introduction to another volume in this series (*Looking at* Antigone), too literal a translation would read disturbingly like A.E. Housman's infamous parody, *A Fragment of a Greek Tragedy*, whose overpowering flavour can be sampled even in its opening line: 'O suitably-attired-in-leather-boots, head of a traveller'. While retaining an awareness of Sophocles' original, I have attempted to render his dialogue (and poetry) in a somewhat more direct style, even though this has inevitably meant sacrificing some of his grandeur.

I have, however, retained one element of Sophocles' original that to us may seem rather alien: the vocalized cries of alarm or distress such as '*io*', '*iou iou*', '*oimoi talaina*' and '*ai ai*'. These piercing cries, discussed by Alyson Melzer in her chapter, 'The Sounds of Ajax's Grief', tear through every surviving Greek tragedy, reminders of the profound emotions that once swept through the theatre and caused the first audience of our play (or so we read) to weep. In our play, they also confront us yet again with the problems of translation, for in one of his great speeches Sophocles links the lamenting cry, '*ai ai*', with Ajax's name, and in doing so reminds us that in Greek both hero and play were called not Ajax (the Latin version, which is ubiquitous today), but Aias (430–1). In the end, all that a poor translator can ever hope to do is fudge (an observation that may not be not as elegant as Frost's, but is equally true nonetheless).

> *aiai*! Who could have known my name would suit my agony so perfectly?
> Aiai! Aiax! My very name's a lamentation stretching out for ever.

## Notes

1  The episode does not appear in extant literature before our play, though it does seem to be alluded to on a *kylix* by the vase-painter Onesimus dating to the early fifth century BC.
2  Early sixth-century BC vase paintings show Greeks confronting one another over Ajax's corpse. Sophocles may have introduced the notion that it was forbidden any burial.
3  Aeschylus' trilogy comprised: *Contest for Arms* (where Ajax loses the armour of Achilles to Odysseus); *Thracian Women* (in which Ajax commits suicide); and *Salaminian Women* (in which Teucer may have been exiled by his father Telamon). Sophocles' other 'Ajax' plays are *Teucer* and *Eurysaces*. There is no evidence that these formed a connected trilogy with our *Ajax*. All of these tragedies survive only in fragments (one word in the case of *Eurysaces*).

# 1

# Some Visual Influences on Sophocles' *Ajax*?

David Stuttard[1]

*Time stretches to eternity. It brings all things into the light and buries them again in darkness. All is inevitable. Nothing can resist – not even the most binding oath or the most steadfast will.*

Sophocles, Ajax, 646–9

For those familiar with the character of Ajax only from his appearances in the *Iliad* and *Odyssey*, his philosophical utterances in Sophocles' play can come as a surprise.[2] In epic, Ajax is the quintessential tight-lipped warrior, second only to Achilles in might and main. In fact, at Troy these two site their tents on either wing of the Greek encampment, those dangerously liminal positions that were potentially so vulnerable to attack (*Iliad*, 8.226; 11.7–9; cf. Sophocles *Ajax*, 4), and, when Achilles withdraws from battle to nurse his slighted honour, it is no coincidence that his cousin Ajax, like him a man of action, is chosen as one of three ambassadors who try (albeit unsuccessfully) to change his mind (*Iliad*, 9.182–668), complementing perfectly the silver-tongued Odysseus and wily old Phoenix, Achilles' erstwhile tutor.

In Achilles' absence, Ajax readily assumes the role of Greece's champion. Several times he pits his strength against Hector, the most courageous of the Trojans, not least when Hector leads a Trojan attack on the Greek ships (*Iliad*, 15.674–745; cf. Sophocles, *Ajax*, 1276–9) or when the two fight as champions in single combat to decide the outcome of the war (*Iliad*, 7.66–305; cf. Sophocles *Ajax*,1286–7).[3] In a hard-fought struggle, Ajax wounds Hector with his spear and knocks him over with a heavy stone, but the god Apollo protects the Trojan, and the battle lasts till nightfall. As darkness draws in, Hector suggests that they not only suspend hostilities but exchange gifts (*Iliad*, 7.299–305):

Come, let us give each other glorious gifts, so that any man, be he Greek or Trojan, will say: 'Each fought the other with heart-gnawing venom, but before they parted they were joined in friendship.' So saying, he gave Ajax his silver-studded sword, together with its scabbard and a well-cut sword belt, while Ajax gave Hector his shining purple battle-belt.

Although the *Iliad* makes little of it, this exchange of gifts becomes a defining moment in the fate of both warriors: in later Greek tradition, Ajax commits suicide with Hector's sword, while, using the battle-belt the Trojan received from Ajax, Achilles ties Hector's corpse to his chariot before dragging it around his friend Patroclus' tomb.

While the action of the *Iliad* ends before the contest for Achilles' armour (in which Odysseus defeats Ajax) and Ajax's resultant suicide, in the *Odyssey* when Odysseus encounters the soul of the still-resentful Ajax in the underworld (11.543–67) both episodes are alluded to in such a way as to suggest that readers (or listeners) were expected to be familiar with them.[4] Indeed, for those who know the story, even the *Iliad* contains hints of things to come. In Book 23, Ajax takes part in two events in the funeral games that Achilles holds in Patroclus' honour: a fight against Diomedes with spears in which neither party wins, and a wrestling contest with Odysseus, which, although Odysseus appears to be gaining the upper hand, Achilles stops early, declaring it a draw.

It is not the only time in these games that Odysseus gets the better of an Ajax. Odysseus wins the footrace with the help of his patron goddess, Athene, who trips his rival, another Ajax, this time the son of Oïleus, sending him face-first into a pile of ox-dung. Realizing the cause of his misfortune, this 'Lesser' Ajax exclaims:

'Damn it! The goddess hobbled my feet – the goddess who always stands by Odysseus like a mother, and helps him.'

*Iliad*, 23, 782–3

Again, this idea of Odysseus gloating over a rival, laid low by his protectress, Athene, will resonate in later episodes of the Trojan War, and inform not just the action of Sophocles' *Ajax* but (as we shall see) the work of vase painters.

As discussed in the Introduction to this book, the *Iliad* and *Odyssey* deal with only two parts of the Trojan War and its aftermath, so in the centuries after their conception a number of other epic poems (of varying quality) were written, drawing on earlier myth, whose subject matter filled in the blanks to complete the story of the war from its first causes to the death of Odysseus. While all survive only in fragments, we know that in the *Aethiopis* (which begins where the *Iliad* ends), when Achilles is shot in the ankle by the Trojan Paris aided by Apollo, Ajax carries his body to safety, while Odysseus beats off assailants.[5] The *Little Iliad* describes what happened next: when Ajax and Odysseus both claim Achilles' armour (forged by the god Hephaestus), the decision is put to a vote; again Athene helps Odysseus to win; Ajax goes mad and, thinking that he is attacking the Greek commanders, slaughters their cattle instead; when his senses return, he is so humiliated that he commits suicide, but, instead of the usual heroic cremation rites, he is buried without honour.[6]

In epic, then, Ajax is an action hero, a mighty warrior, a man of deeds, not words, who fearlessly strikes down his foe, and, when humiliated by both gods and men, turns his blade swiftly and efficiently upon himself. But by the time we meet him in Sophocles' play, he has become transformed. He is still the fearsome warrior, but now he is more: an apparently deep thinker, whose speeches increasingly blend notions of heroic honour with contemplations of the cosmos and man's place in nature.

If we confine ourselves to extant literary tradition, we might be excused for thinking that this transformation was the work of Sophocles alone. Yet literature was not the only medium by which myth might be explored in Ancient Greece. Vase painters, too, drew inspiration from the Trojan War, and some of their treatments suggest that already by the 530s BC they were using episodes from the life and death of Ajax to explore issues that bordered on the metaphysical.

Sixth-century BC artists embraced Ajax.[7] For centuries formulaic scenes had been stamped on Samian amphorae showing a helmeted warrior carrying a fallen comrade – but now, through the use of captions, painters began to identify many of these depictions as representing Ajax rescuing Achilles' corpse from the battlefield. No captions were needed, however, for representations of another popular episode: Ajax's suicide. Painters delighted in showing him impaled on his sword, their composition mirrored in a sculpture from as far away as Southern Italy (a metope from the so-called Temple of Hera in Paestum), while a Corinthian black-figure cup from around 580 BC depicts Greeks including Odysseus apparently debating over Ajax's impaled corpse.

But it was the mid-sixth-century BC Athenian, Exekias, whose work took the visual representation of the myth of Ajax to new heights, using a purely visual vocabulary to explore it with almost literary eloquence and extraordinary profundity. Let us look first at one of his most remarkable paintings (Fig. 1, now held in the Vatican Museum).

Sitting perfectly within the curves of the amphora, it is quite simply a masterpiece. For sheer composition it is second to none in its use of available space, as the diagonals of the spears and of the heroes' arms, not to mention the direction of their gaze, all focus our attention on the board game, while at the same time our eye is directed to the arc of the handles by the spear tips

**Figure 1** Exekias' Board Game.

and the seemingly-so-casually placed shields. It shows a scene for which there is no parallel in earlier literature, so may well be Exekias' own creation: Ajax and Achilles competing for victory and *kudos* not in the kind of athletic games that feature in the *Iliad*, but in a board game. In it, the two cousins, apparently during a lull in the fighting, are bent over the board, their interest completely taken up in it. Both wear elaborately patterned cloaks. Both clutch spears. But only Achilles is helmeted, and we know that he will win. For, beside him, Exekias has written the word, 'Tesara' ('Four'), while beside Ajax appears 'Tria' ('Three').

Further consideration of the composition reveals more. As we have already seen, Ajax and Achilles, the two bravest fighters in the Greek army, positioned their tents at the two flanks of the encampment, trusting, Homer tells us, in their courage and the strength of their hands. Here, too, in our painting, the two heroes flank a contest – this time a board game, but one that is arguably a metaphor for an altogether more serious contest, a contest of which every Greek hero was desperately aware, the contest 'always to be best and to surpass all others' (*Iliad*, 6.208; 11.784). 'Always to be best' means, of course, 'always to win', and here in the board game Ajax and Achilles use 'the strength of their hands' to shift the pieces until one of them should do just that. And we, the onlookers, know the outcome.

Some Visual Influences on Sophocles' Ajax? 19

**Figure 2** Douris: Voting for the Armour of Achilles.

Ajax will lose, but he will lose more than just the board game. Many artists copied Exekias' composition in the years following its execution, and a red-figure cup by the Athenian vase-painter Douris (Fig. 2, dating from 500–480 BC and now in the Kunsthistorisches Museum in Vienna) may, too, be influenced by it.[8] Douris' cup shows on one side Ajax and Odysseus, swords drawn, quarrelling violently over Achilles' armour (undoubtedly the very armour he is wearing in Exekias' board game), while on the other (Fig. 2) the commanders vote to decide which of the two should inherit it, while Athene, helmeted and wearing her aegis complete with Gorgoneion (Gorgon's head), presides. Once more, most mortal eyes are focused on a raised board, which this time bears not the pieces in a game but voting pebbles – and once more the outcome is clear. Count the pebbles, and we can see that the prize goes (by fifteen votes to five) to Odysseus, Athene's favourite, which is why she stretches her right arm towards him, while he throws up his hands in glee. But Ajax's reaction is entirely different: isolated at the extreme right of the composition, he turns away and veils his head in abject humiliation. It is this episode, of course, that leads directly to Ajax's madness and subsequent suicide, the subject of another painting by Exekias (Fig. 3, now in the Château Musée, Boulogne-sur-Mer).

**Figure 3**  Exekias: The Suicide of Ajax.

Here, rather than showing the conventional scene of Ajax's body slumped over the sword, Exekias has chosen to depict the hero in the left half of the composition, his brow furrowed by emotion, preparing for suicide by burying the sword's hilt in the heaped earth (Sophocles' 'soil of Troy, another enemy', *Ajax*, 819), while the right half is dominated by a shield painted with the baleful Gorgon's head, a helmet and two spears. As has been noted, 'these replace the bystanders who often look in on the central scene in black-figure vase paintings, and thus emphasize the loneliness of the warrior.'[9]

But whose armour is it? The accepted interpretation is that it is Ajax's own, and it is, of course, possible that Exekias has placed it here to emphasize Ajax's vulnerability now that he has stripped himself bare. But I think we can do better than this, because it seems to me that, by placing the armour in such a prominent position and in such a way, Exekias is reminding us of past causes, too, specifically the contest over the arms of Achilles, Ajax's defeat in which led directly to his suicide. In this interpretation the armour represents (or at the very least is intended to remind us of) the armour of Achilles.[10]

For the viewer the armour seems to possess great power, and what lends it this power is how it is arranged in such a way as to suggest that it is being worn by an invisible warrior (note that Exekias has made no attempt to show any physical support for the helmet, shield and spears). Indeed, if we compare this painting with that of the board game, we discover a disturbing symmetry. The empty helmet in the suicide scene mirrors the helmet on Achilles' head in the board game, but now it seems ominous and brooding, looming above Ajax as he buries the sword hilt in the sand. At the same time, the angle of the empty armour's leading spear, strikingly similar to the angle of Ajax's leading spear in the board game, once more takes the eye toward the centre of the composition. Now, though, while Ajax's focus on the job in hand exactly parallels his focus on the board game, instead of the game board a sword blade rises from its mound of earth, and instead of Achilles, the empty suit of armour watches on. And as if this were not enough, drawing the eye, and lending the composition an extra frisson of otherworldly menace, from the shield there grins at us the Gorgon's head. While this Gorgoneion does not appear in Homer's description of Achilles' shield, elsewhere in Greek tragedy (Euripides, *Electra*, 452–75) the shield's decoration does include a scene of Perseus carrying the decapitated head. But for Greek viewers the Gorgoneion was most closely connected with Athene. It was a regular part of her iconography, hung over her chest above her aegis as in the representation on the Douris Painter's amphora. So it may well be that by placing the Gorgoneion here on the shield, watching over the right half of the composition, Exekias is reminding us of the role of Athene, 'the goddess who always stands by Odysseus like a mother', in Ajax's defeat in the contest for the armour. If my interpretation is correct, Exekias has created a deeply unsettling depiction of the suicidal Ajax, isolated yet at the same time presided over by the armour and its invisible wearer, imbued with the wrath of Athene, and symbolic of his overwhelming humiliation.

It is not unreasonable to suppose that Exekias painted the 'board game' and 'suicide' amphorae as a pair, perhaps intending their first viewers to compare the images, whose mirroring is so precise, or perhaps to explore ideas of cause and effect within the medium of painting.[11] But what ideas did Exekias expect his viewers to draw from this comparison?

In the 'board game' amphora, Exekias is not just imagining the heroes happily at play, or reminding us of their importance to the army, the bravest of the brave, encamped on either wing. He is reminding us, too, of the future defeat that awaits Ajax, loser in both the game and the contest for Achilles' armour. Indeed, armour is everywhere in this painting – not least the helmet on Achilles' head as he bends over the board, but the helmet behind Ajax's back, too, turned away from the action, perhaps symbolic of the warrior turning his back upon defeat. In this astonishing image Exekias has presented a portal into the world of Trojan epic, embracing past, present and future, relying on its viewers' knowledge of the Trojan War, while creating its own remarkable vocabulary to suggest the inevitability of Ajax's fate. This is true, too, of his depiction of the suicide, where Exekias combines Ajax's past defeat (signified by the empty armour), his present distress (as he prepares the sword) and his future death (which we know must follow shortly). And, while in the board game vase the focus of Ajax and Achilles is on the game, whose outcome will bring the victor *kudos*, in the suicide vase the focus of Ajax, watched over by the empty armour, is on the sword, 'the executioner' that will bring an end to the loser's humiliation.

No god appears in either of Exekias' vases, yet the sense of doom is palpable, especially when they are viewed as a pair. For, while the less imaginative Douris was forced to include Athene in his composition in order to suggest divine or supernatural causation, through his technique of mirroring (the angle of the spear, the empty helmet, Ajax's focus and so on), not to mention iconography (the shield's Gorgoneion), Exekias presents us with a transcendental mystery, setting up parallels that encourage us to pose questions, while never answering them.

But even Exekias' use of the Ajax myth, remarkable as it is, pales when we consider the work of another artist, the so-called Kleophrades Painter (Fig. 4). On a sadly fragmentary belly amphora dating to around 480 BC (now in the Martin von Wagner Museum in Würzburg, Germany) the artist has chosen to explore the scene where, having fought for much of the day, Ajax exchanges gifts with Hector. Each side of the amphora shows two characters: a helmeted warrior and a staff-bearing attendant who seizes the warrior's wrist. One of the warriors, Ajax, holds a sword, the other, Hector, a battle-belt. The exchange of gifts has just taken place.

But what makes the amphora's two faces so remarkable is that they have been painted in such a way that at first glance they seem to show the *same warrior* (flanked by similar but different attendants) viewed from diametrically opposite directions. Indeed, the artist has done everything he can to heighten this impression, from the warriors' identical stance, facial expressions, helmets, spears and shields to tiny details, such as the way in which Hector's left foot, seen from the back, mirrors Ajax's left foot, seen from the front, its toes breaking free from the figurative zone and curling over the band below with its meandering key pattern; or how both helmet plumes hang down the warriors' backs, one seen from the front, the other from behind.

Indeed, when we realize that it is *not* the same warrior, we cannot resist comparing the two faces of the amphora, continually returning from one to the other, experiencing the truth of one of the themes of Sophocles' play (discussed by Hanna Roisman in this volume) that 'one is ... limited in one's capacity to see beyond one's own subjective understanding'. While viewing the amphora side-on allows both warriors to be seen, facing off, glaring at

Some Visual Influences on Sophocles' Ajax? 23

(a)

(b)

**Figure 4** Kleophrades Painter: (a) Ajax and (b) Hector after their exchange of gifts.

each other, only the gods (and readers of books such as this, which reproduce juxtaposed two-dimensional images of both sides) can see the whole picture.

The Kleophrades Painter's concept is stunning, and its execution encapsulates the sublime mystery of the moment in which the two men's fates cross over to bind them inextricably together – as Hector gives Ajax the sword with which he will kill himself, and Ajax gives Hector the belt with which he will be tied to Achilles' chariot. As in Exekias' board game, the future is contained in the present. Until this exchange of gifts the two men have been separate but now they are united as part of one mysterious whole. And it is this unity that the Kleophrades Painter is exploring with such remarkable economy and brilliant imagination: positioned on the two sides of the vase, it appears to the viewer as if (albeit for the merest moment), not only might the fates of Ajax and Hector have been fused together with the exchange of gifts, the two men might somehow have been melded into one, the same person, whose corporeal substance is contained within the vase itself. It is a bold, original image, taking three lines from the *Iliad* and transforming them into something both mysterious and transcendental. Like Exekias, the Kleophrades Painter has used the medium of painting to suggest questions that elevate the scene to the sublime, questions that are repeated by Teucer in our play (1028–35):

> See how the two men's fates are intertwined! Hector was tied to the chariot rail with the battle-belt that Ajax gave him – dragged round till he was shredded raw, until his spirit left him. And Ajax died by falling on this sword, his gift from Hector. Surely it was an Erinys, a fury of revenge, who forged this sword! Surely Death himself, cruel craftsman, made the battle-belt!

In fact, even the *Iliad* contains an oblique suggestion that there is a deeper significance in the exchange of gifts than might at first be apparent. Earlier, I translated the lines describing Hector's gift-giving as: 'so saying, he gave Ajax his silver-studded sword, together with its scabbard and a well-cut sword belt'. What this translation fails to convey, however, is that the Greek for 'sword belt' is 'telamon', which is also, of course, the name of Ajax's father. So, through word play, Hector's gift to Ajax may be considered to contain properties that are both life-giving (the sword belt and Ajax's father share the same name) and death-dealing (it is this sword that will kill him). Like the image on the Kleophrades Painter's amphora, the gift represents two halves of an existential whole.

It is this tradition – both literary and visual – of using Ajax's story to explore deeper truths that, I suggest, Sophocles is both following and developing in our play. At its most basic level the tradition can be seen in passages where Ajax and later Agamemnon, Menelaus and Odysseus pick up on Hector's words in the *Iliad* ('Each fought the other with heart-gnawing venom, but before they parted they were joined in friendship'), as they explore the true nature of friendship and enmity. Indeed, Ajax himself muses on the theme, reflecting upon how the friendship-gift of Hector's sword has become a hostile curse. In his so-called 'deception speech', as he bids farewell to Tecmessa, his son and his comrades, he explains (658–63):

> I'll bury this sword of mine, my nemesis, deep in the earth where no-one will ever see it, but Night and Hades will keep it safe below. Hector was my harshest enemy, and, ever since he gave this sword to me, I've been dishonoured by the Greeks. It's true what they say: a gift's not a gift if an enemy gives it, and no good will come of it.

He develops this theme as he prepares for suicide (815–18):

> The executioner stands ready, razor-sharp, where it will do most harm. And I've still time to work out the connections: this was my gift from Hector, my enemy, the man I hated most, my greatest enemy.

But this is not the only way in which Sophocles explores the fusion of the two heroes' fates. As others (such as Hanna Roisman) explore in this collection, he even goes so far as to model the scene between Ajax, Tecmessa and Eurysaces (*Ajax*, 430–595) on the Iliadic scene between Hector, Andromache and Astyanax (*Iliad*, 6.405–93). Not only is the scenario the same, so are many of the arguments the characters use, albeit with slight variations. For example, both Andromache and Tecmessa claim that, now that their parents have been killed in the war, they have no other protector but their husbands (*Iliad*, 6.411–13; *Ajax*, 511–17) – but Andromache's parents have been killed by Troy's enemy, Achilles, whereas Tecmessa's have been killed by her own husband/master Ajax; both warriors address their sons (*Iliad*, 6. 476–81; *Ajax*, 550–77) – but Hector prays that he will be greater than his father, whereas Ajax prays only that he be his equal ('just more fortunate'); both authors include similar passages imagining the enslavement and humiliation of the mother/wife, when her husband has been killed – but in the *Iliad* it is put into the mouth of the compassionate Hector (450–63), whereas in *Ajax* it is given to Tecmessa as she pleads with the inflexible Ajax to relent (*Ajax*, 490–503); both men will soon die – but Hector will win honour by killing the enemy, while Ajax will win shame by killing himself. Although this mirroring may not be quite so perfect as that on the Kleophrades Painter's amphora (indeed,

Sophocles surely introduces the differences for dramatic emphasis), in our play the two heroes' fates have become so intertwined that even their farewells to their wives and children are uncannily alike.

Nor may this be the only parallel between the two heroes' fates that Sophocles introduces. There is no suggestion in any surviving author prior to Sophocles that Ajax's corpse was temporarily denied burial.[12] It may be Sophocles' own innovation. Even if it is not, in the context of the parallels that we have seen above, his emphasis on the denial of burial is significant, since the only other hero of the Trojan War to be temporarily denied burial was Hector, whose corpse was alternately dragged round Patroclus' grave mound and kept in Achilles' tent, to be released only when Priam appealed to Achilles' humanity in much the same way as Odysseus uses the argument of shared humanity to appeal to Agamemnon in our play.

This is not the place to discuss the two scenes in depth, but suffice it to say that once more there are undoubted ironies in these parallels between the two heroes' fates, not least in the fact that Ajax, who strove to be Achilles' successor by claiming his armour, suffers the very fate (denial of burial) that Achilles inflicted on his enemy, Hector, while Odysseus, who wins Achilles' armour (and so almost literally steps into his shoes), rejects the Achillean punishment of Ajax's corpse, becoming 'the only man alive who wouldn't let his corpse be desecrated' (*Ajax*, 1384–5), declaring (in a sentence that goes to the very heart of one of the play's major themes): 'I was your staunchest enemy; I'm now prepared to be your staunchest friend' (1377–8). The two opposites have been reconciled and we appreciate the profundity of the moment, just as by setting together, reconciling, the two faces of the Kleophrades Painter's amphora we appreciate their profundity, too – indeed, just as in the *Iliad* Hector appreciates the profundity of the moment, when he and Ajax cease fighting and exchange armour: 'each fought the other with heart-gnawing venom, but before they parted they were joined in friendship'.

\* \* \*

To conclude: while the character of Sophocles' Ajax has been shaped in part by literature (and partly, too, no doubt by the tradition of mystery cult, which Richard Seaford discusses in this volume), it also owes much to visual artists, including Exekias and the Kleophrades Painter, whose work we are fortunate still to have, and perhaps many others whose work is now lost. For, while the notion that gods were behind Ajax's destruction appears already in the *Odyssey* (11.547; 555–60), it is these artists who, in the century before our play, began to use the myth of Ajax, the noble warrior reduced to madness and driven to suicide, to explore profound questions – the Kleophrades Painter, developing the relatively conventional Iliadic scene of gift-giving into (quite literally) the uniting of two opposites, where the explosive mystery of the moment is contained within the empty space of the belly amphora itself; Exekias, brilliantly melding present loss and future tragedy not only in his creation of the board game, but in what he may have intended to be a companion vase imbuing the harsh reality of suicide with a troubling sense of otherworldly intervention embodied in the brooding presence of the empty armour.

By the mid-fifth century BC, when our play was first performed, many in the audience may well have been as familiar with such images as they were with descriptions of Ajax from the *Iliad* and *Odyssey* or other literature. Sophocles' genius was to develop these ideas still further, not least through the words his Ajax speaks. So when, addressing his loved-ones for the last time, the once-taciturn Iliadic hero explores ideas of change and development using cosmic imagery, we, who have seen the works of the Kleophrades Painter and Exekias, should no longer be surprised. All things evolve; all things mature; even Ajax. As Ajax himself says (670–7):

> Winter, knee-deep in snow, gives way to the fertility of summer. And all-encircling night is scattered, when day with its white horses flares into light. Storm winds die down. The seas grow calm. And even sleep, which conquers everything, allows his captive to go free, and doesn't keep him chained for ever. So why should I not discover a new understanding?

## Notes

1 I would like to thank Ian Jenkins and Sam Moorhead, both of The British Museum, who read a draft of this chapter, for their excellent suggestions. Such errors and infelicities as remain are entirely the result of my own intransigence.

2 For more on the character of Ajax in Homer and earlier literature see the Introduction to this book. In his article in *Omnibus* 62, 2011, Patrick Finglass (2011a) discusses three vases (including Exekias' suicide vase) exploring the myth of Ajax, concluding that vase artists: 'independently fashioned many of the visual effects that Sophocles would strive to effect many years later on the stage. Sophocles might have been influenced by visual depictions (not necessarily limited to painted pottery) as well as previous literary accounts. Be that as it may, the lazy assumption that pictures are secondary, and text primary, is unsustainable. These images have a profound contribution to make to our understanding of Greek myth, and no-one studying Greek tragedy at any level can afford to neglect them.'

3 For how Sophocles utilizes audiences' knowledge of both these scenes, see Laura Swift's chapter in this collection.

4 See the Introduction to this book.
5 Discussed by Sophie Mills in this volume.
6 See Sophie Mills' chapter in this volume, and especially her note 8.
7 For another discussion of Ajax in art see, for example, Finglass (2011a) 26–33.
8 The Douris cup is one of several to show these scenes juxtaposed in this way.
9 Finglass in his article, 'Sophocles' *Ajax* and the Vase-Painters' (2011a).
10 There is a further possibility that, just as the sword is a 'symbolic representation of Hector' (see Rosie Wyles' chapter in this collection and her discussion of Melissa Mueller's work), so the empty armour, too, may represent Ajax's enemy, Hector. There is, after all, nothing to suggest its ownership. But given both the prominence of Achilles' armour in the myth of Ajax and the similarities in composition to the 'board game' amphora, I consider it more likely that Exekias' intended link is with Achilles and his armour.
11 While the provenance of the suicide amphora is uncertain, both vases were probably found in Vulci, Italy, where they may have been commissioned by a wealthy (Etruscan) resident. However, unless the composition shown on the 'board game' amphora was itself modelled on another, public artwork (which, given how well it fits the amphora's shape and contours, is possibly unlikely), it must have been seen, admired and copied in Athens before being exported, since it subsequently appears to have itself been the model for a surprisingly large number of almost identical treatments of the scene. It is not unreasonable to suppose that the suicide amphora was similarly displayed, albeit briefly, in Exekias' atelier.
12 See Finglass' Introduction to his edition of the play (2011).

# 2

# Ajax the Hero

## Laura Swift

The figure of Ajax, his temperament, decisions and relationships, dominates Sophocles' play. Although Ajax himself dies a little over halfway through the play, even in death he remains the central figure, with the other characters preoccupied with how to treat his body. This chapter will discuss Ajax as a hero in relation to the broader concept of heroism illustrated and debated in the play. I will investigate how Sophocles draws on traditional and especially Homeric models of male heroism in his portrayal of Ajax, and how he adapts them for a fifth-century Athenian audience. Ajax's central dilemma, of whether he can bear to live having lost honour in the eyes of his peers, reflects the tensions faced by Homeric heroes between personal status and their duties to a wider group. I will also explore the different approaches to heroism presented by Ajax and Odysseus, and the broader principles that underpin these. The final part of the chapter will look at a different aspect of heroism that helps make sense of the last part of the play: Ajax's role in Athenian hero-cult.

Calling Ajax a 'hero' appears at first glance self-evident. But when we start to approach the nature of Ajax's heroism, and Greek heroism more generally, this apparent simplicity quickly begins to fracture. The English word 'hero' derives from the Greek *hērōs*, a term used to describe the mythological warriors, such as Ajax, who were believed to have lived in an earlier age, and who surpassed contemporary men in their power and their great deeds. However, the connotations of the two are quite different. In English, the word 'hero' can be used of a central literary character: thus Ajax can be called the 'hero' of his play simply by dint of being the character whose story it follows. But the English term 'hero' also has a strong positive connotation: it usually refers to someone who accomplishes something extraordinary, and usually altruistic. To us, a 'hero' might be someone who risks his or her life to save others, or who endures suffering for the sake of a moral cause. People who are simply powerful or influential do not necessarily strike us as heroes, especially when their actions seem morally questionable. Indeed the superheroes of modern films or comic books are distinguished not only by their exceptional powers, but by their choice to use them to protect others weaker than themselves. Conversely, even a superficial study of Greek literature reveals that this sense of altruism is lacking among ancient heroes. Rather, the heroes of the Greek world are heroic because they are capable of greater things than ordinary mortals, but greater need not necessarily mean kinder or more ethical. The heroes' greatness, which is rooted in excess, can often lead to problems, both for themselves and for others around them. This is particularly apparent in the case of Ajax.

The concept of heroism in Greek literature must be situated against the background of the Homeric epics. The *Iliad* and *Odyssey* act as foundational texts for the nature of heroism, and since *Ajax* is set during the Trojan War and deals with the aftermath of the death of Achilles, the *Iliad* is a continuous backdrop to Sophocles' play. Ajax himself features in the *Iliad* where he is already a blunt man of action and a great warrior, and Sophocles evokes the hero's Homeric portrayal from the first words of the play, where Athena describes Ajax's hut as 'far out on the army's wing' (4). In the *Iliad*, we are told that Achilles and Ajax placed their huts at each end of the Achaean camp, because they were the most powerful warriors and therefore could occupy the most vulnerable position (*Il.* 11.7–9). By starting out with this detail, Sophocles makes it clear that the *Iliad* will be an important intertext. Towards the end of the play, the Iliadic Ajax makes an appearance once more, when Teucer reminds Agamemnon of how he single-handedly defended the Achaean ships against Hector (1276–9):

> He stood his ground, one man alone, and saved you, when the flames were licking the ships' decks, and Hector was leaping high over the trench and would have boarded us.

This scene comes at the high point of Hector's advance against the Achaean camp (*Il.* 15.674–745), and the vivid image of Ajax alone on the deck of the ships trying to ward off the Trojan advances would have been a memorable scene for audiences of Homer. Teucer also recalls another of Ajax's great feats detailed in the *Iliad*: his duel with Hector (1283–7). Teucer praises Ajax for freely volunteering to face Hector in single combat and describes how Ajax was selected because the token he placed in the helmet 'was sure to be the first one picked' (1286–7). This echoes the Iliadic scene where the warriors willing to fight Hector throw their lots into a helmet, and Ajax's is the first to leap out, to the joy of the other Achaeans (*Il.* 7.182–3).

However, these echoes of the *Iliad* are also infused with irony, since an audience familiar with Homer's poem would also be attuned to the ways in which these interludes are not fully representative of their Homeric counterparts. For example, when Teucer speaks of Hector's attack on the Achaean ships, he asks Agamemnon: 'Who stopped him then? Wasn't it Ajax?' (1280). In fact, though Ajax's defence of the ships is presented as a great act of courage in the *Iliad*, he is ultimately unable to withstand Hector's divinely-supported onslaught: Hector destroys Ajax's spear, leaving him armed with only a pole, and Ajax then gives way before the Trojan missiles, allowing Hector to throw fire over the ships (*Il.* 16.114–23). It is this that prompts Achilles to send Patroclus into battle, and it is Patroclus' arrival that forces Hector and the Trojans away from the ships. Similarly, though it is true that Ajax volunteers to face Hector in single combat, he is one of nine warriors to do so (*Il.* 7.161) Nor is it clear that he is universally considered the best combatant, since the Achaeans pray that the lot selected might be that of Ajax, Diomedes or Agamemnon (*Il.* 7.179–80). Agamemnon is of course Teucer's addressee at this point, and so there is an irony to how Teucer effaces Agamemnon's involvement in the scene. Moreover, Ajax's duel with Hector ends in a draw, and although it is clear that Ajax has the upper hand, it is hardly a triumph. It is because of the inconclusive outcome of this duel that Hector and Ajax exchange gifts, so that Ajax comes to have Hector's sword, which he uses as his suicide weapon (816): in a sense, Ajax's failure to defeat Hector is embedded into the central moment of Sophocles' play. An alert audience-member would therefore be able to see how Teucer's narrative fails to recognize the hero's limitations, and the contributions made to events by his fellow-warriors on the Greek side. This sense that Ajax (and his ally Teucer) oversell his importance is clear in Ajax's lyric lament after recovering his sanity, when he describes himself as (423–6):

> a man who
>   it's no empty boast
>   to say
>   was once unequalled
>     in the army
>       of the greeks
>         who sailed to troy

Yet any reader of the *Iliad* would know that it is Achilles, not Ajax, who was the 'best of the Achaeans', and his superiority to all the other warriors is confirmed throughout the poem. Ajax's boast is subtly corrected by Odysseus towards the end of the play: 'So I'm not going to deny that – with the exception of Achilles – Ajax was the best of all Greeks who came to Troy' (1341). Thus the echoes of the *Iliad* do not necessarily cast Ajax in a positive light, and highlight his boastfulness as well as his heroic past.

Comparing Ajax to his Homeric counterpart also highlights the individualistic tendencies that Sophocles has given his hero. Another of Ajax's most important moments in the *Iliad* is his participation in the embassy to Achilles in Book 9, where along with Odysseus and Achilles' old tutor Phoenix, he tries to persuade Achilles to renounce his anger with Agamemnon and return to combat to save the Achaeans. Ajax speaks last, and his speech focuses on Achilles' duty as a soldier to his comrades. He criticizes Achilles to the others (*Il.* 9.628–32):

> Achilles
> has turned the great-hearted spirit in his breast to cruelty,
> hard man, and he has no regard for his companions' love,
> we who used to honour him above all others beside the ships.
> He is without pity.
>
> Trans. Verity

It is therefore ironic that Sophocles gives his Ajax exactly the qualities that the Homeric Ajax criticizes in Achilles: excessive pride, inability to move on from a slight, and putting his own honour above the wellbeing of the wider group. Indeed, the Homeric Achilles is in many ways more of a model for Sophocles' Ajax than is the Ajax of the *Iliad*, since the Sophoclean Ajax, like Achilles, cannot overlook losing honour in the eyes of the community, and ends up bringing about his own ruin through his inability to be persuaded by his friends. Yet here too, Sophocles' portrayal of Ajax pushes these qualities more to the extreme even than Achilles does, and he lacks the elements of compassion and self-awareness that balance Achilles' quickness to anger. While Achilles is willing to let the Achaeans suffer at the hands of the Trojans rather than accept Agamemnon's offer of compensation, Ajax goes further, since he actively seeks to harm his former comrades himself, and does so deceitfully, by attempting to kill and torture them while they sleep. Achilles acknowledges in his reply to Ajax that his criticisms are fair even if he cannot bring himself to act differently (*Il.* 9.644–8) and over the course of the embassy scene shifts his position from wishing to leave Troy immediately to saying that he will not enter battle before the ships are endangered (*Il.* 9.650–3). Conversely, Ajax in his madness gloats over the suffering he has caused the other Greeks, for example responding to Athena's question 'You've soaked your sword nicely in Greek blood?' with the boast 'Indeed I have! I won't deny it' (96–7). When he realizes what he has done, he expresses no remorse for having attempted to murder his fellow-Greeks, and instead laments that his plan was unsuccessful (372–5):

such cruel fate
  to let
    those enemies
      those demons
        whose one wish is
          to crush me
  get away
    while all the time
      instead
        i was attacking
          goats and
            wide-horned cattle

Ajax's lack of respect for his community thus exceeds Achilles', and so too does his disrespect for the gods. Achilles first becomes enraged in Book 1 of the *Iliad*, where he contemplates killing Agamemnon, but when Athena intervenes he is quickly persuaded not to do this, telling her 'Goddess, a man must respect the words of you both [i.e. Athena and Hera], however great the anger in his heart' (*Il.* 1.216–17). This scene too is mirrored by Athena's request that Ajax should stop torturing Odysseus, an order which Ajax refuses to obey (112–13). Thus while Ajax and Achilles share certain basic qualities, both positive (excellence in combat, courage on the battlefield) and negative (anger and pride), the portrayal of Ajax focuses more on these negative qualities, and also makes little attempt to mitigate their full effects on those around him. While we are told of Ajax's prowess in battle, it is only as background to the events of the play, and thus these facets of his personality are given less weight than his behaviour to his family and comrades.

Ajax's basic dilemma is whether he can live on and accept the shame he has incurred by his actions in attacking the Greek flocks. In a culture where personal honour is of paramount importance, any attack on a man's honour is a serious matter. Repellent as Ajax's decision to attack his comrades in the night seems to us, to Ajax it is an act of vengeance against a community which has (he feels) devalued him by failing to reward his military prowess. When he still believes that he has killed Agamemnon and Menelaus, he justifies this to Athena as necessary to preserve his honour: 'They'll not dishonour me again' (98). The desire for vengeance, especially to avenge personal slights, was widely accepted in Greek ethics, as summarized by Aristotle, who writes 'To take vengeance on one's enemies is nobler than to come to terms with them; for to retaliate is just, and what is just is noble; and a real man does not allow himself to be beaten' (*Rhetoric* 1367a24). While most Greeks would probably not have condoned the manner in which Ajax sought his vengeance, they might well sympathize with his basic desire to seek redress for a perceived wrong. The failure of Ajax's plan, and the humiliating realization that he has attacked the Greek herds, means that he has been further shamed. Suicide therefore seems to him to offer the only remaining chance to recover his honour, as he explains after rejecting all other options: 'But a hero has two options: to live in glory or die in glory' (479–80).

Ajax's suicide is a further example of how Sophocles takes a Homeric precedent and pushes it to the extreme. Ajax's death will endanger his family, as made apparent by Tecmessa's speech in which she imagines her fate, and that of her son Eurysaces, after his death (485–524). Tecmessa's speech strongly evokes the scene between Hector and Andromache in Book 6 of the *Iliad*, in which Andromache anticipates how her husband's death will mean her enslavement and risk the safety of their son (*Il.* 6.407–65, see Roisman in this volume). Yet in Hector's case, the audience of the *Iliad* can appreciate that as the strongest fighter in a city at war, he has little option but to risk his life on the battlefield, and his duties to his family must be balanced against those to the soldiers he leads. While Hector couches his desire to fight in terms of personal honour and shame, it is also apparent that he has conflicting duties to different groups. In the case of Ajax, his decision to kill himself is purely driven by his sense of shame and anger: as he acknowledges, his grudge against the Atreids prevents him from reclaiming his honour by an act of daring on the battlefield, as this would benefit the Greek army (467–70). Thus Hector's complicated situation is resolved into a simple dichotomy, as Ajax must choose between personal status and the safety of his loved ones.

The model of the hero as touchy, proud, and self-obsessed is often spoken of as though it was the only or truest concept of what it means to be a hero in Greek literature. Yet already in the *Iliad*, the poet presents a range of heroes, so that the form of heroism represented by Achilles is balanced by, for example, Odysseus, who excels in his command of language and persuasive skills, or Agamemnon, who possesses in wealth and kingly status what he lacks in martial ability. Other heroes such as Diomedes are moderate characters and good all-rounders, and so demonstrate that it is possible to be a brave warrior and skilled fighter without excessive pride or lack of respect for the wider social good. The potential tension between these different approaches to what it means to be a hero is apparent in Achilles' terse response to Odysseus' lengthy speech 'that man is as hateful to me as the gates of Hades who has one thing in his mind but says another' (*Il.* 9.312–13, trans. Verity). In Sophocles' *Ajax* the tension between the Achillean and Odyssean form of heroism is one of the play's major themes. Ajax, as the blunt man of action, stands in opposition to the more flexible Odysseus. The background to the play is that the Greeks have voted to award the arms of Achilles to Odysseus rather than to Ajax. The choice between the two heroes takes on broader symbolic connotations, as expressed by Ajax himself (441–6):

One thing I think I know: if Achilles had been still alive to judge the contest for the armour and award it as a prize for bravery, no-one would have taken it but me. But as it was, my bravery meant nothing to the sons of Atreus, so they gave my armour to a shameless cheat.

Thus Ajax sees himself as the natural heir to Achilles, and believes that the arms should have been awarded on the basis of bravery on the battlefield, a quality in which he excels. His description of Odysseus as a 'shameless cheat' is partly a response to the fact that Ajax perceives the victory as intrinsically unfair, but also evokes Odysseus' own traditional qualities of slipperiness and cunning. In fact, the Odysseus we see in this play is presented as not so much devious as moderate, and though Ajax presents the contrast between them as courage versus duplicity, from the audience's perspective the clearer distinction is between Ajax's individualism and Odysseus' ability to consider others, or Ajax's stubbornness and Odysseus' open-mindedness.

Sophocles confounds the audience's expectations by presenting an Odysseus who is surprisingly straightforward in his language, in contrast to the great deceiver of the *Odyssey*, or the manipulative rhetorician we find in other plays such as Sophocles' *Philoctetes* and Euripides' *Iphigenia at Aulis*. The quality that sets Odysseus apart in *Ajax* is his empathy and his sense of belonging to a greater human community, and these qualities are presented as alien to the values of the world in which he lives. At the start of the play Athena says to Odysseus 'And isn't it the loveliest of things to mock our enemies?' (79). This is an ethical system familiar from the Homeric world and from elsewhere in Greek literature, whereby an honourable man's duty is not only to help his friends but actively to cause harm to his enemies. In Plato's *Republic*, this is one of the first definitions given of justice (1.332d), suggesting that it is thought to be a common-sense approach, and we regularly find references to the delight that an enemy's downfall is thought to cause. This morality is accepted by other characters in the play. When Ajax recovers his sanity, he perceives himself as a 'laughing stock' (367), and assumes that his enemy Odysseus in particular takes pleasure at his misfortunes (381):

how
   he'll be laughing
now

       and
           gloating
               at my ruin

Similarly, the Chorus initially believe that the stories circulating in the Achaean camp about Ajax's attack on the flocks are malicious lies spread by Odysseus to dishonour and mock his enemy (148–53):

odysseus
is whispering
this story
    moulding it
    adorning it
    implanting it
         into the ears
         of all he meets
    and they
         so readily
    believe him

he is so easy
    to believe
and anyone
    who hears him
         smiles
         and laughs
         and mocks
              your misery

The Chorus draws on the mythological tradition of Odysseus as a manipulative speaker who uses his rhetorical powers to advance his own agenda. Yet the audience already know that the story is a true one, and not invented or embellished by Odysseus. Far from mocking Ajax, Odysseus in fact expressed deep discomfort at the prospect of seeing him in his madness, and when forced to do so by Athena, feels pity for Ajax's plight, recognizing that his fall from greatness is illustrative of the fragility of human fortune (120–6):

And although we're enemies, I pity him. Poor man! Deranged. Demented. But I can see myself in him. Yes, I can see us all, all human beings. We're nothing but delusions, empty shadows.

After Ajax has killed himself, his friends continue to assume that Odysseus will rejoice in his downfall and mock their grief. The Chorus and Tecmessa's immediate response to discovering Ajax's corpse is to imagine Odysseus' mocking laughter directed at their expense (955-73). Yet Odysseus in fact acts supportively towards his former enemy, arguing that Agamemnon must allow Ajax to receive honourable burial on the basis that this basic ethical requirement supersedes personal enmities: 'it's the gods' laws you'd be desecrating, not Ajax' (1343-4). A consequence of Odysseus' commitment to this depersonalized moral framework is that he must put personal friendship and enmity aside in favour of broader concerns. Thus he acknowledges the hatred between himself and Ajax, but argues that Ajax's standing as a great hero must supersede these private matters: 'He was my enemy. But more than that, he was a noble man' (1355). Agamemnon is suspicious of this willingness to put aside old enmities and criticizes Odysseus as 'inconstant' (1358). Like Ajax and Athena, he adheres to the traditional ethic of helping friends and harming enemies, and so perceives Odysseus' flexibility as showing a lack of moral fibre. This exchange engages with one of the play's central questions: whether changeability should be viewed as a positive or negative quality. When Agamemnon presses Odysseus on why he is now willing to help Ajax, Odysseus admits that at the core of his empathy lies self-interest: 'one day I'll need to be buried, too' (1365), a comment which Agamemnon sees as showing Odysseus' ultimate selfishness (1366). Thus Odysseus' view of heroism is pragmatic, and his principles are underpinned by his assessment of what will best serve his own interests. This exchange evokes contemporary fifth-century concerns about the opportunistic speaker who will advocate any cause he believes to be beneficial to his own interests. Yet the audience can also see the great social benefits of this flexibility, which enables Odysseus to break the stalemate over Ajax's burial and to put an end to the grudges that have caused rifts within the Achaean army. Ironically, it is this flexibility which secures Ajax's honour.

This tension between principle and flexibility is also brought out in Ajax's 'deception' speech, where after his previous implacability he appears to have had a change of heart. Ajax speaks of how change is itself an irresistible process, comparing his new mindset with the natural alternation of the seasons (669-77). A careful reading of Ajax's words may reveal that they are not quite as they seem: for example his statement that he will 'bury this sword of mine, my nemesis, deep in the earth' (658-9) may foreshadow how he first buries the hilt of the sword to fix it in place, and then buries the blade in his own body. Nevertheless, even if Ajax does not lie outright, his speech is intentionally deceptive, and leads Tecmessa and the Chorus to believe that he no longer intends to kill himself. It is therefore ironic that it is he, rather than

Odysseus, who turns out to be the most manipulative speaker of this play. At the end of his speech, Ajax claims to have adopted a more flexible approach to friendship and enmities, saying 'I've learned just recently that an enemy should be treated as an enemy only in the knowledge that one day he might become a friend' (678–9). These words foreshadow Odysseus' argument with Agamemnon at the end of the play, and his words to Teucer 'I was your staunchest enemy; I'm now prepared to be your staunchest friend' (1377). Yet this mindset of adaptability is ultimately not compatible with Ajax's personality, and far from becoming reconciled to his enemies, he dies with a curse that the Furies should 'spare no-one from all the army' (844). Here too, Ajax reflects the stubbornness of the Homeric Achilles, yet pushes it further, with destructive consequences. Achilles is ultimately able to give up his anger when he accepts his enemy Hector's right to an honourable burial, and, like Odysseus in Sophocles' play, recognizes the claims of a shared humanity which surpasses individual grudges, in his case with his enemy's father Priam (*Il.* 24.485–551). Conversely, Ajax is never able to become reconciled with Odysseus, even in death, and Teucer rejects Odysseus' request to attend Ajax's funeral 'in case I offend the dead' (1395).

Sophocles, then, takes a longstanding concern with the role of the great individual and how he should behave in his community, and explores it through a character who pushes his desire to maintain personal honour to the extreme. As we have seen, Ajax's characteristics are inspired by the Homeric Achilles, yet the negative aspects of this type of heroism are foregrounded even more clearly. In order to understand this, it is vital to read *Ajax* in its cultural context, the democratic society of fifth-century Athens. Athenian ideology placed great emphasis on the idea that one should act for the common good, and that a good leader put the group interest above personal concerns. Nevertheless, aristocratic families remained powerful in the democracy. Their leisure and education gave them the ability to dominate institutions such as the assembly, while their wealth enabled them to succeed in public life through funding public benefits, or 'liturgies', including tragedy itself. The position of aristocrats was therefore a source of tension, since they were both essential to the operation of Athenian society and a threat to its democratic ethos. Heroes such as Ajax therefore provide an opportunity for an Athenian audience to reflect upon these tensions from the safe distance provided by the mythological setting.

In the play, we see how Ajax's brand of heroism is fundamentally incompatible with communal values. The mutually beneficial relationship that ought to exist between leaders and the people is expressed by the Chorus in the *parodos* (157–61):

> petty envies
>   cling
>     to great men
>
> and yet
>   without them
>   how could we
>     average men
> protect
>   our cities
>
> the best thing's
> to work in harmony
>   the weak
>         depending on
>            the strong
>   the strong
>     relying on
>       the weak

However, Ajax's excessive nature means that this sense of balance is never evidenced in the relationships we see onstage. Rather, Ajax expresses little concern for the impact that his decisions will have on those around him, though the audience can see that the potential consequences are severe. Thus Tecmessa fears that his death will mean that both she and Ajax's son will be passed as slaves to another of the Greeks and maltreated (496–9, see Roisman in this volume), while the Chorus fear for their own safety if they are associated with Ajax (254–6: see McCallum-Barry in this volume), and Teucer imagines that Ajax's death will lead to his own disgrace and exile when he reports the news to their father (1019–20). Despite being adult males (who in an Athenian context would be citizens), the Chorus seem to have little agency, and are dependent on Ajax for their wellbeing and status. From an Athenian perspective, Ajax's lack of regard for others in his community reinforces the dangers of an oligarchic or autocratic system. Admirable as Ajax may be for his strength, courage and single-mindedness, as a member of a *polis*, he is a liability.

The other side of Ajax's anti-social behaviour in life is his reconciliation with the wider community in death, since the play ends with the Greek camp united once more around the task of his burial. The focus on Ajax's burial site and tomb evokes a final aspect of Greek heroes, their role in cult as civic protectors. Greeks believed that the heroes of myth really did live once upon a time, and that they continued to have power after their death. This power was centred on the site of their tomb, or relics associated with their physical remains, and possession of a hero's cult site or his bones could offer protection or success in war. In myth, heroes are frequently given these powers in compensation for the suffering that they have had to endure in life, and this is a common pattern in tragedy. Ajax held a particularly important status for Athenians because he was one of the ten heroes who gave their names to the tribes of Athens, meaning that a tenth of the audience could believe themselves to have a special connection with him. He was honoured with a statue in the *agora*, the centre of Athenian public life, and received a festival at his shrine on the island of Salamis, which had been part of Athens' power-base since the sixth century. Thus the second part of the play, with its focus on Ajax's corpse and its burial, allows Ajax to transition from being a Homeric style hero to a cultic one, and explores how his negative qualities in life can be compensated for in death by his new powers. Teucer imagines that Ajax continues to have abiding power even as a corpse, and so advises Eurysaces to kneel and take his hand in supplication (1172–5). By suggesting this action, Teucer imagines Ajax's body as though it is already the hero-tomb that it will later occupy, and so a suitable location for suppliants to offer their prayers. The body offers shelter and protection to Tecmessa and Eurysaces, and Teucer envisages that a supernatural curse will befall anyone who tries to remove them from it (1175–9):

> If any man at all in all the army tries to drag you off his body, may he die in shame, may he lie unburied on the earth, and may he and all his family shrivel to their roots, cut down as I cut off this lock of hair from my own head.

Teucer's curse contains its own religious power, as does his ritual cutting of a lock of hair, an action which is both associated with funerary ritual (for example, Sophocles' *Electra* 52) and with religious dedication (as in *Iliad* 23.142–7, where Achilles had promised to dedicate a lock of his hair to the river-god Spercheios). Ajax's body effectively becomes a religious sanctuary which offers protection to the weak and needy, and Teucer's advice to Tecmessa and Eurysaces evokes the tradition that those persecuted could seek shelter at a shrine, and could not be forcibly removed without incurring divine punishment. In death Ajax is able to protect his family in a way that he was not capable of in life (when he rejected Tecmessa's appeals), just as he is able to become a force for reconciliation rather than division among the Greeks.

In conclusion, *Ajax* offers a fine example of tragedy's creative use of epic and the heroic tradition. In taking Iliadic characters and setting his play in the Greek camp at Troy, Sophocles makes a deliberate choice to engage with the *Iliad*, which by his day was established as the foundational text of Greek poetry and of the values and ethos of the heroic world. His portrayal of Ajax as a proud and stubborn hero reflects the central conflict of the *Iliad*, which also revolves around the question of what it will take to make a hero who has been slighted give up his anger. Yet by making Ajax outstrip even the Homeric Achilles in his stubbornness, and by focusing on the negative aspects of his pride, Sophocles invites his audience to question the role that powerful individuals play in society, and to consider how their greatness can be accommodated without social damage. Ajax is a troubling figure to a democratic Athenian audience, yet he is also admirable for his brilliance and his uncompromising adherence to his principles, and the play would not be successful if the audience did not regret his death, and empathize with the grief felt by Teucer, Tecmessa and the Chorus. The final part of the play suggests a partial solution to the difficult question of how a community can incorporate excessively powerful individuals, and after his death, Ajax's admirable qualities become more apparent, with even his enemy Odysseus offering warm words about his greatness. By hinting at Ajax's ongoing role in hero-cult, Sophocles not only anticipates his transformation into a protector of Athens, but also looks to cult as a mechanism for reconciling the power and the anger of the heroes, who in death can finally become socially beneficent figures.

3

# 'Shield of the Achaeans'

Sophie Mills

Ajax is the Greeks' best defensive warrior. In the *Iliad*, he is the *herkos Achaiōn*, often translated as 'bulwark of the Achaeans' (*Iliad* 3.229, 6.5, 7.211). The word *herkos* typically denotes the idea of defence against attack (*Iliad* 5.316), or a wall around a city (*Iliad* 15.567, Herodotus 7.191), or a house or a garden (Homer *Odyssey* 7.113, *Iliad* 5.90, 18.564). Ajax is therefore strongly identified with the supremely defensive weapon of his shield in the *Iliad*, where his shield is a weapon apparently like no other warrior's. It is huge, made of seven cow-hides with a layer of bronze around it (*Iliad* 7.220-23, 245-6) and even in the thick of battle, Ajax is recognizable because of it (*Iliad* 11.526-7). Whereas other Iliadic shields are described as 'round', or 'equally balanced' (*Iliad* 13.405, 20.274), Ajax is described as holding his shield as a wall or tower (*Iliad* 7.219. 11.485, 17.128), implying that it is large enough to cover his whole body,[1] and at *Iliad* 8.268-72 he actually sets it on the ground so that his half-brother Teucer can shoot deadly arrows at the Trojans while hiding behind the wall of Ajax's shield. This shield, unlike any other, was so heavy that Ajax himself sometimes needed attendants to carry it when he was tired (*Iliad* 13.709-11). The shield of Ajax is very different from the hoplite shield,[2] which was designed not only to protect the person holding it, but also to overlap with the shield of the next man, so that defence against the enemy could be carried out in community with others, rather than on the more individual basis which a shield like that of Ajax necessitates.

His shield is highly successful in defending him. Ajax is the only major hero on the Greeks' side to avoid being wounded in the Trojan War. Interestingly, apart from Agamemnon, Ajax is also the only major hero in the *Iliad* who receives no significant help from the gods on the battlefield,[3] apart from the fairly general encouragement Poseidon offers him and other Greeks, at *Iliad* 13.59-60. Of course Ajax is a superb warrior: notably, he takes on Hector (*Iliad* 7.181-312)[4] and gets the better of the fight as he knocks Hector out with a huge stone (cf. *Iliad* 14.410-39) so that Apollo must intervene to help Hector (*Iliad* 7.270-2) before heralds stop the combat. Hector will one day have his revenge, since his gift of a sword to him after the contest will be ultimately Ajax's means of suicide (*Iliad* 7.303; *Ajax* 660–66). But though he gets the better of Hector here, and is responsible for the deaths of many Trojans, the brilliance of Ajax as a warrior is essentially in defence,[5] and unlike some other heroes such as Diomedes or Achilles, Homer gives him no defined *aristeia* in which he is on the offensive. The function of the Iliadic Ajax is essentially as the army's shield rather than its spear.[6]

Ajax and Odysseus are a pair of natural opposites, even though in the course of the Trojan War they work together well at first, both in the *Iliad*, where Ajax even rescues Odysseus (*Iliad* 11.473–88), and in post-Iliadic Trojan War narratives. The pair are the two close associates of Agamemnon who have the crucial task of attempting to persuade Achilles to return to the fighting in *Iliad* 9. Here, Odysseus is characterized as outgoing, verbally fluent and mentally flexible, offering many different inducements to Achilles, even though the impetuous young hero considers Odysseus' verbal fluency tantamount to sheer dishonesty (*Iliad* 9.312–3). The speech of Ajax contrasts with that of Odysseus, being just eighteen lines long (*Iliad* 9.624–42) and direct, so that he seems less intelligent than Odysseus, but it is more effective on Achilles. In post-Iliadic tradition, when Achilles is killed by Paris, and the Greeks are trying to recover his body, the pair act as a team again: Odysseus fights off the Trojans while Ajax uses his great shield and spear to recover the body and get it to the ships.[7] When the two vie for possession of Achilles' armour after his death, early sources are unanimous that Odysseus wins it and Ajax kills himself, and Pindar, possibly reflecting earlier sources, states that Odysseus used his superior eloquence in a competition that he considers crooked, to persuade the Greeks to favour him over the less eloquent, but braver Ajax.[8] It is certain that Homer knew of the contest between them and certainly possible that he knew of a story in which Odysseus, with Athena's help, was able to seduce his listeners with brilliant talk that put Ajax in the shade: at any rate, Ajax's rage at Odysseus endures even in the underworld, and his innate lack of eloquence extends to a refusal to say anything at all to him when they meet there (*Odyssey* 11.543–67).

To be effective in protecting the warrior who uses it, a shield must be strong, hard and unyielding, an item that is essentially inwardly-directed as a protection to ward off the attacks that come from outside.[9] Sophocles' Ajax has many of the qualities of his pre-Sophoclean characterization, and there are many analogies and connections between the hero and his shield.[10] Ajax's singular shield has the qualities of great defensive value and effective protection, and so too Sophocles' Ajax is strong, tough and unyielding, excelling in defence and warding off outside attacks. He is the protector of Teucer, Tecmessa, his son and the Chorus, who specifically describe him as their shield (1213), while early in the play (155–61), they express their own dependence on him and (164–71) lament their own inability to protect him from the charges which they loyally consider slander cooked up by Odysseus.[11] But once a shield is broken, it is useless, and when the Chorus learn that the rumours they had feared are true, they fear that they will be vulnerable to stoning by the rest of the Greek army as punishment for their master's crimes (255; Teucer narrowly avoids this fate at 720–34). Later in the play, they regard Ajax's suicide as their own death (900–5). Ajax himself feels defenceless once he realizes what he has done (275–6) and his shame is compounded by his need to wail aloud (317–21, 333–9), though he had once believed that only cowards acted like this. To wail aloud so that others can hear is the antithesis of the strength and inwardly-directed defensive power[12] that has been central to Ajax's previous behaviour.

The defensive power of Ajax's shield comes at a cost of heaviness and a lack of flexibility. Protected by his shield, and as the Greeks' supreme defensive fighter, Ajax has acquired the belief that he is somehow invulnerable[13] and, like his shield, he is rigid in his relationship to the world, which, in the ever-changing, uncertainties of human life that the play expresses, proves to be his undoing.[14] Yielding is not in his nature,[15] and he is called 'iron-willed' (914, 929). By contrast, Odysseus shows a notable flexibility and sensitivity to ambiguity in his first speech. Although it is entirely clear that Ajax is the perpetrator of the crime against the flocks, since there is even a witness to what he has done, Odysseus expresses caution (21–3) in assuming that the doer of the deed is Ajax. His strongest expressions of certainty are those in which he allies himself with Athena, since the help of the gods is the only certainty a human being can have (86): Athena's emphasis on her power to humiliate Ajax and pleasure in doing so (66–7, 79) shows both the necessity of Odysseus' beliefs but also her darker side, since it is not until later that we learn the reasons for her apparently sadistic behaviour to Ajax here.[16] Odysseus is aware of the great gap between humans and gods, and will not fully endorse Athena's claim at 79 that it is sweet to mock enemies. By contrast, Ajax takes Athena's claim further, not merely by mocking supposed enemies but hideously abusing them, with sadistic physical punishments that he imagines he is inflicting on Odysseus: significantly, these punishments incorporate rigidity, so that he imagines that he has tied Odysseus to a pillar[17] and is whipping him (105–10; 239–42.) This is the deed of someone so convinced of his own rightness and his own invulnerability that he feels compelled to restore justice by punishing his opponents' supposed wickedness in dishonouring him (98). For such a person, those who failed to give him what he considers deserved are unquestionably wrong because it is impossible that he is wrong in his self-assessment, and thus punishment is the only option: 'just let them try to take away my armour now' (100). At 372–6, even in the depths of his degradation he is still sure that he is right and that Odysseus and the Atreidae deserve punishment, in spite of the disaster that overtook him when he tried to punish them before, and even though he knows Athena is his enemy (401–3).[18] Though he is an enemy of the gods, he keeps on requesting them to do his bidding, convinced that he is right, whereas all those around him see that he is not. In contrast to Odysseus' slightly wary, occasionally dissenting, but thoroughly respectful interactions with Athena as mortal to god (74–86), Ajax speaks to her as an equal (113, 116–17; cf. 774–6). Like Athena (cf. 133), he has a rigid sense of right and wrong and no pity on those he considers his enemies,[19] whereas at 121–6, Odysseus' awareness of human vulnerability leads him to pity, and a necessary flexibility, aware of change and uncertainty: Ajax may hate him, but human beings are feeble and their prosperity can change in a day, as Athena reminds Odysseus (127–33).[20] But Ajax, previously invulnerable thanks to his shield, imagines that he is invulnerable to the changing conditions of human life. We learn only halfway through the play[21] why Athena has punished him so cruelly, and it is because he considers himself too good to need help from the gods. When his father reminds him that victory in battle requires divine aid (765–9), he rejects its necessity for someone of his calibre, stating that even a worthless man can find victory with the gods' help (cf. 456), and he is too great to need them. Similarly, when Athena offered him help and encouragement, he rejected it: 'Lady, go stand with the other Greeks. The line won't break when I'm here' (774–5). Ajax's huge sense of his own worth is connected with his rigidity in considering categories in human life: one is worthy, like him, or base, and so he is deprived of any broader insight into his sufferings.

The shield that has made him invulnerable up until now could only ever give him temporary or partial invulnerability, given the impossibility of complete invulnerability for human beings. It has also had an isolating factor, as the shield that covers him alone, unlike a hoplite shield.[22] Ajax's shield protects him, and also separates him from others, and there is a loneliness and hardness about him.[23] At 348–50 and 362 he emphasizes that only the sailors in the Chorus are still his friends, since he has become alienated from the rest of the Greeks, though the Chorus too will later complain of his isolation (614, 620), and he expresses his isolation even more powerfully at 457–9, where he complains, 'It's obvious the gods hate me. The Greek army hates me too – and Troy, yes, and the plain of Troy', in contrast with his claims to perfectly self-sufficient power at 764–70, separated from gods and men alike by his supposed superiority on the battlefield. At 412–36, he calls upon inanimate nature and says 'you/will not see me/in this life again/a man who/it's no empty boast/to say/was once unequalled/in the army/of the greeks/who sailed to troy/but now/dishonoured/broken' (cf. 440). This claim is objectively true, yet it cannot be the whole story because of his appalling attempt to damage the Greek community: his relationship to them is different now, and honour cannot be given unreservedly to him. On the one hand, he has been deprived of honour, so he cannot go home to his father, but to redeem himself by attacking the Trojans in lone combat, which he is confident he can do, is no use because it would just gladden the Atreidae (466-9): because of his complete isolation and rigidity, his position in the Greek community is untenable. In contrast, Tecmessa has learned the need for flexibility through her own fall from royal honour to slavery, and now she is all too vulnerable when the shield provided her by Ajax has disappeared, in a speech (485-524) whose clear and multiple echoes of the Hector and Andromache scene in *Iliad* 6.391-493 underline the great differences between Hector and Ajax,[24] between the supremely community-minded Trojan whose care is for his family and the utterly alienated Ajax who cares only for himself, and even denies that he owes any service to the gods (589-90), a clearly mistaken claim in the light of his fate. She emphasizes remembrance and kindness, which demand a relationship with others, as the only true nobility (524) and they are the antithesis of the isolation that defines Ajax.[25] Ajax ignores her pleas and instead demands to see his son, but not with expressions of love, but rather (545-79) to exhort him to promote his own father's claims to glory, since he is named for the shield that is so central to Ajax's own identity (574-6.)

Even that shield, which protected him throughout the Trojan War, will fail him ultimately, since it will be the sword from his deadly enemy Hector that will have its revenge on him, as the inflexible man is impaled upon the inflexible sword. His isolation has been his undoing and it is sadly appropriate that he will kill himself in the ultimate isolated act of suicide where a person deliberately cuts himself off from his living community (906). It is also a violent end (917-19, 411-13) whose violence echoes the violence he wreaked on the flocks at the beginning of the play (231-44, 295-310).

In his great dissembling speech, Ajax does acknowledge the necessity of accepting change in the uncertainty of human existence and even uses himself as an example: 'I was strong once, as strong as toughened iron, but what she said – this woman – has undone me.' Tecmessa's appeals to pity have touched him, but he describes the sensation as being 'turned into a woman',[26] thus as something that he must harden himself against, shielding himself from the dangerous implications of such emotions.[27] All he can do is turn his sword upon himself now that his function of shield for the Greek army is over. He is right when he compares the natural processes of change to men's lives (670-6) but because his vision is much more fixed, a life in which neither enmity nor friendship are fixed and eternal (679–82) is impossible for him.[28]

In his final speech, he is still obsessed with the enemies who have done him wrong (815–20), making no attempt to examine his own part in his disaster, and, as before, he assumes that he can call on the gods to do his bidding. Here he invokes the Erinyes, asking them to punish the Atreidae to avenge his death. The man of the shield made of seven oxhides is unable to accept change and ambiguity even in death: later, Teucer will refuse to let Odysseus take part in his burial, fearing Ajax's anger even beyond the grave (1394), while quite some time after his death, the blood is still pouring out of his corpse (1412–13), symbolizing even now the continued rage of Ajax and his inability to imagine any other explanation of events than his own.

The structure of the play forces the audience as well to reject rigidity. It is full of action and intrigue, and gradually incorporates new strands of information through which we have to rethink our previous impressions. Notably, we only learn halfway through the play why Athena is punishing Ajax (758–75), which certainly helps to reframe her interaction with him at the start of the play. The middle section of the play is also full of suspense, especially for those familiar with the story that Ajax commits suicide: at 595, Ajax's harsh words as he exits hint that he is about to kill himself already.[29] When instead he reappears on stage and apparently recants, a joyous and relieved choral song (693–718)[30] is immediately followed by the revelation (741–2) that he must not be allowed to leave his tent on this day. The warning comes from Calchas, who is the mouthpiece of the gods, emphasizing the great gulf between gods and men to which Ajax wrongly thinks that he is invulnerable.

The interactions between Teucer, the Atreidae and Odysseus in the last part of the play offer us a many-faceted and complex account of the Greek army's relationship to Ajax, in which no single perspective is the full story. Menelaus is right to be hostile to Ajax, because of his attempt to destroy his fellow Greeks (1045–60), and yet he is unsympathetic to deny burial to a dead and now vulnerable enemy (1065–70, 1130–1): in fact, he resembles Ajax in seeking a greater degree of control than a human being can have.[31] Ajax had rendered many great services to the Greeks: had he not done, he would not even have been in contention for the prize of Achilles' armour, and this too must be recognized. No less than Ajax, Menelaus divides humans into the base and the worthy, but the play shows clearly that such absolute judgements are impossible.[32] Equally, his insistence that the success of cities and armies depends on respect for the law (1073–6) is reasonable. Agamemnon's arguments similarly balance reasonable arguments and their opposite: he too judges others through an appeal to a fixed nature,[33] considering Teucer's arguments worthless because he is a mere captive slave's son (1225–30), calling him 'a nobody standing up for a nobody'. Whatever else Ajax is, he is certainly not a nobody.[34] Teucer had claimed – again, a surprising twist – that the Greeks' vote to award the arms of Achilles to Odysseus was fraudulent (1135–6): Sophocles gives no hint as to whether we should believe him, but if it is not true, then Agamemnon is right to say that the majority vote ought to be respected (1243–6). Right until Odysseus brings the argument to a halt, the audience is made to engage with multiple, shifting perspectives.

Ajax is the son of Telamon: Odysseus is described as Sisyphus' son (191), but also as Laertes' son (101, 381, 1394), and he is not the tricky, deceitful Odysseus, whose brilliant eloquence has its shadow side of deception and dishonesty, but the one who can do the sort of adaptive thinking that Ajax cannot. Similarly, for all the terrible acts that he has performed, and though Ajax hates him (20), in Odysseus' eyes, Ajax remains 'noble' in spite of it all (1355), a neat recognition of the two opposites in human life, change and certainty, and also a paradoxical endorsement of the constancy that is elsewhere questioned in the play. Odysseus can acknowledge that both are true, while Ajax kills himself in inability to acknowledge such ambiguities. He is like the metal that is unable to bend but shatters under too much pressure.

In his hardness, Ajax resembles his grim father Telamon, of whose insults his bastard son Teucer is afraid (1010–18): with Ajax dead, Teucer is scared to go home and scared to stay among so many enemies. In this, too, Ajax has finally failed as a shield for him. For Ajax there is a fixed line of heroic nature that connects his father, himself and his son, and part of his shame is because he has broken that line by his failure to repeat his father's success in winning the supreme prize of valour (434–48, 462–5). Again, there is an element of resistance to change here that is fundamentally opposed to the changeable conditions of human life. Ajax had hoped to reduplicate his father's heroic brilliance and then, by naming his son Eurysaces after his shield (574–5), to reduplicate his own identity through his son. At 575–6, Ajax invites his son to hold this shield, his only inheritance from his father, a huge and unmanageable burden for such a young child.[35] In his relationship with his son no less than in his other relationships, Ajax is hard and isolated from ordinary human relations. Again, Sophocles invokes the Iliadic Hector to underline Ajax's deficiencies as a member of a family and a community. While Hector hopes for his son to be even more glorious than he is (*Iliad* 6.479–81), Ajax hopes merely that he will be luckier (550). And whereas Hector acknowledges his little son's fear of his helmet and comforts him (*Iliad* 6.472–4), Ajax states that if this infant is his true-born son, he will not mind looking on the bloodied corpses of animals (545–7) and that he must at once be broken in like a young horse to his father's harsh ways and moulded to be just like him in nature (548–9).³⁶ Even when he briefly acknowledges Eurysaces' sweet youth and innocence (554–5), he claims that life is sweetest when one lacks sense until one comes to know joy or pain, again preferring isolation from the world to entering into it.

While it might seem that Ajax is condemning his son to an unlucky life like his own, if he must follow the hard, unyielding pattern of reacting to life's circumstances that have done his father no good at all, there is a chance that his father's prayer for greater luck for him will be answered. At 1168–81, Teucer urges him to come and take hold of his father's body as a suppliant to guard it from the Greek army. In effect, he is to be his shield, not of bronze and oxhide but one of flesh and blood, of a son's care for his father and a suppliant's prayers to the gods.³⁷ In the final action of the play the child is enjoined by Teucer to lay loving (1410) hands on his father and help his uncle with the corpse. Many commentators (including Richard Seaford and Laura Swift in this volume)³⁸ have noted that Sophocles is hinting at the future cult of Ajax at Athens, where he will be honoured as one of the ten eponymous heroes of Athens. It is generally thought that Eurysaces was worshipped at Athens (in the district of Melite) earlier than Ajax (whose Salaminian ties always remained strong), and that Ajax was joined with his son only later, perhaps during Athens' long dispute with its neighbour Megara in the sixth century over the possession of Salamis. If this is right, then the image of the son's care for his father at the end of Sophocles' play finds an analogue with Ajax's gradual assimilation into Athenian cult and society via Eurysaces.³⁹ Though the end of the play is sombre for Ajax and his family, life's changes will continue and eventually, he will be restored to his shield-like persona as an honoured hero of Athens and the rest of the Greeks, summoned with Telamon to their aid at the Battle of Salamis in 480 BCE and even thanked for his services after the battle, with the dedication to him of a captured foreign warship.⁴⁰

## Notes

1 Mueller (2016) 135–6 notes the specialness of Ajax's weapon, which is given its own 'biography'.
2 Though note 575–6 in which Eurysaces is enjoined to hold it by its handle (*porpax*), which may suggest that Sophocles is conflating Homeric and hoplite shields: Mueller (2016) 148; Finglass (2011) 307.
3 And his shield is made by a man (*Iliad* 7.220), not (like Achilles', 19.368) a god: Mueller (2016) 136.
4 On the centrality of his shield in this fight see Mueller (2016) 137–8 who notes that it is considerably more effective than Hector's.

5 For example, *Iliad* 15.730-45, 16.358-63, 17.115-39; also the two similes at *Iliad* 11.548-66 which emphasize his dogged determination never to give way to attackers.
6 Trapp (1961) 273 argues for a more active and intelligent Ajax than commentators typically conceive of, citing *Iliad* 6.5-11, 12.330-471, 14.402-41, 15.674-746, but even so, the general impression that emerges from Homer is that of a strong, relatively reticent defender, in contrast to the portrayals of warriors like Achilles or Odysseus: Mueller (2016) 136.
7 Arctinus' *Aethiopis* fragment 3: Davis (1989) 56-7.
8 Pindar *Nemean Ode* 8.25-34 with Davis (1989) 57-8. The contrast between the two is worked out in detail in Ovid *Metamorphoses* 13.1-398. Other earlier sources for Odysseus' victory over Ajax include Lesches *Little Iliad* fragment 2 who connects the victory with Athena's intervention (cf. *Odyssey* 11.547) and refers to the slaughter of the cattle: Davis (1989) 61-3. Stories of Ajax including his suicide were popular in art long before Sophocles: Finglass (2011) 26-33.
9 Mueller (2016) 135 describes it as Ajax's 'second skin' that 'extends the natural limits of Ajax's biological agency'.
10 Shield and warriors' nature are often connected, though more commonly via the designs on their shields: Corradi (2011)
11 For their dependent relationship with Ajax, see also 134-40, 245-53, 1211-16: Hesk (2003) 48-9.
12 While the eloquent Odysseus knows what to say to have a persuasive effect on those around him, directing his words outwards, Ajax's relative inability at speaking may be seen as analogous with his defensive prowess: see also Segal (1981) 133-8.
13 His shield prevents him from being wounded but isolates him so that he acquires a psychological wound which will cause him to wound himself: Hesk (2003) 29.
14 Nielsen (1978) 24 who notes that the code by which Ajax lives matches his shield, as 'substantial invincible and changeless'.
15 To yield is the ultimate failure in defence. Ajax, like many Sophoclean heroes, is commanded, and refuses, to yield (371, 667, 670): Knox (1964) 17.
16 In particular in the exchange between them, 90-115, where she pretends to be his ally and lures him into a fantasy about physical punishment of Odysseus.
17 Itself an analogy for his towering shield. On Ajax the tower, compare *Iliad* 7.219, 11.485 *Odyssey* 11.556; Sophocles *Ajax* 159: Hesk (2003) 28-9.
18 Similarly, at 450-5 he recognizes Athena's role in bringing him down just as he was about to take revenge on the Atreidae, but still believes in his own rightness.
19 Nielsen (1978) 22.
20 Burian (2012) 72-3.
21 This information is placed after the great speech in which he pretends to endorse a more Odysseus-like relationship to the world: evidently, he has

gained no new insights from his terrible experiences. The complexities of Ajax's speech here, though it is clear from his subsequent actions that it cannot ultimately represent his thinking, lie outside this paper: see Lardinois (2006) 213–23; Hesk (2003) 74–95; Finglass (2011) 328–9.

22 Mueller (2016) 139, commenting on the Iliadic Ajax, states 'The *sakos* almost supernaturally extends Ajax's human agency, allowing him to enact the role – and to assume the identity – of the *herkos Achaiōn* (something he would not be able to do without his shield)' but, as she goes on to say, 'the feeling of being unbounded cannot last forever'.

23 The play emphasizes Ajax's aloneness: e.g. 29, 45–7, 294, 348–9, 359, 461, 467, 657, 796, 1276, 1283. See also Seaford in this volume. On the isolation of the hero that is typical in Sophocles, see Knox (1964) 32–4.

24 Compare especially *Ajax* 496–505 with *Iliad* 6.458–65: Reinhardt (1979) 20–22; Burian (2012) 75–7; Schein (2012) 429–31.

25 On the importance of reciprocity in the play see Hesk (2003) 48–9.

26 *Ajax* 651, '*ethēlunthēn*': this phrase is not directly represented in Stuttard's translation.

27 Heiden (1993) 146 suggests that the very practice of acting in Athens was a voluntarily accepted humbling, a public recognition of one's own fragile mortality which could encourage a feeling of solidarity among the Athenians, to cultivate self-criticism, to facilitate an honest flexibility in the conduct of civic business – all things that a character like Ajax cannot do.

28 It is typical of the Sophoclean hero to wish to transcend the conditions of time, an impossible task given human limitation: Knox (1964) 26–7.

29 Mueller (2016) 21.

30 Those familiar with Ajax's story or Sophocles' techniques would doubtless know that their joy is likely to be short-lived and be in suspense as to what will really happen.

31 Hesk (2003) 110–11.

32 His claim at 1089, that he was once the attacker but now it is his turn to glory is a kind of perversion of the natural processes of change to which Odysseus gives proper expression, and is deeply problematic, as the Chorus note, 1091.

33 Teucer refutes Agamemnon's similar reliance on such a view of the world by pointing out his own barbarian ancestry and the unsavoury history of the house of Atreus, 1290–9.

34 Teucer uses the authority of broadly Iliadic material to refute such claims (1270–85); compare *Iliad* 15.415–515, 9.241–3, 16.123–4.

35 I take it that the shield is an actual prop on stage: though for some scholars the staging problems are insurmountable, the relationship of the young child with the huge, grim shield would have great visual power. I agree with Mueller that it is probably taken off at 596, since there is no reason for Ajax to bring it on for his suicide speech, when the sword demands the audience's full focus. But it is an attractive idea that it returns on stage at some point and forms a bier for Ajax: Mueller (2016) 141, 152–3.

36 Hesk (2003) 70–1.

37 Cf. Heiden (1993) 159.
38 Burian (1972); Henrichs (1993); Mueller (2016) 149–53 among others.
39 Pausanias 1.35.3, Plutarch *Solon* 10: Kearns (1989) 81–2, 141–2; Mueller (2016) 147–50.
40 Herodotus 8.64, 121: Hesk (2003) 21–3.

4

# The Power of Ajax's Sword

Rosie Wyles[1]

The power of Ajax's sword within Sophocles' tragedy is indisputable. The dramatic action hinges on this prop: without it, there would be no nocturnal slaughter, no crisis and no suicide. The sword exerts a 'chilling and powerful stage-presence' in the suicide scene affecting not only the spectators but perhaps even Ajax himself.[2] The culmination of the prop's power is expressed in Ajax's action of throwing himself upon it. The impact of this stage moment was already noted within antiquity (recorded in scholarly notes, known as *scholia*); one ancient commentator reflects that Sophocles innovated in the staging of this scene and muses that perhaps the playwright wished to 'shock' through it.[3] Another ancient commentator tells us that the actor Timotheus of Zacynthos enjoyed particular fame for the skills he displayed enacting this scene, gaining the nickname 'Slayer' (*sphageus*, the term used by Ajax to describe the sword).[4] This claim about Timotheus points to the perceived dramatic impact of the scene, its prominence in performance, and the extraordinary status of its central prop (which, the nickname suggests, became an iconic symbol of the play's power). A proper understanding of Sophocles' *Ajax* therefore depends on an appreciation of the sword's significance. The following discussion includes insights from the work of Oliver Taplin, Charles Segal and Melissa Mueller, and pushes some aspects of their analyses further to enrich our understanding of this prop's power.[5] The first section summarizes the sword's four symbolic associations which are then explored further in the following sections.

## 1. The Sword's evolving symbolism

Ajax's sword demonstrates the capacity for props in ancient Greek drama to gain multiple and complex meanings during a production. The verbal references to the sword in the play reveal the symbolism constructed for it. Even before the prop is visible to the audience, descriptions of it prime the spectators to view it in a certain way and begin to establish its significance within the play. The sword may not have been onstage before the 'deception speech' episode at line 646 (though scholars have suggested that it could have been visible when Athena forces Odysseus to look at Ajax or when Tecmessa opens the doors at the Chorus' request), but multiple verbal references in the first 325 lines of the play forge its association with Ajax's regrettable acts the night before.[6] Athena tells us that his hands have 'slaughtered with the sword' (lines 9–10),[7] Odysseus reports that Ajax was seen by a scout 'rushing alone across the plain with dripping sword' (lines 29–31) and Athena offers graphic details of Ajax hacking apart beasts (lines 50–8), before later asking Ajax whether he stained his sword with the blood of the Argive army (lines 94–5). Further comments from the Chorus about the animals killed with flashing iron (line 147) and slaughtered with dark blades (lines 229–32) as well as the explicit details in Tecmessa's account of Ajax's actions – his butchering of the animals (lines 235–9 and 295–300), his departure from the tent with his 'two-edged sword' (lines 285–7), and the reference again to beasts 'slaughtered by the iron' (323–5) – reinforce the symbolic association of the prop with these events. The verbal references collectively load the sword with meaning and enforce its intimate connection with the slaughter of the beasts and foiled attack on the Argives.

A key element to the power of the sword as a prop in *Ajax*, however, is the way in which its symbolism gradually shifts and becomes more complex as the play unfolds. In Ajax's 'deception speech' (beginning at 646), two further verbal references invite the audience to reinterpret the prop (now present onstage), deepening the layers to its symbolic meaning. Firstly, Ajax's comparison of his earlier attitude to 'iron when it has been dipped' (line 651) prompts a symbolic association between the hero and this prop (since the iron-dipping process refers to metal working, and by extension the sword). Then in a more direct reference to it, Ajax tells us that he will bury his sword which is 'most hostile' of all weapons (line 659) and that no good has come to him since receiving it as a gift from Hector (lines 660–3). Both details add further complexity to the sword's symbolism. While before this scene the sword had been symbolically linked to past violence, the ambiguity of Ajax's description of it as 'most hostile' and his desire to bury it associate the prop with current or future danger. The revelation of this sword's earlier history (i.e. beyond the events of the night before) creates additional meaning, evoking the duel between Hector and Ajax (*Iliad* 7. 206–312) and establishing further disquiet from its paradoxical status as a 'gift' from an enemy. Although Ajax refers to it as 'my sword' (line 659), the audience is made aware just lines later of the previous owner and his extreme hostility (line 662). From the moment that Ajax alludes to the sword's origin, it becomes a 'Hector-haunted' prop for the audience; an association asserted twice more: in Ajax's suicide speech (lines 817–820) and then by Teucer after Ajax's death (line 1027).[8] Finally, the sword gains the symbolic status of 'agent' or 'actor' since it is named first by Ajax as 'slayer' (*sphageus*, line 815) and then by Teucer as 'killer' (*phoneus*, line 1027); these terms bestow the prop with the characteristics of 'human agency' pushing perceptions of its capabilities beyond the boundaries of a mere 'object'.[9] The idea of its agency is furthered by Ajax using the term 'kindly disposed' (normally applied to people, line 822) and Tecmessa's reference to it testifying (as a human might) that Ajax killed himself (lines 905–7).[10] Ajax's sword thus gains four symbolic associations in the play, coming to represent: Ajax's shameful acts, Ajax as a hero, Hector, and the power of objects. These associations, and their intersection with the drama's themes, are explored further below.

## 2. The Sword as symbolic representative of Ajax

The complex network of symbolic associations, outlined above, communicates (with growing intensity as the play progresses) that the sword is intricately bound up with Ajax's fate. This finds its ultimate expression in the literal intertwining of the two as the sword pierces through Ajax. An arresting image of Ajax impaled by his sword (used to illustrate the cover of this book) is depicted by the Brygos Painter in the interior of one of his red-figure cups, dated to around 490 BC and now in the Getty museum (86.AE.286).

The extent to which the audience saw a stage image equivalent of the depiction on the cup is uncertain. The precise logistics of the staging of Ajax's suicide, and whether the audience could see the sword, have been much debated by scholars and remain contentious.[11] While the audience may not have seen the suicide take place, the text of the play certainly puts emphasis on the image of Ajax being pierced through. Ajax himself anticipates the effect of his action, describing how he will leap 'piercing through' his side with the sword (line 834), Tecmessa draws further attention to the way in which he is 'folded round' the sword (line 865), and Teucer, finally and most graphically, reinforces the idea of the two being intertwined as he asks how he can tear Ajax away from the point of the sword (lines 1024–5). These references may draw attention to what the audience can see onstage. Tecmessa's use of a deictic at line 907 ('*this* sword', implying a gesture towards the object) could reinforce the case for the sword being visible before she covers the body, at lines 915–19, and after it is uncovered at Teucer's request, lines 1003–5.[12] Alternatively, and at the very least, the verbal references may have evoked images from art (such as the Brygos cup) in the minds of the audience.

The idea of Ajax and the sword being one, as encapsulated by this image, is in fact established from the very beginning of the play. In Athena's opening speech, the goddess uses a compound adjective to describe Ajax's hands as 'sword-slaying' (i.e. they slay with a sword, line 10). The effect is to blur the lines between Ajax and his weapon. It is an impression which continues to be reinforced through the opening scenes as Ajax's hands and his sword are interchangeably described as blood-stained (hands: lines 43, 453; sword: line 95) and as the instruments of killing (sword: lines 147, 231, 325; hands: lines 57, 115, 219, 232). The sword as a prop is closely aligned to the protagonist through this verbal equation. This effect of merging between protagonist and prop is furthered, as noted earlier, through Ajax's description of himself as being hard like dipped iron (lines 650–2). He volunteers this comparison in his 'deception speech' in the context of a claim to have been softened and to have changed his views. The sincerity of his speech has been much debated by scholars, with some arguing that Ajax speaks in earnest, others that he is deliberately deceptive, and yet others suggesting that he unintentionally misleads his audience.[13] The issue of whether his claim to have changed is genuine or not, however, does not affect the veracity or symbolic potency of his description of his past self as being like iron. The subsequent events demonstrate that Ajax and his sword are inextricably bound together (so either his claim to have been softened was insincere or it was deluded). The 'doublespeak' of the 'deception speech' hints at this proleptically as Ajax describes burying the sword and yet he will be the one who is (eventually) buried.[14] Charles Segal has argued that in the suicide scene the sword, as a paradigm for persistency in hatred, becomes a symbol of Ajax's rigidity and his refusal to change (in contrast to the opposite approach taken by Tecmessa and embodied in her soft enveloping cloak).[15] The sword, in the end, represents Ajax, according to Segal's interpretation.

## 3. The Sword as symbolic representative of Hector

Melissa Mueller, on the other hand, has made a persuasive case for interpreting the sword as a symbolic representation of Hector.[16] She applies the anthropological concept of 'distributed personhood' to the prop and argues that it takes on Hector's character (as its previous owner), allowing him to be metonymically present onstage. This enables Mueller to offer a fresh interpretation of the 'deception speech' which acknowledges the importance of the prop's presence to the delivery of that speech and its ability to inflect Ajax's decision making. The sword, Mueller argues, is responsible for turning Ajax's innocent words into 'doublespeak' as the audience hears the sword's voice undermining his words. So, while Ajax does not intend to kill himself when he makes the 'deception speech', the prop is, according to Mueller, powerful enough to change his mind subsequently. When it comes to the suicide scene, Hector's presence is conjured, Mueller argues, through Ajax's personifying use of masculine forms (such as 'slayer'). This constructs the suicide as a reworking of the earlier Homeric duel between Hector and Ajax. Mueller goes on to suggest that while in the Homeric duel Hector uses *words* to cheat Ajax of his victory, this time it is the 'Hector-haunted' weapon which seems to dictate Ajax's actions. After Ajax's death, all of this is spelt out by Teucer's unambiguous interpretation of events (line 1027): 'Do you see how in the end Hector even in death was to be your killer?'

A further effect of the sword's agency, Mueller argues, is that it blurs the line between human and object in the play. We can add to Mueller's argument by returning to the tradition about Timotheus as it points to the importance and prominence of this effect within the play. It is revealing that the nickname he gains from acting Ajax's suicide scene effectively is not 'Ajax' but is instead 'Slayer' (*sphageus*). The choice of nickname highlights the blurring of the line between human and object in the play since it was this term (*sphageus*) which bestowed human agency onto the prop in performance. The tradition therefore celebrates not only the actor but also a key feature of the tragedy's dramatic effect generated from Sophocles' handling of props. A further aspect of the performance which may have contributed to this blurring effect is the likely use of a dummy to represent Ajax's corpse; this 'demonstrates an aggressive substitution, as an actor is replaced by a stage property' and it offers another example of the line between object and human being dissolved.[17] The blurring of this line, as well as the ability for the prop to shift meaning (at one point it seems to represent Ajax and yet at another it symbolizes Hector) reflects one of the central themes in the tragedy: that of change and mutability.

We can also take the argument further by pursuing the question of how the sword attains its agency as this has implications both for the interpretation of the play and our understanding of props in general. While earlier descriptions of the sword in the play already seem to blur the line between object and human, it is Ajax himself who creates the symbolic association with Hector by twice mentioning that it was a gift from him (first in the 'deception speech' and later in the suicide speech). This demonstrates Ajax's utter incompetence in using the 'language of costume'. I have argued elsewhere that pieces of costume or props, when endowed with certain symbolic meanings, have the ability to 'determine' the fate of a character in a drama.[18] In light of this, Ajax's choice to bring out the sword's association with his enemy Hector is fatal. He mistakenly thinks that he can resolve, or 'neutralise', the sword's hostility through action (by burying it), but in fact within the dramatic frame the way in which a prop's power can be transformed is through offering a fresh interpretation of it (a competing symbolism). If we look at Aeschylus' *Suppliant Women*, a play which was staged years before *Ajax*, we are offered an example of a female chorus who demonstrate complete control over their costume and an awareness of the importance of manipulating its symbolic meaning through words. In that play, another male character (the Argive King Pelasgus) is shown, like Ajax, to lack an understanding of how costume and its symbolism work.[19] The consequences for Pelasgus are ultimately fatal (he died in a subsequent part of the now lost trilogy). It seems possible therefore that one of the effects of Ajax's ill-conceived references to the sword's former owner would be to generate tragic *pathos* amongst the audience who would, from their previous experience in the theatre, be fully aware of the dangers of creating such symbolic associations.

## 4. The Sword's Homeric power

Yet are Ajax's articulations about the sword within his control? The idea that the sword has the capability to influence the words and behaviour of those around it, is worth exploring further. It seems possible that the Homeric 'resonances' in the text could be understood to be generated from the sword. Ajax's, and then Teucer's, reference to the sword's origin make its status as an object belonging to, or carried over from, Homeric epic explicit. Even before these articulations, however, its presence (whether narrated or onstage) seems to be able to impose Homeric behaviour on those around it. The first example is offered by Tecmessa's account of Ajax leaving the tent in the night (lines 285–94):

> Since you have a share in it, you shall learn everything that happened. At dead of night, when the evening lamps no longer burned, he took his two-edged sword and made as though to start out, for no reason. And I objected, saying, 'What are you doing, Ajax? Why are you starting on this expedition unbidden, when you have not been summoned by messengers nor heard any trumpet? Why, now all the army is asleep!' But the words he spoke to me were few and hackneyed: 'Woman, silence makes a woman beautiful.' Hearing this, I ceased, and he sped off alone.

Tecmessa offers advice on military affairs and is told by Ajax to be quiet. There are broad resonances with the Homeric scene in *Iliad* 6 in which

Andromache too offers military advice (lines 433–9) but is ultimately silenced by being sent back to her loom and told to leave war to men (lines 490–3). The parallels with *Iliad* 6 continue in the onstage interactions, as scholars have noted, between Tecmessa and Ajax (lines 485–505; as she, like Andromache, begs him not to leave her a widow) and then between Ajax and Eurysaces (lines 545–77; speculating on his son's future, compared to Hector and Astyanax).[20] If the sword is present onstage during these interactions, then perhaps we should adjust the way in which we understand this engagement with Homer. Rather than thinking about such allusions as a literary game played between Sophocles and the audience, we might consider the possibility that in performance it is the prop that is understood to exert its Homeric influence over those in its vicinity, resulting in characters framing their responses through the lens of the *Iliad*. If so, then this lays the ground for the later scenes in which the sword's past is acknowledged explicitly and the consequences of a more malign aspect to its influence can be witnessed as the allusions shift from *Iliad* 6 to *Iliad* 7 (and the reworking of the duel, resulting in Ajax's death).

## 5. The Sword and the contest of arms

The contest over Achilles' arms is as important a spectre from the past in the play as episodes from the *Iliad* as it offers a further context for understanding the sword's significance. The decision to award Odysseus the armour of Achilles and Ajax's insistence that there had been foul play in this contest is presented by some characters as the beginning of all the trouble. Even though this event occurred before the beginning of the play's action, it is repeatedly brought into view through characters' references to it; so, for example, it is mentioned by Athena (41), Ajax (obliquely 572–7), Teucer (1135), Agamemnon (1239–45), and Odysseus (1336–7). The final reference is particularly telling since Odysseus' turn of phrase about gaining Achilles' weapons echoes Ajax's comment about receiving the sword from Hector. Odysseus says (lines 1336–7): 'For me too he [Ajax] was once my chief enemy in the army, *ever since* I became the owner of the arms of Achilles'. Earlier Ajax had said (lines 661–2): '*For since* I received this gift from Hector, the deadliest of my enemies, never have I had any good thing from the Argives'. The italicized terms in the translation of these lines are expressed using the same phrase in Greek. This sets up an equivalence between the two events: Ajax receiving the sword from Hector, and Odysseus gaining the arms of Achilles. This has implications for the sword's symbolism. On the surface, Ajax's victory against Hector resulted in the reward and recognition which he was subsequently denied by the outcome of the contest of the arms. Yet gaining the sword will prove to be just as destructive to Ajax as not gaining the arms of Achilles. By equating the two episodes in these terms, Sophocles enables the sword to become symbolically associated with Ajax's failure in the contest of arms. This doubling of the sword's meaning (representing both the false victory against Hector, as well as the failure in the contest of the arms) may be extended further by recognizing that beyond its associations with the duel or contest, the sword is also an instrument performing Athena's will. This framing of it becomes clear from the herald's report of Calchas' prophecy (lines 748–83) which reveals that the ultimate force determining events is not Hector's hostility from beyond the grave or Ajax's grievance about the contest, but Athena's anger over Ajax's boasts about winning glory for himself. Ajax's suicide using the sword represents the ultimate expression of Athena's anger. This network of symbolic associations (the duel, the contest, Athena's will – all bound together in the symbol of the sword) enables this prop to take on a complex meaning and pushes its dramatic purpose far beyond the play's action.

## 6. The Sword in Athenian context

Toph Marshall, in his discussion of Sophocles' stagecraft, suggests that too many props can diffuse the intended effect and gives the example of *Ajax*, noting that alongside Ajax's sword, there is also his whip, perhaps his shield, and Tecmessa's veil.[21] The competing attention of other props onstage, however, is not necessarily problematic and can even be helpful in creating meaning through juxtaposition. Charles Segal, for example, brings out the symbolism of Ajax's sword very effectively by considering it alongside Tecmessa's cloak/veil.[22] Melissa Mueller defines the symbolism of the sword in part by comparing it to the shield; concluding that the sword belongs to the epic past whereas the shield is a 'future-focused weapon' (because of its link to cult in Athens).[23] Another prop, not considered by these scholars, which might further define the sword's symbolism is Teucer's bow and arrows. While the text of the play does not explicitly confirm the inclusion of Teucer's bow as a prop, his status as an archer gains special attention, and denigration, in his debate with Menelaus (lines 1120–4). This verbal attack would have been more effective in performance, if Teucer were carrying his bow. What are the implications of this prop? While Teucer may win some of the audience's empathy as he argues that Ajax deserves burial, in terms of weaponry, the audience would identify with Ajax over Teucer.[24] The sword may belong to the epic past but it was also a feature of the Athenian present forming a part of a hoplite's armour.

If we re-visit Teucer's speech over Ajax's uncovered body and the attention which he gives the sword: 'How shall I tug you from the gleaming point of this cruel sword? What a killer has extinguished your life, wretched man!' (lines 1024–7), then the scene becomes far more impactful if Teucer has his bow with him. This would draw attention to his lack of experience with swords and by extension invite the audience, or some of them at least, to reflect on their own expertise by comparison. If we go further back in the action of the play, then Ajax's speculation about how the sword would strike him (lines 823–4) and Tecmessa's description of the wound (lines 918–19) take on a different resonance when we consider the experience of spectators who had fought as hoplites for Athens. The sword, however, could also have resonated beyond the personal experience of individual soldiers, since the hoplite's armour had likely become, by the time of *Ajax*, a prominent symbol of broader Athenian identity. The demand, usually assumed to date to the 440s, for Athenian allies to send a cow and a 'panoply' (a hoplite's full suit of armour which included a sword) to be offered to Athena at the Greater Panathenaea festival would have heightened the symbolic status of these objects for Athenians.[25] It would also have extended the Athenian associations of the sword beyond the hoplites who owned one (and fought with it on behalf of Athens) to all Athenians who were now in a sense recipients of such weapons, through Athena, from the city's allies.

This Athenian civic association complicates the potential emotional response of the audience to the sword within the play since this prop is presented as far from innocent. In the first place, it is closely associated with Ajax's mad rampage against his fellow Greeks which engenders further violence (as those in the camp are reported to have unsheathed their swords at Teucer's arrival, lines 729–30) and then it becomes the instrument of his own death, creating further disputes amongst the Greeks. The sword is likely to have evoked a complex and ambiguous response from the audience since within the context of the play it is presented as deeply problematic, while in their own life it perhaps carried more positive connotations as part of their civic identity. The response is further complicated by the Chorus' reflection that the man who showed Greeks how to join in war with hateful weapons should have died first (1194–7). This sentiment extends the negative view of the sword in the play to weapons in general and so dissolves the distinction between past and present, appearing (to some of the audience perhaps) to be just as pertinent to the Athenian present as to the Trojan war.[26] These lines prevent the sword from being comfortably relegated to the past. The sword prop, we might therefore conclude, presents the Athenian audience with a complex view of both the past and their present. This 'double vision' of the sword (as past and present) is consistent with its ability to represent both

Ajax and Hector at different times in the play's action and it also correlates with the ambiguous handling of other themes within the tragedy (such as, for example, the ever-shifting view of friendship and enmity which, even at the end, is not resolved).[27]

## Conclusion

The complexity of the sword's symbolism within *Ajax* is testament both to Sophocles' skill as a playwright and the remarkable dramatic potential of props in ancient Greek tragedy in general. The sword's significance within the play shifts as the action unfolds but the importance of this prop is made clear from the beginning. This primes the audience to pay attention to the sword which (as some may already anticipate from their familiarity with the myth) will be the instrument of Ajax's suicide. Audience members with a heightened awareness of the prop's destined end would presumably have appreciated Sophocles' skill in developing a highly complex symbolism for the sword along the way. The spectators in the audience might, of course, have had different views of the prop's meaning and, rather like the scholars who write about the play now, could have prized different aspects of its symbolism. The power of the prop, however, is that it allows for this multiplicity of meanings without losing any of its dramatic force within the play.

## Notes

1 I am grateful to David Stuttard for his invitation to contribute this chapter and for his comments on it.
2 The quotation is from Segal (1980–1) 127; for the idea of the prop affecting Ajax's behaviour see Mueller (2016) 15–41, discussed further below. I follow both Segal and Mueller in the assumption that the same sword was used throughout the play.
3 Σ 815 in Falkner (2002) 355.
4 Σ 864a in Christodoulou (1977); I owe both *scholia* references to Mueller (2016) 17 and 30.
5 Taplin (1978) 85–8, Segal (1980–1), and Mueller (2016) 15–41.
6 Taplin (1989) 85 and Segal (1980–1) 127 for Odysseus viewing it; by contrast, Mueller (2016) 20 suggests line 346 (Tecmessa opening door).
7 All translations are from Lloyd-Jones (1994) unless otherwise stated.
8 'Hector-haunted' Mueller (2016) 31; Teucer may elaborate further on this association in lines 1028–39, but some scholars doubt the authenticity of these lines, see for example Finglass (2011) *ad loc.*

9 Mueller (2016) explores the concept in full.
10 Taplin (1989) 86 makes the point about 'kindly disposed'.
11 There is an entire volume dedicated to the topic: Most and Ozbek (2015). Finglass (2011) p. 377–9 summarizes the scholarship; he argues (there and at Finglass (2015)) that the sword is not visible and that the suicide takes place in the *skene* building, p. 376. Taplin (1989) 86 suggests that the sword blade is visible to the audience.
12 Though Finglass (2015) argues against this assumption for the deictics at 828 and 834.
13 For an overview of the scholarship see Garvie (1998) 184–6. Finglass (2011) nn. 646–92 pp. 328–9.
14 Mueller (2016) 29.
15 Segal (1980–1) 127–9.
16 Mueller (2016) 15–30.
17 Marshall (2012) 194. Finglass (2011) 376 on dummy.
18 For the concept of costume's 'determinism' see Wyles (2011) 69–76.
19 Wyles (2011) esp. 71–73.
20 Finglass (2011) *ad loc.*
21 Marshall (2012) 193. On the whip see Taplin (1989) 85 with n. 7 (p. 188).
22 Segal (1980–1) 127–9. Finglass (2009) argues that Tecmessa covers Ajax with her 'veil' rather than 'cloak', though the conceptual fluidity of ancient Greek clothing terms poses a challenge to rigid distinctions.
23 Mueller (2016) 149.
24 While the later evidence of Aristotle, *Athenian Constitution* 42.2–5 points to the inclusion of archery in the training of ephebes, Finglass (2011) nn. 1120–3, p. 454 notes its association in Athens at the time of the play with the Persian enemy and potentially also (if the play pre-dates them) the Scythian slaves who made up the 'police force'.
25 On this demand see Parker (2008) 146.
26 This suggestion is further reinforced by the choice of language to describe fighters which could resonate with the contemporary audience: see Mueller (2016) 142 and 146 on the reference to the Chorus as shield-bearing and sailors at line 565 and the use of a fifth-century term for shield strap at lines 575–6.
27 On friendship in the play see Finglass (2011) 55–6.

5

# The Sounds of Ajax's Grief

## Alyson Melzer

In the first book of the *Politics*, Aristotle argues that one fundamental quality differentiating human from beast is speech (*logos*). Many animals have a voice (*phōnē*) that expresses pain or pleasure, but only human beings create language with which to conceptualize morality, strategy, philosophy and politics (1253a11–19). Through *logos* we explore and share our sense of self and our place in the world. Any animal is capable of emoting – man alone, according to Aristotle, is able to articulate.

Verbalization was central to diagnosing illness in the ancient Greek world, and its loss was considered symptomatic of the loss of vitality and sanity, even humanity.[1] So what happens when a person is reduced to *phōnē* and, in a moment of extreme pain, loses the faculty of speech, limited instead to noises that bring him closer to the inarticulacy of animals? What humanity or meaning is salvageable in this moment of incoherent grief? In *The Body in Pain*, Elaine Scarry explores this question and the experience of trauma by describing the effects of pain on speech: 'pain does not simply resist language but actively destroys it, bringing about an immediate reversion to a state anterior to language'.[2] Extreme pain is vocalized in Greek tragedy through shattered language, nonverbal screams of existential horror by characters who are unable to put words to their suffering. After Creon learns that his actions have caused his son's death, he cries out '*pheu iō*' (*Antigone*, 1276); when Orestes proclaims that he has killed his own mother, the Chorus respond in sorrowful horror with '*aiai*' (*Libation Bearers*, 1007); Cadmus screams '*oimoi*' as he watches his daughter unknowingly present her own son's head as a hunting prize (*Bacchae*, 1248). Our eponymous hero Ajax also grieves with such noises, '*iō moi*' and '*aiai aiai*' (333, 370), his inhuman misery echoing the livestock he slaughtered.

These exclamations contain no formal lexical or grammatical meaning in their original Greek form, and are traditionally understood by scholars to be *phōnē* extending beyond the regular boundaries of *logos* into clamours of emotion and pain.[3] They likely reflect real Greek lamentation practices of spontaneous wailing which were incorporated into formal dirge performances.[4]

Because they are not easily definable (at least as a noun or a verb is definable), they present a distinct challenge for translators.[5] Some render these cries as 'woe is me!' or 'alas!' In modern contexts, however, these exclamations sound more archaic and highfalutin than vulnerably emotional. In an attempt to evoke the spirit of the Greek cry more directly, some translators opt for English cries of 'ah!' or 'oh!' which appropriately maintain the vowels central to Greek interjections, and do not add lexical meaning where there is none (as translations of 'woe' or 'no' do). Other editions conscious of reperformance include stage directions instead of translations, such as '*cries in distress*' or '*groans miserably*', leaving the delivery of the cry up to the actor or the reader's imagination. And finally, there are translators who choose to leave the cries out entirely and rob their audience of these passionate interjections altogether.[6]

To circumvent these adaptation problems, some translators (including David Stuttard in the translation featured in this volume) elect to represent the original expression by transliterating the Greek into English letters.[7] While cries like *aiai* or *oimoi* may initially strike the modern ear as 'overintrusively alien', as Oliver Taplin claims,[8] I believe this is exactly what they are meant to do: to disrupt *logos* and communicate the incoherence of trauma, to jolt us to attention and to grate on our ears so that we feel some of the pain their vocalizer feels. In their Greek form, these screams offer unnervingly raw expression, and as I will explore in what follows, they also contain a great deal of interpretive significance that should not be taken for granted. In the introductory essay to her translation of Sophocles' *Electra*, Anne Carson justifies her decision to transliterate the cries by outlining what we can learn about Electra from the particular aural characteristics of her pain – something impossible to do when the cries are translated or omitted.[9]

So too will we be 'listening to Ajax' in this chapter for what we can learn from his sounds of grief. When he wakes from madness, Ajax loses the *logos* which Aristotle ties to humanity, and instead expresses his pain through *phōnē*. His cries not only vocalize emotional distress for dramatic effect, but also provide insight into his suffering and his attempt to recover from it. I will trace Ajax's experience of trauma not through the content of his or other characters' speeches, but through his grieving voice. In their sound alone, his groans and shrieks depict a hero severed from his austere heroic identity. They become gaping wounds, literally opening up the once self-contained hero to exposure and vulnerability, revealing his devastating anguish to everyone listening.

As we shall see, however, Ajax eventually tries to delimit his misery and impede his emotional outpour by transforming his *phōnē* into *logos*. He imposes meaning onto his seemingly meaningless cries, sculpting them into something almost articulate, rationalizing his trauma and thereby gaining some authority over it. Scarry describes this process of recovering articulation while dealing with trauma as a 'remaking' of the language that was 'unmade' by pain: 'to be present when a person moves up out of that pre-language [expression of pain] and projects the facts of sentience into speech is almost to have been permitted to be present at the birth of language itself.'[10] I argue that Ajax remakes his heroic subjectivity and authority *by means of his inarticulate cries,* particularly the exclamation *'aiai'*. His noises of grief therefore both disclose *and* reconstruct the hero's disrupted autonomy.

\* \* \*

Tecmessa first draws our attention to the central role sound plays in understanding Ajax's trauma. Before he re-emerges onto the stage, she sorrowfully recounts the atrocities that transpired in the night, describing Ajax's initial reaction when reawakening to sanity (317–22):

> He groaned so agonizingly, so desperately – I've never heard him groan like that before. He'd always said that crying was for cowards, and when he grieved it was in silence, not like a woman, no – no, like the rumbling of a bull.

On the battlefield, Ajax was accustomed to responding to pain with a taurine reverberation that was inaudibly deep (*hypostenazein,* literally 'sighing from under', 322). This is an appropriate pitch range for a man: in Greek lament tradition, shrill high-pitch sounds were associated with female wailing, whereas lower drones were thought to be better suited for men.[11] That Ajax 'had always said' this about lament suggests that his subaudible grief was a consistent aspect of his heroic persona, separating him from cowards and women. In his current state, however, the line between him and both of these groups has become disturbingly blurry. Ajax can no longer uphold his personal doctrine of silent suffering, having lost control of his own expression after losing control of his mind and actions. Tecmessa's observation signals how dramatically Ajax's temperament has shifted as a result of his trauma: he now laments with a vulnerability entirely unnatural to his austere character.[12]

Prompted by Ajax's uncharacteristic lament, Tecmessa fears 'he's planning something terrible... somehow I can tell from *how* he's muttering and sobbing' (326–7, emphasis added). The audience soon experiences the sounds of Ajax's trauma for themselves: his first lines after the mad scene are two cries of '*iō moi moi!*' from offstage (333, 336). At their most basic level, these howls evoke intense panic and loss of self-containment as the *phōnē* spills out of Ajax's mouth and tent, filling the theatre. Tecmessa initially described Ajax's mad deeds as 'unspeakable' (*logon arrhēton,* 214), too terrible to put into words, and Ajax himself now exemplifies this impossibility of communication by mourning his crisis with sounds rather than speech. Because he is offstage out of the sight of the audience and his companions, in these two cries Ajax is completely severed from his physical body and represented only as disembodied sonic agony.

Like the noises Tecmessa reports in her earlier speech, Ajax's first sounds are shocking and unnatural. But after the two cries of '*iō moi moi!*' he attempts to find some sense in his wailing, to 'remake' his screams into language. He thus transitions from a wordless expression of anguish into a lament for his child when he exclaims '*iō!* My son! My son!' three lines later (339). The Greek is '*iō pai pai*', a phrase that contains significant sonic similarities with '*iō moi moi*' in the initial *iō*, the total number of syllables, and the two labial consonants (*mu* and *pi*) followed by diphthongs ending in *iota* (*oi* and *ai*). Ajax's lament has infected his regular speech to the point that an invocation of his son is interwoven with screams of anguish. Simultaneously, Ajax reaches towards sense, forging lexical meaning from inarticulate noise by grasping at the word closest to his scream as he grasps at the person closest to his heart, Eurysaces. This progression out of grief towards meaning and *logos* is accomplished in his subsequent line: after '*iō pai pai*' Ajax calls out for his brother, saying 'Teucer! Where's Teucer!' (342). He drops the exclamation *iō* altogether and delivers his first fully coherent sentence ('Will he never come back from his cattle-raid?' 342–3). The evolution of Ajax's cries into speech leads the Chorus to conclude that he is now 'rational enough' to be confronted (344).

With at least some of his emotions contained again within the expressible confines of language, Ajax finally appears onstage. But Tecmessa undoes his containment as she opens up the tent and floods the theatre with the sight, now in addition to the sound, of Ajax's pain. As he emerges he collapses back into the sheer noise of grief with '*iō*' at line 348. He repeats this cry as the opening refrain of five verses in his ensuing lament (348, 356, 379, 394 and 412). Of the many exclamations available to the tragic Greek playwright, these *iō* cries are significant for their pronunciation: they begin with the mouth constricted by the *iota* then opening up into the long *omega*, as if the lips strain at first to compress the outpouring of emotion within the mouth but eventually unleash everything out through the broad opening demanded by the *omega*.[13] As Ajax confronts his trauma, he wants to restrict his vulnerability but fails to do so. This process is mimetically performed by his cries of *iō*.

In addition to these repeated cries and another *iō moi moi* at 385, the lament Ajax performs when he first appears onstage (348–427) contains two other sonic features that mark his emotional unravelling. First, while

Tecmessa and the Chorus speak their lines throughout this passage, Ajax sings.[14] Although singing a lament is not in itself antiheroic or unmanly in tragedy, it does display an emotive desperation which is markedly different from what is expected of the sombre hero who once followed a strict code of restrained lamentation. It also enacts his solitude, as he begins the deadly process of physical and emotional isolation from Tecmessa and the Chorus with audible separation from them.

The second aural feature of Ajax's destabilized self-containment is his frequent repetition that in this context sounds like the stammer of a sob spilling out of an unbarred mouth. His first line onstage after he cries *iō* is an address to the Chorus of his comrades that repeats 'only' (*monoi*) and 'friends' (*philoi*) twice: 'my only friends, you sailed with me, and only you, friends, have stayed loyal and true' (348–9). The doubling of *monoi* emphasizes Ajax's isolation, while the repetition of *philoi* frantically grasps at a connection to others. Ten lines later Ajax stutters a similar craving for the support of the Chorus: 'you were my crewmen, you sailed us here... you are the only people I can turn to now' (*se toi se toi monon*, 359–60). But he soon turns away from them with three successive reprises of the command that darkness 'come, come, come to me' (*helesth' helesthe m'... helesthe m'*, 396–9). This desperate plea does not invoke his companions, but rather the blackness of death and community of the underworld towards which he gradually turns. His vocal stutters therefore display not only his emotional instability, but also his alienation and mounting notion that death is his best solution. Ajax continues his repetitive lament when asking 'where can anyone escape, where can I find rest?' (*poi... poi*, 403–4), and concluding with an address not to any human group, but the Trojan landscape, a place that has kept him away from home 'so long, too long' (*polun polun*, 414) but 'no longer, no longer' (*ouketi m' ouket'*, 416). In his complete emotional desolation, Ajax rejects the very land he stands on as well as the people around him.

From his singing, stammering and cries of agony, we hear Ajax process his trauma, moving from hysterically incoherent grief to lonely depression. We come now to a cry that seems to express the core of Ajax's pain. At 370, still in the midst of his extended lament song, Ajax shouts out '*aiai aiai*' with the repetition we have seen in this song as a symptom of his fraught isolation. Nicole Loraux describes the cry *aiai* as one 'in which grief seems to be expressed in perfect immediacy without the mediation of articulated speech... a naked cry of sorrow, mourning transformed into pure vocal emission.'[15] It creates the inverse mouth shape of the *iō* cry, with the lips constricted by the *iota* after the long *alpha* vowel rather than at the beginning of the syllable. The mouth begins completely open but draws itself in tightly for the end of each syllable, preventing full openness. Whereas the *iō* cry seemed to mirror Ajax's attempt to restrict his expression before it was inevitably ripped open, the *aiai* cry oppositely struggles to close up a mouth agape like an open wound, curbing the outpour of the *alpha* with the choking *iota* and imitating Ajax's looming decision to close off his own vulnerability through suicide.

He does eventually stymie his grief when he stops singing at line 430 and speaks a monologue in which he contemplates what to do next. This is the apex of his transition away from unaccustomed mourning towards a reacquisition of self-containment. As he shifts from song back into deliberative speech he vocalizes his intention to abandon unguarded lamenting and re-establish the sombre autonomous heroic persona he lost. He accomplishes this re-establishment, ironically, through the cry *aiai* that opens the speech (430–1):

> *aiai!* Who could have known my name would suit my agony so perfectly?
> Aiai! Ajax! My very name's a lamentation stretching out for ever.

Unlike his previous cries of *iō* and *aiai* which were detached from the content of the song that followed, this *aiai* is incorporated into his speech as the introduction to a meditation on his existential dilemma. Ajax provides an etymology of his own name, now believing it to mean 'the one who says *aiai*'. This makes better sense in the original language, since our eponymous hero's name in Greek is actually *Aias* (the spelling 'Ajax' commonly used today is a Latinized translation).[16] Name as a reflection of a person's fate and nature was a common trope in ancient Greek literature, as in *Odyssey* 19 when Odysseus' grandfather names him for the hate he will incur (*odyssamenos*, 'the odious one', 407).

While inarticulate cries such as *aiai* have been largely interpreted as expressive only of emotion and not lexical or interpretive meaning, several recent studies look for sense beyond pain in nonverbal cries (as we see in Ajax's speech). Sean Gurd describes how 'in such cries language strained toward its own limits', not beyond; they are a kind of invented language rather than a lack of language, 'transforming the open, agonized mouth into a channel for liberated melodies' that are both 'a form of high vocal control' and concurrently 'the voice out of control'. Naomi Weiss argues that ancient lament in tragedy is both nonverbal noise and a skilful song performance, and that the slippage between these two poles is fundamental to the drama of tragedy and practices of ancient lament which is simultaneously *logos* and *alogos*, articulate and inarticulate expression. For Sarah Nooter, Ajax appropriates marked lyrical style for the recreation of his heroic identity and authority, delivering the performances of a poet in control of his language in an attempt to regain control of his life.[17]

According to these three scholars, elements of tragic speech that seem to express only raw emotion can actually be artful features of performance that contain meaning and intentionality beyond a reaction to pain. In his exclamation of *aiai* at line 430, we hear Ajax's 'rebirth' out of speechless grief into language and into a new sense of self: he articulates his newfound identity as someone fated to lament through his previously inarticulate cry. As we have seen, however, excessive lament is otherwise completely alien to his character and disposition. He thus discovers a terrible paradox at the centre of his selfhood, but refuses to submit to it and instead remakes his mourning into *logos* with etymological significance. *Aiai* is thus no longer only an unintelligible *phōnē* of pain, but now an emblem of his identity and an explanation of his crisis even if it is also inevitably and inescapably a manifestation of vulnerability and uncharacteristic lament. This paradox of *aiai* is representative of Ajax's trauma, since he struggles both to understand and express his pain while simultaneously distancing himself from others and eventually sealing off the expression of his pain permanently. He is both the embodiment and rejection of grief, an irreconcilable identity that can only be resolved through death.

For the remainder of his life, Ajax strains to distance himself from the mourning embedded in his identity by continuing to remake his grief into language. At line 545, when his son Eurysaces is presented onstage Ajax calls for the attendant to 'lift him! lift him!' In the Greek this is '*air' aire*' (545), a sonic echo of *aiai*. As with the etymology of *Aias*, here too Ajax turns a sound of emotion into something intelligible. His tragic noises infect his speech, as with *iō moi moi* and *iō pai pai*. In this case, the infection is even more controlled because it is redirected to a constructive imperative and contains only the echoes of an inarticulate exclamation rather than the cry itself.

Ajax continues to reject mourning and vocal excess by refraining from all tragic cries and anguished lament in his remaining speeches, in which there is no singing, no anaphora and no dramatic expression of agony. He uses his recovered verbal steadfastness to deliver the infamous 'deception speech' (646–92), where he displays impressive rhetorical skill to convince the Chorus and Tecmessa of his feigned willingness to let go of his suicidal intentions. As he later prepares for his death, he delivers a final speech that is relatively calm, oratorically elegant and without inarticulate cries (815–65).[18] He does not even sing a lament for himself, as Sophoclean characters sometimes do when death is imminent but they are isolated from community and consequently have no-one to sing their funeral dirge.[19]

He concludes his final speech by saying 'these are Ajax's last words' (864). The only other time he refers to himself in the third person is in the mad scene (98), when he has been driven out of his own mind and addresses himself as if another person. In this final speech, Ajax uses the third person with a similar tone of self-estrangement, having detached himself from the vulnerability signified by his name and the aspects of his identity that have predestined him to grieve excessively. The closest utterance to *aiai* Ajax makes before his death is here with his own name, *Aias*, and another name which is sonically similar, *Haidēs* ('Hades' or 'the dead', 865). Ajax denies *aiai* its significance as a pure grief noise and instead incorporates it into language, refusing to open himself up again to the vulnerability of lament and securing his authority over his previously uncontrollable grief. Although he has gained some power over the cry contained within his name, it is nevertheless inescapable in life.

With his last words, Ajax declares that 'from now on I shall speak only with the dead' (865). That Ajax will save any speech for the underworld is saturated with tremendous irony given the illustrious 'Silence of Ajax' in *Odyssey* 11.541ff. While Odysseus converses with deceased heroes and family members in the underworld, he sees Ajax standing apart from the others, persistent in his isolation even now. Odysseus tries to talk with him, pleading for reconciliation, but Ajax provides no words of peace or understanding: he turns his back on Odysseus in silence and walks away. In this moment, the anguish of Ajax's silence rings louder than any cry ever could.[20]

\* \* \*

In Sophocles' *Ajax*, we hear sounds of self-alienation and pain that 'unmakes' language, triggering a deluge of inarticulate emotion; we also hear sounds that grasp at a 'remaking' of identity and meaning. Ajax's cries, as they fluctuate between sense and nonsense, ask us to question what language is and how it signifies. If a word is not definable, is it necessarily meaningless? The spectrum between speech and sound invites a re-evaluation of Aristotle's argument that *logos* defines our humanity since there are ideas and experiences best conveyed through pure *phōnē*.

In their profound albeit mercurial connotations, these cries reveal the phases of Ajax's trauma, his relationship to and eventual rejection of others (including himself) and his ineffable inner turmoil. He is not the only character in the play to make these noises of grief, of course. After Tecmessa and the Chorus discover his body, they dissolve into exchanges of *iō moi moi* and *iō* which are vigorously renewed when Teucer joins them. Within each of their screams is the echo of Ajax's mourning voice. Even when the Chorus rejoices with elated cries of '*iō iō*' in a very brief moment of hope after the 'deception speech' (694, 707), it is impossible not to hear the ominous foreshadowing of Ajax's destruction within those sounds that remind us of his desperate lament when first exiting the tent covered in the blood of his animal victims.[21]

Given its significance, it is noticeable that *aiai* is never uttered among the many cries of grief vocalized after Ajax's death. Perhaps it is too individually expressive of one person's suffering in its intimate connection to his identity, and thus cannot be transferred into another mouth. Perhaps the severity of Ajax's isolation extends even to his wailing, and *aiai* represents his secluded pain. Or perhaps in his death, Ajax also kills this particular cry, successfully managing to stanch the open wound of his lament, but only by opening another wound in his side.

## Notes

1 Holmes (2010) 157.
2 Scarry (1985) 4.
3 Perdicoyianni-Paléologue (2002), Stanford (1983) 56–60, Nooter (2017) 41–48. '*Moi*' is an exception to this, since it originates from the dative singular first person pronoun and therefore does suggest lexical meaning (though it is still usually not deployed as both a cry and a pronoun at the same time).
4 Alexiou (2002); on the complex legal, gendered and artistic issues of lament in ancient Greek society, see also Suter (2008), Dué (2006) 30–56, Foley (2001) 19–55.
5 Walton (2006) 79–84, Carson (2001).
6 In Jebb (1896) and Storr (1913) the most common exclamations are 'ah me!' and 'woe is me!' Storr is more likely to leave some cries out of his translation, where Jebb will use 'alas' or 'o'. Moore (1957) usually opts for 'oh!' or 'ah!', with several cries of 'oh! no!' or 'o God!' Tipton (2008) most often uses 'no!' but does have a few rather liberal uses of 'FUCK!' and 'Damn it!' and leaves other cries out of the translation. Taplin (2015) uses stage directions, as does Moore (1957) occasionally. For examples of cries left out entirely: Storr (1913) lines 339, 348, 356, 379, 412, Moore (1957) line 339, Tipton (2008) and Taplin (2015) lines 339 and 379.
7 Golder and Pevear (1999), Dutta (2001) and Esposito (2010) also do this.
8 Taplin (2015) xxxii.
9 Carson (2001).
10 Scarry (1985) 6.
11 For more on female lament in ancient Greece, see Alexiou (2002). As Suter (2008) argues, lament in tragedy is not necessarily in and of itself a markedly feminine act; the distinction here is one of style rather than activity.
12 For more on Ajax's isolated and severe heroic persona, see Laura Swift, Carmel McCallum-Barry, Sophie Mills and Richard Seaford in this volume.
13 The first-century BC Greek literary critic Dionysius of Halicarnassus provides us with an extensive account of Greek alphabet pronunciation in his essay *On the Composition of Words*. In Chapter 14, he ranks the vowels in order of

most euphonic to least: *omega* is in third place because it rounds out the mouth but still contracts the corners of the lips, while the *iota* is the least pleasing because the mouth is barely open at all. His favourite letter is the long *alpha*, since it opens the mouth to its fullest extent.
14 This would have been apparent for Sophocles' audience, anyway, since it is yet another acoustic element often lost in translation and silent reading. Jebb (1896) and Finglass (2011) provide a full outline of the metres that indicate what lines are sung or spoken in this passage.
15 Loraux (2002) 35–6.
16 Finglass (2011) 265; Svenbro (2004) explores the etymology of *Aias* and its connections to *aietos* or 'eagle,' as well as *aiai*. Loraux (2002) 35–39 argues for a sonic connection between *Aias* and *ania*, 'pain', as well as *aei*, 'always': Ajax is thus doomed to always be in pain. See also Nooter (2012) 40.
17 Gurd (2016) 62, Weiss (2017), Nooter (2012) 31–55. Nooter's study deals more with the content and rhetorical devices than the sounds and exclamations of Ajax's lament; her subsequent book (2017) explores inarticulate cries in Aeschylus in more detail.
18 Nooter (2012) 31–55.
19 As in *Antigone* (806ff.) and *Philoctetes* (1081ff.).
20 As the Greek literary critic Longinus describes it in *On the Sublime* 9.3.
21 As previously discussed, the *omega* in this cry broadly opens the mouth after the constricting *iota*: in celebration, the release of the *iota*'s tension enacts a release from anxiety. The openness of the final *omega* also evokes the vulnerability of the speakers, as it does when expressing grief, but in the context of joy their vulnerability stems from the fragility of this happy moment which the audience knows will not last. For more on the invocation to Pan in this cry, see Finglass (2011) 343.

6

# Ajax's Suicide

Robert Garland

The Greeks had no words for what are considered to be chronic disorders such as schizophrenia, paranoia and borderline personality, or for temporary psychological impairments such as anxiety, depression and loss of self-esteem. But though they lacked the scientific terminology by which neurotic and pathological states of consciousness are systematized by contemporary clinicians, they were still fully capable of exposing the interior life of the individual to intense scrutiny.

Nor is there any reason for supposing that Greek society, any more than any other ancient society, was incapable of subjecting its members to as much psychological pressure and damage as our own, even though it is only occasionally that we gain a glimpse into the response of the human psyche to this pressure and damage. The first vignette of a suicide in the Western literary tradition is provided by Homer. She is Epicaste, the mother and wife of Oedipus, who hanged herself from a roof beam on discovering that she had unknowingly had intercourse with her son. Homer neither condones nor condemns her act. He merely reports that her restless spirit, through the intervention of the Avenging Furies, will forever plague her son (*Od*. 271–80). Additionally, Achilles, under the stress of overwhelming guilt at the death of Patroclus, entertains suicidal thoughts – so much so that Antilochus is forced to restrain him (*Il*. 18.34).[1]

Our major source of insight into suicide is, however, Greek tragedy.[2] Though we might justifiably argue that the tragedians, since their plots derive from mythology, are hardly responsible for the high incidence of suicide that we find in their plays, it is difficult to resist the conclusion that the suicidal state of mind and the circumstances that contribute to it preoccupied them to a high degree. In addition to Ajax, Deianeira in Sophocles' *Women of Trachis*, Jocasta in his *Oedipus Tyrannus*, and both Haemon and Eurydice in his *Antigone* commit suicide. The list in Euripides includes Evadne in *Suppliants*, Iphigenia in *Iphigenia at Aulis*, Macaria in *Heracleidae*, Menoeceus in *Phoenician Women*, and the daughters of King Erechtheus in his lost play *Erechtheus*. In all these cases the suicide is reported by a messenger. Aeschylus' lost play *Thracian Women* also deals with Ajax's suicide, likewise reported by a messenger.

However, no other surviving tragedy explores the stages by which the decision to take one's own life is reached with greater precision than Sophocles' *Ajax*. Only here, moreover, is there a possibility that the act may have taken place on stage. Sophocles also analyses with considerable subtlety the response to Ajax's threat to commit suicide from his family and friends. The play concludes with an acrimonious debate in which his supporters and detractors argue whether he is entitled to burial. The fact of his having taken his own life plays no part in their deliberations.

Ajax is the archetypal product of a shame culture. 'A hero has two options: to live in glory or die in glory,' he declares (479–80). By failing to achieve the honour to which he aspired, he has been humiliated and not once but twice – first by being beaten in the competition for the arms of Achilles, and second by directing his venom against brute beasts rather than his intended target, the judges. Henceforth, he concludes, he will be an object of mockery and contempt. Today we might characterize him as clinically depressed, his condition contingent upon a catastrophic loss of self-esteem that resulted from an intense devaluation of his social self. As is often true of those manifesting suicidal impulses, moreover, Ajax is both highly manipulative and self-obsessed. He deceives his well-wishers (and possibly himself) into believing that he has dismissed the thought of taking his own life.

Sophocles did not invent Ajax's suicide. On the contrary, the story appears at least two centuries earlier. Two of the poems in the Epic Cycle, namely the *Aethiopis* and the *Little Iliad*, describe Ajax's suicide.[3] The event is also depicted in the figurative arts dating to the same period. Nor did Sophocles invent the detail of Ajax falling on his sword, which appears in artistic representations already in the mid-seventh century and in literature as early as Pindar. The most famous depiction is on a black-figure amphora by Exekias dated *c.* 540 BCE, which shows him fixing his sword in the ground, his brow furrowed. Other scenes related to the myth also occur. For instance, a fragmentary red-figure kylix dated *c.* 500–480 by Onesimus depicts the cattle he killed.[4] It follows that Sophocles' audience would have been fully expecting that his tragedy would deal with his suicide.

\* \* \*

To understand the causes behind Ajax's suicide, we need to analyse the statements he makes about his mental condition and the reaction that those statements evoke in others. The play opens with Athena informing Odysseus that the reason why Ajax has mistakenly slaughtered livestock and their herdsmen is because she cast 'evil notions of insatiable joy over Ajax's eyes' (51–2), though a few lines later she claims she afflicted him 'with maddening sickness'. 'Madness (*mania*)' and its cognates are used repeatedly, as is 'sickness' (*nosos*) and its cognates. Along with *atê*, 'delusion', these are the only terms the characters in the play have at their disposal to explain Ajax's mental condition, which, they believe, is the result of divine intervention. It is unclear whether they believe that Athena merely distorted his vision or went further and tampered with his mental faculties.[5]

From Ajax's perspective, and that of the heroic code by which he lives, his intention to kill his enemies is a perfectly reasonable response to the humiliation he feels at having lost the competition for the arms of Achilles. That is why he does not question the morality of attempting to slay his enemies when he returns to his senses. It is the failure of the attempt, not the attempt itself, which prompts his decision to commit suicide.

Athena boasts of her power to deceive humans and invites Odysseus to gloat over his enemy's disgrace. 'Isn't it the loveliest of things to mock our enemies?' she enquires, assuring him that she will prevent Ajax from recognizing him by darkening his vision (78–9, 85). Ajax emerges from the *skênê* or scene building that represents his hut (99–117). He is so out of touch with reality that he believes Athena has assisted him in killing his enemies (90–3; cf. 117). When invited by Athena to gloat, however, Odysseus expresses pity for Ajax's delusional state (*atê*) and reflects on the fragility of human existence (121–6). His reaction is in stark contrast to the delight that the goddess takes in the havoc she has wreaked.

Athena and Odysseus depart and the Chorus speculates about the truth of the rumour that Ajax has slaughtered cattle (154–7). Tecmessa informs them that 'a madness (*mania*) fell on him in the night' (216–17). She describes in chilling detail how Ajax tore animals apart with his bare hands and tortured a ram, believing it to be Odysseus. He is now, she informs the Chorus, *phronimos*, 'of his right mind'. In a striking paradox that demonstrates deep insight into the human condition, she declares, 'When the sickness (*nosos*) was upon him, he rejoiced in his wretchedness ... but now that he has recovered from it and breathes easily, he is racked by terrible anguish' (271–5). Reality, in other words, is worse than fantasy. She describes how he gives vent to low moans like a bull, refuses all food and drink, and is sitting in a catatonic state. She concludes by saying, 'He's planning something terrible. I can tell' (326). Does she expect him to make a second attempt to murder his enemies?

The doors of the *skênê* open and the audience sees the tableau that Tecmessa has just described, namely Ajax sitting among the slaughtered cattle (346–7). Probably this effect was achieved by means of the *ekkyklêma* or 'object that is rolled out'. Recognizing his comrades, Ajax cries out, 'Kill me now!' (361). The Chorus is shocked and urges him to speak words of good omen. Ajax bemoans the fact that he has become an object of derision (367, 379–81). He prays to Zeus to give him advice about how to slay the Greek chiefs before he dies, but, though he predicts his death, he refrains from suggesting that he will take his own life (387–91). He realizes that Athena is his enemy and invokes the darkness of the underworld (394–403).

In the first of his three great speeches Ajax characterizes his condition with unsparing clarity. 'So what now?' he demands. 'It's obvious the gods hate me. The Greek army hates me too – and Troy, yes, and the plain of Troy!' (457–9). If he returns home, how could he and his father look each other in the eye? What makes his condition all the more intolerable is that he has become the exact antithesis of his father, who won the prize for his martial prowess at Troy a generation earlier. Hatred and humiliation beset him on all sides. True, he could hurl himself into the fray and die fighting gloriously, but this would merely bring satisfaction to his enemies (466–9). 'Only a coward wants long life, when everything's against him,' he concludes (473–4). Ajax's entire speech is focused on himself. He shows no capacity to think of others. It is a characteristic that never deserts him, no matter what others are having to endure.

Though the audience would have realized that he is set on taking his own life, the Chorus clings to the hope that all is not lost. It compliments him for speaking truthfully and urges him to accept guidance from his friends (481–4). Tecmessa, who fully gathers his meaning, encourages him to imagine the consequences of his death for others. Using the same argument that Hector's wife Andromache employs in Homer's *Iliad* Book 6 (407–39) in an effort to dissuade her husband from risking his life in battle, she pleads with him to reflect upon the miserable life to which she and their son Eurysaces will be consigned if he dies. She reminds him of his obligations to his elderly parents. Above all, she invites him to take pity on their son. She points out that there is no-one else to whom she can turn for protection, since he captured her in war and killed her parents. She ends by reminding him of the debt of kindness he owes in return for the happy life they have shared (523–4).

All to no avail. Ajax remains obsessed by his own sense of ill-usage. He asks to see Eurysaces, whom Tecmessa has removed for fear that he might do him injury. 'Be like your father in all ways, but be luckier,' he instructs (550–1). Even when contemplating Eurysaces' future, Ajax can only think of his own ego. He orders the Chorus to tell his brother Teucer to accompany Eurysaces back home so that he can look after his elderly parents – a task which should have devolved upon him (567–71). He bequeaths his shield to Eurysaces, but instructs the Chorus to bury him in his armour.

The audience would have understood that Ajax has put his affairs in order preparatory to taking his own life. Tecmessa, too, senses this, though she does not give up hope altogether. 'I owe the gods nothing! Can't you see that?' he replies (589), his evident point being that he has the right to die. 'Don't speak ill-omened words,' she replies, using the same expression as the Chorus had done earlier, when he asked it to help him to die (591). The Chorus claims that Ajax 'shares with the god's madness (*mania*)', though nowhere does Sophocles provide any indication that he is anything but rational and sane (611). It conjures up the image of Ajax's white-haired old mother deeply afflicted by the news of his mental sickness (*nosos*). Finally, it recklessly suggests that a man who is suffering sickness – *nosos* again – to no good purpose, one who has inherited great wealth from his father, who is unable to control his rage, and who is 'uselessly sick (*nosôn*),' would actually be better off dead, though it refrains from drawing the conclusion that he should take his own life (635, 639–40).

Given the testamentary arrangements that Ajax has just made, the audience would have been expecting the entry of a messenger bearing news of his suicide. Instead Ajax reappears to deliver his second great speech, the so-called 'deception speech'. Though he does not disavow his intention to take his own life, he intimates that he has had a profound revelation. 'Time stretches to eternity,' he declares. 'It brings all things into the light and buries them again in darkness . . . I was strong once, as strong as toughened iron, but what she said – this woman – has undone me. I feel such pity for her, left alone, a widow, and my orphaned boy, surrounded by my enemies' (647–54). He will yield to the gods and respect the sons of Atreus. He will purify himself to escape Athena's wrath and bury his sword in the ground where it cannot be seen – a mordant allusion to the manner of his suicide. 'Why should men like us not learn our limits?' he enquires (677).

Ajax's lines are permeated with a bitter irony. His true revelation, the audience will soon discover, is the opposite of the one he claims: he of all mortals will be unchanged by time, since his hatred of Agamemnon and Menelaus is immutable. He is therefore not merely outside the human fold, but outside the natural order of things as well. The question to address, however, is whether there is anything to suggest that Ajax has been temporarily softened by Tecmessa's appeal. Does he now recognize his responsibility towards his dependents? Or is he lying? And if he is lying, what is his purpose, given the fact that Tecmessa and the Chorus will now have to deal not only with his suicide but also with the fact that he has made them his dupes?[6] Another possibility: is he deceiving himself? Is he demonstrating the behaviour of a manic-depressive? In the end there is no way we can definitively choose between these various interpretations.[7] On a theatrical level the speech serves the practical purpose of enabling Ajax to part from Tecmessa and the Chorus, ostensibly to purify himself but in reality to die alone.

Thoroughly deluded, the Chorus is ecstatic to learn that Ajax is no longer bent on self-slaughter. 'Ares, the war god,' it declares, 'has dissolved the black pain blinding me' (706) – a deeply ironic line that recalls Athena's boast of having obscured his vision at the beginning of the play. It takes comfort from the fact that Ajax has performed rites in honour of the gods, which it interprets as a sign that he has recovered his wits.

A messenger reports that Teucer has just arrived and that the soldiers jeered at him for being 'the brother of a madman' (724). Calchas, the Greek seer, has warned him to confine his brother to his tent for twenty-four hours. We might suspect that the reason for this is that Ajax needs to be put on suicide watch, but instead he has to be protected from Athena, who will destroy him if she sees him. And now, finally, we learn of the cause of Athena's hatred: when she offered him encouragement, he boastfully claimed that he had no need of the gods to win fame on the battlefield, even though his father had warned him against excessive pride (762–77).

In his final speech Ajax invites the audience to visualize the act he is about to perform and be privy to his last thoughts on earth. He describes the care that he has taken in inserting the newly whetted sword into the ground – the same sword, he reveals, that he used to slaughter the cattle (819–22). He castigates Agamemnon and Menelaus for provoking him to take his own life and invokes the wrath of the Furies upon their heads. His desire for vengeance now extends to the whole Greek army, whose blood he ghoulishly urges the Furies to drink (844). He imagines his elderly parents receiving the news of his death, but checks himself with the recollection that he has an urgent task to fulfil. He remains thoroughly self-absorbed. He has no parting thoughts either for Tecmessa or for Eurysaces or for his fellow-sailors. Had he been inclined to write a suicide note, it would perhaps have been to Teucer alone, reminding him to carry out his last wishes. 'Death! Death! Come here, now! Look at me...' he cries (854). After invoking Helios, Salamis, Athens and Troy, he falls on his sword. Even if the actor playing Ajax did not enact his suicide on stage, many members of the audience might well have been expecting that he would.

How Sophocles handled Ajax's suicide is a notoriously vexed issue.[8] There are many possibilities. The actor playing Ajax may have fallen on a retractable sword in full or partial view of the audience. Or he may have left the stage either through the *skênê* or through a temporary screen that was erected to conceal his act from public view. If he did act out the suicide in view of the audience, this may have been the first occasion when a violent death was performed on stage.

There are further uncertainties regarding the revelation of Ajax's corpse, which is visible to Tecmessa at l. 891 and to Teucer by l. 1003 at the latest. If Ajax committed suicide on stage, a dummy must have been substituted for the actor playing Ajax, as he would have been required to play the part of Teucer, there being a seemingly inflexible convention that only three actors had speaking parts. But when and how was the dummy substituted? Perhaps it was wheeled out on the *ekkyklêma* just after Tecmessa found it. This second use of this device would have balanced the tableau at the beginning of the play, in which Ajax sat among the slaughtered cattle. However, since the *skênê* had been used earlier to identify Ajax's tent, the audience would have been required to envisage a scene change at l. 814 – another vexed issue. Admittedly a scene change occurs in Aeschylus' *Eumenides*, from the sanctuary of Apollo at Delphi to that of Athens on the Acropolis. But here the audience's imagination would have had to transition from Ajax's tent or hut to a lonely grove – the only occasion in Greek tragedy, so far as we know, when the *skênê* was used to represent an outdoor space.[9]

As soon as Tecmessa discovers Ajax's corpse, the Chorus runs towards her and asks her the cause of his death. Was it expecting to learn that Ajax had been murdered? Learning he has taken his own life, the Chorus blames itself for having failed to note the warning signs. It even accuses itself of delusion (*atê*), employing the same word that Odysseus used of Ajax' condition at the beginning of the play. To spare his friends from witnessing such a distressing sight, Tecmessa covers his corpse with her mantle. She asserts that Athena is to blame for Ajax's death and that her purpose was to give pleasure to Odysseus. The Chorus speculates that Odysseus will exult in Ajax's death (955–60). Tecmessa agrees, accusing Odysseus of hubris.

The remainder of the play deals with the consequences of Ajax's death. Around l. 936 Ajax's corpse, an almost living presence, becomes visible to the audience. Henceforth it 'silently holds stage for the rest of the play' (Rehm 2002, 131); that is to say, for approximately one-third of its length. The characters debate whether Ajax has forfeited his right to burial, during which time the corpse becomes a silent witness at its own trial.

Ajax's brother Teucer arrives and sends Tecmessa off to fetch Eurysaces in case Ajax's enemies might harm him. He does not have a single word of sympathy for her. Indeed he does not even greet her. Once she has departed, he exposes Ajax's corpse, thereby countermanding her order to leave it covered. He is distraught at the thought of reporting the news to his father Telamon, who, it turns out, is a morose old so-and-so. Very likely he will heap scorn on his one surviving son, whom he holds in less esteem than Ajax. Teucer, we now discover, has his own issues with self-esteem. He speculates that Telamon will accuse him of having conspired to kill his brother, with a view to usurping his inheritance. He will be thrown out of the house and accused of being a slave. To make matters worse, his few friends have all deserted him. 'And all because you died,' he glumly observes (1023). Self-absorption runs in the family.

Menelaus enters and orders that Ajax's body be left unburied, accusing the deceased of attempted murder and insubordination. He threatens that anyone who disobeys his command will be summarily executed. Teucer dismisses the claim of insubordination by pointing out that Ajax came to Troy voluntarily. The argument degenerates into a trading of insults and Menelaus departs. Preparations for Ajax's burial get underway. Teucer orders Eurysaces to watch over the body, which has now acquired a kind of sanctity (1171–2).

Next to arrive is Agamemnon, who abuses Teucer because of his lowly origins. Teucer insults Agamemnon in turn and reminds him of his father's and brother's distinguished military record. This senseless altercation serves no purpose and might be thought insulting to the dead, whose corpse awaits the outcome of the argument. It is interrupted by Odysseus, who argues in support of Ajax's burial on account of his service in the Greek cause. To deny him burial would violate gods' laws. Agamemnon reluctantly concedes and departs.

The play ends with Odysseus declaring his friendship with Teucer and expressing his desire to participate in the burial. Teucer accepts his offer, but forbids him from touching the corpse for fear of offending the dead (1393–5).

A curiosity is that Ajax's corpse, present on stage for the last third of the play as we have seen, is invested with a numinous power capable of protecting the living. Just as Oedipus' body in Sophocles' *Oedipus at Colonus* is destined to become a source of protection to his Athenian allies, so Ajax's body now becomes powerful in its own right, capable of 'guarding its guardians' (Sommerstein 2015, 246). Very possibly Sophocles' audience would have inferred that Ajax has acquired heroic status. In later times his tomb was identified as a mound on a promontory near Troy, and it may be that already in Sophocles' day it was a centre of worship (Taplin 2015, 189). Heroic status could be accorded to individuals because of the enormity of their sufferings and Ajax, given the trajectory of his life, unquestionably qualified. His posthumous elevation is a clear indication that his suicide in no way diminished the esteem in which he was held.

\* \* \*

'The act of suicide,' as Faber (1970, 16) wrote, 'is an ambivalent act, an act in which a great many forces are at work, forces which contribute to an emotive pattern of considerable complexity and which attest to the kaleidoscopic nature of human motivation.' Irrespective that the characters in the drama consistently ascribe Ajax's fate to divine intervention, Sophocles' play constructs a complex picture of the kaleidoscopic nature of human motivation. It also indicates, with textbook clarity, how the hero rejects the efforts of family and friends to put meaning back into his life and further how he deceives them – or at the very least deceives himself – into the belief that he is on the road to recovery.

The fact that the Greek language lacked the technical vocabulary to identify Ajax's condition in terms that we would use today in no way undermines the sensitivity with which Sophocles explores the subject of suicide. The French nineteenth-century sociologist Emile Durkheim identified three principal categories of suicide, which he labelled as egoistic, altruistic and anomic. Ajax's decision to take his own life is so complex that it contains elements of all three. His suicide is egoistic because it does not take into account the feelings of all his immediate family, particularly those of his wife Tecmessa, who will be reduced to the status of slave in the event of her husband's death. It is altruistic – Durkheim's terminology is confusing to us due to the fact that the word is used in a more restricted sense in English – because the implacability of his hatred shows him straining for identification with an absolute, ideal value, outside a world of constant ebb and flow. And finally it is anomic – the word is derived from the Greek word *anomos*, meaning 'lawless' – because Ajax is an outsider and a loner, a man who has no abiding links with the society around him, neither with the members of his own family, nor with his compatriots in the Greek army.

Ajax's suicide also gives Freudians much to ponder about. His father Telamon had previously won the competition for best soldier, in which he, Ajax, was defeated by Odysseus. His prize was a captive girl, who subsequently gave birth to Ajax. Ajax feels not only outclassed and humiliated by his father, therefore, but in all probability also rejected by his mother, a former captive – and intensely guilt-ridden in consequence. It is hardly surprising that he cannot face going back home to see his parents for fear of appearing naked in their sight. Suicide is therefore the way to reconcile himself with his father, whose forgiveness he seeks for having sullied the family name.[10]

Ajax is the victim of a culture in which the competitive stakes were astronomically high. We might think of it as one where it was impossible to function without a high sense of self-esteem. Once he has been humiliated, he sees no way to lessen his sense of failure. Only by taking his own life will he be able to escape his disgrace, prove that he was no coward, and re-integrate himself posthumously into society. It is therefore a means – the only means – to restore his reputation and self-image, albeit at the cost of his life.

Yet despite the psychological insight that the portrait of Ajax displays, we should not ignore the fact that the play also incorporates a traditional mythological explanation for Ajax's suicide. While Sophocles explores Ajax's psychological state with deep understanding, he provides no explanation for the onset of his original delusion other than the intervention of Athena, who feels a deep personal insult at his contemptuous rejection of her. From a clinical perspective, however, his failure to be awarded the arms of Achilles would have been sufficient to cause him temporarily to go berserk.

There is more to it than that, however. Ajax is more isolated than any other character who commits suicide in Greek tragedy. He is isolated not only from the army and its leadership, which he detests, but also from his family and friends, whose love he rejects, and from the gods, who, he believes, hate him (ll. 457-8, 614-15). We should also note that Ajax is cast in the mould of the typical Sophoclean hero, to which he shows a close family resemblance – isolated, unyielding and impervious to advice. It is a mindset that fascinated the playwright.

Sophocles' play also presents a detailed analysis of the consequences for others of Ajax's act of self-destruction. The Chorus expresses its guilt at having failed to recognize his intention earlier. Teucer is buried in self-pity at the prospect of having to break the tragic news to his parents. Tecmessa demonstrates a fatalistic acceptance of the fact that this is both what heaven willed and what the victim sought. She does not criticize suicide from a moral standpoint. On the contrary, she bases her opposition to it on the adverse consequences that it will have upon his family and friends. As moderns, we are likely to be struck by the matter-of-factness of it all. Suicide is presented as a socio-economic loss to the community, chiefly to the suicide's family, which now lacks his protection.

The debate as to whether Ajax is entitled to a proper burial presents an interesting picture of Greek, specifically Athenian, cultural norms. Hostility towards suicide in Classical Athens seems to have been muted – a possible reflection of the fact that pessimism pervaded Greek culture. 'Call no man happy until he is dead,' remarked the sixth-century BCE Athenian lawgiver Solon (Herodotus 1.32.7). The fourth-century BCE orator Aeschines records that it was the practice in Athens to bury a suicide's hand apart from the body, but that may have been generated by fear of the suicide rather than a judgement on the act itself (Aeschines 3.244). As we have seen in the debate in Sophocles' *Ajax* about whether the hero is entitled to funeral rites, no-one mentions the fact that he has committed suicide. Nor did it disqualify him from achieving heroic status. This is consistent with Aristotle, who claims that Athenian law did not explicitly condemn suicide, though de facto it treated it as illegal, since a person who made an unsuccessful attempt upon her or his life was fined and deprived of citizenship. In seeking to explain the rationale behind the law, he reaches the conclusion that suicide 'wrongs the state'. In other words, it is what we might call an act of social irresponsibility (*Nicomachean Ethics* 5.1138a), rather as Tecmessa suggests.

Broadly speaking tolerance of suicide, albeit at times grudging, at other times tinged with admiration, endured in the West for nearly a thousand years after Sophocles wrote his play. Only with the rise of Christianity did the situation change, and when it did this was primarily due to the influence of philosophy, not religion. The principal posthumous instigator, so to speak, was Plato, since it was his interpretation of the *psyche* or soul that Christianity chiefly absorbed. Even so, Plato was not judgemental about suicide. In *Phaedo* (62b) Socrates in his death cell commends the Orphics for teaching that the body was a prison from which it was unlawful to escape. 'It is not unreasonable', he goes on to say, 'to assume that we should not take our own lives.' But he importantly adds, 'unless the god has sent some necessity upon him, like the one I'm facing' – a reference perhaps to the fact that he saw himself as a martyr to the truth – in which case suicide was excusable.

There is one last point. Though *Ajax* concentrates single-mindedly upon the fate of its central character, Odysseus plays a highly significant framing role. Both in the opening scene and at the conclusion, Odysseus rises above self-interest by expressing his deep sympathy for a manic-depressive who, according to his clear-sighted gaze, is not a shred less human for his profoundly disturbed psychological condition. It was not until 1823 that the practice of driving a stake through the body of a suicide and burying it at the crossroads was finally abandoned in Britain, and it was not until 1961 that the Suicide Act finally abrogated a law that had been in force in England and Wales since 1554 declaring suicide to be a criminal act. In the USA some states, including Virginia, still technically regard attempted suicide as a common law crime.

# Notes

1 Shay (1994) identifies Achilles as a sufferer from post-traumatic stress disorder. See also Emma Cole's chapter in the present collection.
2 As Zanetto (2015) 278–9 points out, suicide is common in the Greek novel as well, though it uses the literary model inherited from tragedy.
3 Finglass (2011) 26–36 gives a full account of the mythical tradition surrounding Ajax.
4 For the iconographic tradition relating to Ajax's suicide, see Catoni (2015) 15–28.

5 See Finglass' discussion of the phraseology (2011) 153–4, 156.
6 Knox (1961) 44 argued that the first thirty-nine lines of this speech were a soliloquy and that he was trying to understand the world 'in which he has now lost his way.'
7 For a useful summary of the competing arguments, see Garvie (1998) 184–6 and Finglass (2011) 328–9.
8 In 2013 an international conference was devoted to the staging of Ajax's suicide without reaching consensus about any of the problems this raises (Most and Ozbek 2015).
9 For discussion of the *skênê* in tragedy with special emphasis on its use in *Ajax*, see Garvie (2015) 34–42. Scholars are in sharp disagreement as to whether Ajax's suicide was preceded by a change of scene (Most and Ozbek 2015).
10 Ajax's suicide can be explored on so many levels, and I do not pretend to have exhausted the list of contributing factors. Faber (1970) 20 offers this 'partial summary', viz. 'the crumbling of his grandiose self-image, his fear of derision, his capacity for magical thought, his relationship to his father, and his own self-hatred,' to which he later adds 'anger at his mother'.

# 7

# Looking at the Isolation of Ajax

## Richard Seaford

For some time now it has been clear to many that the meaning of Athenian tragedy had (and has) an important visual dimension. What is less often recognized however is that – to approach the visual meaning of the original performance – we should not limit ourselves to working out (so far as we can) how it was enacted. There is no such thing as purely objective seeing. How we see art and drama (and everything else) is determined by preconceptions and associations, a fact which becomes especially important when we try to approach the visual meanings of a very different culture. Here is a simple example from Athenian tragedy. In Aeschylus' *Agamemnon* a man (Agamemnon) and a young woman (Cassandra) arrive in a chariot at a space, just outside his house, where there stands a welcoming woman (Clytemnestra). Is it irrelevant that the same configuration of figures occurs in Athenian vase-paintings of the *wedding*? Given the undoubted familiarity of Athenians with the dramatic public spectacle of the wedding procession, might they not have seen the *Agamemnon* scene differently from how we do? Might their seeing have been influenced by the verbal evocations of the wedding in this very scene?

It is of course impossible to reconstruct the myriad associations and preconceptions (religious or otherwise) that influenced how the Athenians saw tragic performances. But this is no excuse for ignoring what we can know. Every tragedy was performed in a particular emotional and intellectual (as well as a physical) landscape. I have elsewhere described the importance of some major features of this landscape for understanding *Ajax*: mystery-cult, hero-cult (also discussed in this volume by Laura Swift), and pre-Socratic cosmology.[1] Here I will not repeat the detail of the argument, but rather extend it into the visual dimension. This will not involve the much-discussed but insoluble questions of how the action was staged. Instead I will make connections between the visual impact of the performance and three interconnected features that in general distinguish tragedy from Homer: focus on the extreme isolation of the individual; the evocation of mystery-cult; and the anticipation of hero-cult.

## 1. Individual isolation

The opening of the play is marked by seeing and not-seeing. Odysseus hears Athena but cannot see her (14–17), and can see Ajax. Athena made Ajax see animals as his human enemies (51–4), prevents him from seeing Odysseus (69–70, 85), and can see and hear both men. The distortion or failure of looking, imposed by deity, may set the individual in a world shared by nobody else. The isolation of Ajax is emphasized: he used to fight the Trojans 'alone' (*monos*: 467, 1276, 1283), and considers doing so again (467). To kill his Greek enemies he rushed out *monos* (47, 294), and after killing the animals was seen bounding *monos* over the plain (29). Realizing what he has done, he suffers the pain of 'seeing his own sufferings, with nobody else having contributed to them' (260); he 'pastures his thoughts alone' (*phrenos oiobōtas*, 614).

Isolation of the individual does occur in Homer, but never in the extreme form that is a central feature of tragedy. There are several instances in tragedy of the individual being alienated from his own family, society, and the gods (Pentheus, Oedipus and Kreon are just the best known examples). Ajax himself declares that he is hated by the gods and by the Greek army, and that he cannot return home because his father will not bear to see him (457–65).

What of his other family members? He requires (688–9, 827) – and after his death receives – the assistance of his half-brother Teucer. Towards his 'spear-won bride' (894) Tecmessa (discussed in this volume by Hanna Roisman) he exhibits – despite her expressions of dependence on him and of grief at his calamity – imperiousness (293, 527–8, 586), hostility (312–13, 369, 594), striking indifference, but eventually pity (652–3); and he praises her for protecting his infant son (536), the family member to whom Ajax feels closest. Although he does not suffer or perpetrate the kin-killing that is a central theme of tragedy (and studiously avoided by Homer), he does say, interestingly, that to have killed his own son 'would have been appropriate to my fate' (534): suicide was associated (probably by an interpolator) with kin-killing later in the text of the play (839–42), as well as by Plato (*Laws* 873c).

Of course individuals may be isolated in Homer too. Odysseus loses all his companions far from home, and Achilles is alienated from the Greek army. But neither of them is alienated from their family or from the gods. Indeed, the constant protection of the Homeric Odysseus by Athena is evoked in the opening of *Ajax* (1, 14, etc.), providing a striking *visible* contrast with the hostility of deity that on Ajax imposes isolation-in-delusion.

Visible expressions of the isolation of Ajax continue. The second episode (646–92), which consists entirely of Ajax's famous speech in which he says he will yield to the ruling Atreidae, 'contains no entrance or exit apart from his own, a rare occurrence ... the effect is to isolate the protagonist' (Finglass). Moreover, in the second part of the third episode (815–65), 'the sense of isolation is still greater, since Ajax appears on stage alone' (Finglass), without the Chorus, and kills himself. The isolation of Ajax preparing his suicide is also expressed in vase-painting (discussed in this volume by David Stuttard).[2]

The absence of the Chorus from this episode is crucial. The departure of the chorus in the course of a drama occurs elsewhere in extant tragedy only four times, and only here in *Ajax* does it accord with the desire of a character to be alone (659). Sophocles could have chosen to report the discovery of the impaled corpse in a messenger speech (as often occurs with tragic violence), but instead he has Ajax – alone in a deserted place (657) – delivering a speech which ends with his suicide.[3] Meanwhile, the Chorus is laboriously *searching* for him (813–14, 866–78), a point to which we will return.

## 2. Mystery-cult

Ajax's insight into the cosmic unity or alternation of opposites – winter and summer, night and day, storm and calm, sleep and waking – seems to reconcile him to his enemies and to death (646–92). I have argued elsewhere that the key to understanding this otherwise baffling speech is to recognize the allusions in it to mystic initiation, in which – as a later epigram[4] puts it – 'death is not only not bad, but good', which is what Ajax has come to realize. The speech is sometimes called the 'deception speech', which is misleading. I call it the 'mystic speech'. Here I confine myself to two points about *visual* meaning.

Firstly, there is a connection here with his isolation. The individual initiand was, before being joyfully integrated into the group of initiates, subjected to suffering and *isolation*.[5] But he or she also acquired understanding of the cosmic unity of opposites, for instance of death with life.[6] Similarly, Ajax is – we have seen – profoundly isolated, and in 646–92 unexpectedly expresses a general understanding of the cosmic unity of opposites. It is as if isolation, detachment from all human relationships, is a precondition for integration into the cosmos. The fact that he is not fully understood by his hearers, which has so baffled and divided scholars, coheres with the secrecy of mystic doctrine and the riddling obscurity[7] of its ritual exposition, as well as itself intensifying his isolation.

Earlier, shortly after being released from the isolating vision inflicted on him by Athena, he expresses another isolating vision, this time of a cosmic unity of opposites: '*Io* darkness, my light, o Erebus, most bright for me, take me, take me as your inhabitant' (394–6). The sudden appearance of salvational bright light in the darkness was a central feature of the death-like experience of mystic initiation that so many of the audience had experienced.[8] Those who have read my piece in *Looking at Bacchae* will know that a bright light in the darkness is revealed to Pentheus as one of his mystic experiences within the house. And just as Pentheus is profoundly isolated, so too Ajax, in his sudden access to darkness as light (expressed as a unity of opposites), is profoundly isolated by his vision. He alone is on the point of death: it is 'darkness, *my* light, Erebos brightest *for me*'.

This isolation takes us to the contrasting solidarity of the choral group. When Ajax ends his mystic speech by saying that he is, despite his current misfortune, 'saved', the Chorus react by bursting into song: 'I shuddered with passionate desire' (*ephrix' erōti*). Passionate desire (*erōs*) for *what*? The phrase *ephrix' erōti* occurs elsewhere only in a fragment of Aeschylus, where it is desire for 'this mystic *telos*'. *Telos* (and its verb *telein*) can refer to mystic initiation (even without the adjective 'mystic'), and has the general meaning 'completion'. Ajax himself has just asked Tecmessa to pray for the 'completion' (he uses both *telos* and *telein*) of what his heart 'passionately desires' (*erān*, the verb of *erōs*).

Consider now the very next words of the Chorus: 'and with great joy I flew up'. Several ancient texts suggests that the idea of the dying soul as a fluttering bird, anxious to escape, was present in the preliminary, fearful state of the mystic rehearsal for death.[9] Mystic initiation was generally a group experience, or – to be more precise – a ritual in which anxious isolated individuals were eventually joyfully integrated into a group, sometimes a chorus.[10] This mystic dynamic is evoked, in Euripides' *Bacchae*, in the interaction of individual (Pentheus) and chorus in the scene in which the royal house is demolished.[11] It is also evoked – differently – in *Ajax*. In the *Bacchae* scene the Chorus represent mystic initiates emerging from their initial despair, whereas Pentheus exhibits all the anxieties and actions of the isolated mystic initiand. These actions include 'wearisome wanderings around' (cf. *Bacchae* 625, 634–5), which in the Eleusinian mysteries were probably envisaged as a search for Persephone.[12] The choral search for Ajax is brief, but goes everywhere (868) and is extremely troublesome (866–76: 'toil brings toil on toil ... a mass of toil'), ending not (as at Eleusis) in the joyful discovery of Persephone returned from Hades but of Ajax just departed for Hades.

I am not claiming that Ajax or the Chorus, or Pentheus and the Chorus, enact the sequence of mystic initiation, but rather that the emotional response to the dramas (especially of the many initiated spectators) was influenced by various evocations of mystic ritual, which might include the horrifying failure or reversal of the mystic sequence. But even if we ignore mystic initiation, there was a special place in the Greek mythological imagination for the positive transition from troublesome wandering to permanent fixity. One of many examples is the wandering of Demeter that led to her founding of mystery-cult at Eleusis, another is the wandering of Orestes that led to his trial that established the Areopagus at Athens. In *Ajax* this transition occurs, in miniature, in the visual impact of the troublesome wandering that leads to the discovery of what dominates – visually as well as verbally – the rest of the play, the corpse of Ajax. But how can a corpse dominate? Here there would for the audience have been another association – with a cult that frequently interpenetrated with mystery-cult, namely hero-cult.[13]

## 3. Hero-cult

Greatness and power, transgression, isolated and piteous death, and enduring hostility to the enemies of Athens: all these features of the Sophoclean Ajax are typical of the aetiological myths of hero-cult. In other tragedies, Sophocles' *Oedipus at Colonus* for instance or Euripides' *Herakleidai*, they lead within the drama to the actual establishment of hero-cult. Each of these features has its socio-political function: his greatness and power provides the protection offered by the tomb of the hero, his isolated piteous death (resulting from transgression) ensures the enduring communal emotion needed to perpetuate the cult, his hostility to Athens' enemies ensures confidence in battle. Even the good will to enemies embraced in Sophocles' drama by both Ajax and Odysseus (contrasting so dramatically with the Peloponnesian Atreidae) would assist the socio-political cohesion engendered by the communal cult of heroes. The political significance of Odysseus' view is discussed in this volume by Brad Levett.

Hero-cult was generally a perpetuation of death ritual centred on the hero's *tomb*. The Chorus predict that Ajax 'will possess the dank tomb that will always be remembered among mortals' (1166–7). There was indeed a tomb and cult of Ajax in the Troad,[14] but he and his son Eurysaces also had an important cult in Attica, in which we know from inscriptions that a key role was played by the *genos* (clan) called 'Salaminians'. In the drama the Chorus of the Salaminian Ajax's Salaminian[15] followers, who are called a *genos* (357), plays a key role in Ajax's burial. His last words include addresses to the three places of his cult: Salamis, Athens – and the Troad (859–63), where Ajax's tomb may perhaps have bolstered the Athenians' (emotional, and military) appropriation of the area.

My focus here is, again, on the visual effect of the cultic associations. The pitiful sight of the corpse of Ajax dominates the last third of the play, and from 1171 the corpse is joined by his infant son Eurysaces. But the effect is not one of mere pathos. Pathos is just one of the necessary ingredients of hero-cult. Another is the *power* exercised by the dead hero. Eurysaces is told to make physical contact, as a 'suppliant', with his father's corpse. This makes sense only if the corpse has retained power, as in hero-cult.[16] This tableau, threatened but ultimately enduring, manifests the visually absorbing combination of pathos, weakness and supernatural power.

There are many parallels between the Ajax–Tecmessa–Eurysaces family in *Ajax* and the Hector–Andromache–Astyanax family famously depicted in the sixth book of the *Iliad*. But the Greeks did not allow Astyanax, as the 'son of an *aristos* (best) father' (Euripides, *Troades* 723) to live, thereby pre-empting future revenge; whereas Eurysaces, whose future seemed so precarious if Ajax were to die,[17] lived to be made an Athenian and to hand over Salamis to Athens:[18] this may have been the theme of Sophocles' (lost) *Eurysaces*, in which there may have been established (or predicted) his cult with its benefit for Athens – a common pattern of Athenian tragedy.

The suicidal Ajax had proudly addressed his son, whose survival and return to Salamis he predicted (545–70). He then told him to 'take hold of the very thing that gives you your name, Eurysaces [Broad Shield]' (574–5), and also predicted that 'my other arms will be buried with me' (577). The sword – with which Ajax killed Trojans, the animals and himself – presumably remains visible after Teucer pulls his corpse from it (1024–35); and the shield bequeathed to Eurysaces (discussed in this volume by Sophie Mills) may well come with him when he is brought back to the stage after 1171. That is why it is (only) the 'body-armour' that Teucer orders to be brought out (and may actually appear) while the corpse is carried out for burial at the end of the play. Here yet another detail from the cult of Ajax at Athens is relevant: ancient scholarship[19] tells us that the Athenians adorned a *klinē* (bed, couch or bier) for Ajax 'with a full set of arms (*panoplia*)'. During the Battle of Salamis, in which the survival of Athens was at stake, the Athenians summoned Ajax and his father Telamon from Salamis (Herodotus 8.64).

The tableau – of Eurysaces, the dead Ajax and (probably) the armour – remains fixed from 1171 until, with the burial of Ajax and the survival of Eurysaces secured, it moves off in the final procession. This fixity, with its cultic combination of heroic pathos and heroic power, contrasts with the dramatic mutability that characterizes all the previous action of the play, as well as with the toilsome search for Ajax by the Chorus, and with the demeaning tirades – delivered by Menelaos, 'king of Sparta' (1102) and then – accompanying the tableau – by his brother Agamemnon, both of whom maintain their extreme hostility to Ajax (1160, 1373) just as he did for them (838–44). By contrast the triumph of the tableau over the hostility (in the sense that it processes to the establishment of Ajax's tomb) is also the triumph of the principle earlier derived by Ajax himself from his cosmological insight into the cosmic alternation of opposites: 'our enemy is to be hated as one who will later be friendly' (679): in urging Ajax's burial Odysseus says 'to the extent that I was then an enemy, I am now a friend' (1377). The principle accords with the social cohesion promoted by the enduring performance of collective death ritual in hero-cult, which might also however celebrate the enduring hostility of the hero to *external* enemies, just as Ajax also finally expresses enduring hostility to the (Peloponnesian) Atreidae: the contradiction with his earlier attitude cannot be explained from within the text, but derives from the contradictory functions of hero-cult.[20]

Besides all this, the dramatic prominence of the sword has a further dimension, as a visible embodiment of the general unity of opposites expressed by Ajax in his mystic speech. Since receiving it as a gift from Hector he has had nothing good from the Greeks: 'the gifts of enemies are not gifts' (658–65). With it he fought the Trojans, killed the sheep, and kills himself. It is the 'most hated/hostile (*echthiston*) of weapons' (658), made perhaps by a Fury (1034), but 'most friendly' (*eunoustaton*) in giving him a quick death (822), the death he passionately desires. Like many other tragic props,[21] the sword is ambivalent.

There is a further aspect of its ambivalence. In his mystic speech Ajax compares his earlier steadfastness to iron that has been hardened by being dipped (in water), but now he has been transformed into his opposite (a woman): 'I was feminized in my *stoma*' (651), which means *mouth* but also *blade*. Ajax, intimately and visibly associated for good or ill throughout the drama with his sword, is here as if identified with it (that the sword has power beyond an ordinary inanimate object is argued in this volume by Rosie Wyles). The iron of the sword was once hardened, and so – it is then implied – can become soft again: the principle of the alternation or unity of opposites is manifest in Ajax himself and in his sword. The salvational unity of opposites pervades not only the cosmos but also what we see on stage.

# Notes

1 Seaford (1994b); there is a good summary of my argument by Hesk (2003) 86–9.
2 Finglass (2011) 30.
3 Where precisely the act occurred has been a matter of controversy.
4 *Inscriptiones Graecae* ii/iii[2] 3661, 6; Clinton (1974) 42. Cf. *Ajax* 684–6, 692, 966–9.
5 E.g. Plutarch, *fragment* 178.
6 Seaford (2003).

7 References in Seaford (2004) 226 n. 36.
8 All this is made clear and explicit in e.g. Plutarch, fragment 178. On the large number of Eleusinian initiates see the references in Seaford (2012) 45.
9 Seaford (2009).
10 Seaford (2013).
11 Again, see my paper in *Looking at Bacchae* (2016). I add here that the initiatory transformation of Pentheus has the following in common with Ajax's: (1) transition from excited aggression to meek subordination to the former enemy; (2) feminization; (3) the acquisition of mystic insight (*Bacchae* 918–24); (4) the mystic image of the harbour (*Bacchae* 902–3); (5) an implicit contrast between the instability of human hostilities and the permanence of mystic happiness (*Bacchae* 897–911).
12 References in Seaford (2012) 28.
13 Seaford (1994a) 123–39, 398–9.
14 Strabo 13.1.32; Pausanias 1.35.5.
15 At 202 they are called descendants of Erechtheus, which expresses the Athenian claim to Salamis: see also 1222.
16 Cf. supplication at the heroic tomb at Aeschylus, *Choephoroi* 334–5 and Euripides, *Helen* 800, with Burian (1972) 154.
17 510–12, 588, 944–5, 985–7.
18 Pausanias 1.35.2; Plutarch, *Life of Solon* 10.
19 Scholiast on Pindar, *Nemeans* 2.19.
20 Another detail that may perhaps be aetiological of the cult is Teucer's rejection of Odysseus' wish to participate in the burial ('I hesitate to allow you to touch this burial, in case my action is repulsive to the dead man'), though he does then encourage Odysseus and the other Greeks to participate in other ways (1394–7). This (otherwise arbitrary) punctilious detail may prefigure the special role for the Salaminioi in the cult.
21 Seaford (1994a) 388–94.

8

# Tecmessa

Hanna M. Roisman

## Introduction

Tecmessa, Ajax's captive wife/concubine, is one of the most powerful secondary figures in extant Sophoclean drama. She is not named in the Homeric epics and seems to be largely an innovation by Sophocles. Surviving fragments indicate that Aeschylus produced an Ajax trilogy that included *The Award of the Arms*, *The Thracian Women* and *The Women of Salamis*, but no evidence exists as to whether Tecmessa appeared in them.[1] The female figure on the Brygos kylix (500–475 BCE) who is shown covering the corpse of Ajax may be a representation of Tecmessa, and thus a possible precedent to Sophocles' character.[2] Within Sophocles' *Ajax* the character of Tecmessa undergoes a remarkable evolution during the course of the play, from a passionate wife/spear-bride who takes an active role in trying to dissuade her husband/master from taking his own life to a self-possessed figure standing silently by his lifeless body.

Tecmessa's time onstage almost equals that of Ajax. Out of the 1,420 lines of the play she is visible to the audience for a total of 805 (56 per cent) lines; she engages with others during 556 (39 per cent) lines, while during the last 249 (17 per cent) lines she is inactive and played by an 'extra'.[3] By comparison, although Ajax is present onstage for 903 lines (64.5 per cent), he only engages with others for 384 lines (27 per cent versus Tecmessa's 39 per cent), and for 519 lines (37 per cent) he lies dead, the focus of a confrontation between Teucer, the Atreidae (i.e. the sons of Atreus: Agamemnon and Menelaus), and Odysseus, with Tecmessa silently standing by. Although Ajax is the central character of the play, dramatically Tecmessa is more active and involved.

The events depicted in Sophocles' *Ajax* take place directly after Odysseus has been awarded the arms of Achilles. Since Ajax regarded the arms as rightfully his, this judgement was such a denigrating insult to his honour, *timē*, that it has driven him to the edge of insanity. In his mind, granting Achilles' arms to Odysseus not only nullified every heroic act that he, Ajax, had ever performed, together with every public accolade he had ever received, but also lionized a man whom Ajax regarded as both unscrupulous and unheroic. Enraged by the perceived injustice, Ajax had set out to the Greek camp in the middle of the night, intending to kill the Atreidae, Odysseus, and possibly many of the Greek army too. It was only Athena's intervention that prevented Ajax from carrying out his plan. She afflicted him with madness, befuddling him to the extent that he mistook the captured herds, flocks and their guards for the Achaean army and their commanders. While honour, *timē*, was recognized as one of the most important values to a Homeric hero, the spectators, well versed in the epics, would know that shedding the blood of comrades in arms out of revenge, even for lost honour, is not a Homeric value. In the *Iliad* Athena did not allow Achilles to draw his sword and kill Agamemnon as revenge for Agamemnon's taking Briseis from him. She instructed him to taunt Agamemnon with words instead, and Achilles listened to the goddess (*Il.* 1.188–218). The spectators, who do not know exactly why Athena has maddened Ajax, might well think that it is the potential shedding of blood that brought the goddess to the defence of the other Achaeans, but they might also ask themselves why she did not prevent it in the same way as in the case of Achilles. Nevertheless, beyond his desire for a bloody revenge, there are no extenuating circumstances for his wish to kill his fellow warriors.[4]

From Tecmessa's first interaction with the Chorus of Salaminian sailors, the audience learns that while she was not privy to Ajax's murderous intentions, she did try to prevent him from going out in the middle of the night with his sword (288–91). Although she was silenced and ignored by Ajax, the fact that she questioned his actions suggests the nature of the relationship between them. The sailors address her as one whom Ajax loves, albeit a spear-won mate; Ajax and Tecmessa, although they may technically be master and concubine, share real affection for each other. The essence of their bond may not immediately be clear, partly because of the ambiguity of the words used to describe it and partly because of Ajax's terse nature. It is no mean feat for Tecmessa to repeatedly stand up to Ajax, the mightiest of all Greek warriors after Achilles, and argue her case despite his frequent commands to desist and remove herself from his presence. Indeed, only in considering the 'larger than life' characteristics of Ajax, can one truly appreciate Tecmessa's qualities. The extent to which Ajax represents the Homeric hero has been discussed extensively elsewhere, along with the idea that he was indeed the last of the heroes, incapable of adapting to a new world governed by different social rules. Nevertheless, in order to make any sense of Sophocles' intentions in depicting the relationship between Tecmessa and Ajax, which is our primary concern, the heroic and uncompromising nature of Ajax must be kept in mind.

## Portrayals of Ajax

In portraying Ajax, Sophocles faced a difficult task. As Ajax was known from the *Iliad* for his conciseness of speech, it would have been dramatically unwise to make him prolix. Sophocles chooses to give three quite different portrayals of Ajax at the start of the play: one from Athena, one from the sailors, and one from Tecmessa, with these three portraits also reflecting back on those who describe him. The image of Ajax presented by Athena is the least flattering of the three. It is she who intervened, preventing Ajax from carrying out his revenge against the Atreidae and Odysseus. It later transpires that Athena's anger against Ajax is of long standing, dating back to his expressions of arrogance years earlier when he rejected the gods' help (762-77). Either way, Athena's objective is not to show Ajax's emotions, but only to disparage him so that his madness, whether imposed by her or arising from his own nature, may serve as a lesson on why humans should honour the divine.

A contrasting view of Ajax is presented in the *parodos* (134-200) sung by the sailors under his command as they march into the *orchestra*. While the sailors express their horror at the rumour of Ajax breaking into the grazing grounds and killing the captured animals, the common booty of the Greeks (144-7), they also convey the respect, confidence and love that Ajax has earned among the soldiers he led to Troy from Salamis. Four times they describe him, either directly or by implication, as 'great' (*megas*, 154, 158, 160-1, 169). If the rumours they have heard are true, that must mean a loss of honour for Ajax, and the sailors are naturally worried. As is traditional, disgrace for Ajax is marked by the laughter of his enemies (198-9). The sailors do not want to believe the rumour, which they hope is gossip spread by Odysseus and the Atreidae. They ask Ajax to come out of his tent and dispel the rumour, even though they are semi-resigned to hearing that the unbelievable has happened. They ascribe the slaughter of the animals to madness caused either by Artemis Tauropolos (related to the bulls) or by Ares, for some misdeed of Ajax. As they end their song, they repeat their appeal to Ajax to come out; but Sophocles surprises the audience by bringing on Tecmessa instead.

Tecmessa is the only person with firsthand knowledge of what Ajax went through the previous night, and she presents her version of the events with none of Athena's vengeful malice. As far as the dramaturgical role Tecmessa plays in this part, it matters little whether she is a concubine, i.e. regarded by Ajax as a slave, or a rightful wife.[5] What matters is how much she cares for him as her consort and father of her son. And she does care. She describes Ajax's whereabouts before his delusion and during it. She also describes in detail and with compassion Ajax's utter devastation as the realization of his diminished honour slowly dawns upon him after he awakens from his madness in total bewilderment. Throughout her recitation Tecmessa displays the ability to report calmly and accurately on highly disturbing events. Although she emphasizes the grisly nature of Ajax's deeds, she never once indicates anything but understanding for him. While we will see later on the considerable ingenuity Tecmessa displays in trying to convince Ajax to rethink his intended suicide, her poise and self-control are already evident in her earliest speeches, when she stands in for Ajax in explaining the situation to the sailors, and then invites them to try to help him at this time of distress.

The first episode starts with her appearance in line 201. Tecmessa provides information about Ajax's acts while the Chorus imagine the consequences. Once the sailors realize the rumour about Ajax is correct, their reaction is swift. They now worry less about Ajax's future than their own. They are afraid that they might share his fate in being stoned. However, on hearing from Tecmessa that Ajax has regained his sanity, they rejoice, thinking simplistically that the trouble is over, not anticipating the danger looming ahead with this regained sanity.

As the exchanges between Tecmessa and the Chorus continue, the audience learns the extent to which Tecmessa empathizes with Ajax's misfortune (265–83). While the sailors only consider themselves, she explains to the Chorus how her misery doubled once Ajax came back to his senses. When demented, he enjoyed what he was doing, while she was grief stricken at seeing him in the throes of delusion. But once Ajax regained his reason, 'and he's returned to his old self, he's mortified' (275), and Tecmessa is equally distressed, because now 'both parties are unhappy, not just one' (277). Tecmessa, unlike the sailors, identifies herself completely with Ajax's affliction, and her following description of him only underscores the deep affection and concern she feels for him.

In reply to the Chorus' question about how Ajax's trouble started, Tecmessa gives a detailed description (284–330) of what she has witnessed. She describes how Ajax, without being summoned, took his sword and ventured out in the depths of the night. Tecmessa tried to stop him, but he dismissed her with a curt rebuke often used when a man wants to silence a woman: '[Woman/Wife,[6]] a woman's greatest gift is silence' (293). She gives up. She does not follow him, and so does not see what happens away from their tent, but she now describes in graphic detail the horrific scene of his return: the beheadings, broken spines and twisted throats of 'bulls and sheep and sheep-dogs' (296–7), brought inside the hut. She describes how Ajax slaughtered them, assaulting some as if they were men. The sailors also hear how Ajax darted out and spoke to some sort of shadow (301–2). He raves about the

Atreidae and Odysseus, and laughing aloud he tells this shadow what payment he inflicted on them for their insults. Tecmessa is baffled by this, but the audience would know that the 'shadow' Ajax was talking to is Athena. The Prologue does not mention Ajax's mad laughter; however, we might well recognize here what Kamerbeek described as 'an excellent stage-direction for the scene 91–117' (1963: on line 303). Kamerbeek supposes that Ajax might have laughed before line 108 or 105, which is very likely and probably referred to by Athena in line 114, when she says to Ajax: 'If it gives you so much pleasure (*terpsis*), go to it. See your plan through to the end.' Tecmessa's mention of the laughter must have aroused in the audience respect for her perceptive acuity and attention to detail. Ajax might have dismissed her as 'just' a woman, but she is proving herself a reliably factual messenger. She has heard and interpreted correctly what the audience has actually seen. From this point on, the audience is unlikely to doubt anything she tells them.

We learn next from her that immediately after Ajax's brief encounter with Athena he returns to his senses:

And when he finished, he came crashing back inside the tent.
And somehow slowly, slowly he regained his sanity.

305–6

Tecmessa goes on to describe Ajax's ghastly awakening, how he cried aloud, sitting among the carcasses and tearing his hair with his nails, and how he threatened her terribly, forcing her to reveal the whole train of events. Her thorough description serves as a substitute for the audience watching the scene themselves.

Tecmessa admits that she told Ajax all that had happened through fear. He then broke into a bitter cry, groaning and wailing, behaviour he normally considered a mark of a coward (317–20). Tecmessa adds, as befits her caring role, that Ajax refuses food and drink, sitting inert among the carcasses of the cattle he has slain. As if predicting what Ajax will soon decide, she says she fears Ajax may harm himself, and asks the sailors for their help, recognizing that Ajax is most likely to listen to those he has fought alongside: 'Men like him can be won over by their friends' (329–30). Tecmessa's initiative might have reminded the audience of Nestor's attempt at convincing Patroclus to persuade Achilles to return to the battlefield in *Iliad* 11.793, stating that 'persuasion of a comrade is a good thing'. They also may think of how in Book Fifteen (404), after seeing the Danaans retreating from their fight with the Trojans, Patroclus rushes back to Achilles, hoping now to prevail upon him to join the battle and remember Nestor's advice. By having Tecmessa use parallels with the *Iliad*, Sophocles enhances her standing in the eyes of the audience. However, the spectators would also have been aware that in both cases the persuasion failed, which does not bode well for her effort.

Tecmessa's description of the events to the Chorus allows both the inner and outer audiences to gain an insider's perspective as to Ajax's state of mind. His current devastation is not primarily because he was maddened by Athena and killed flocks, but because in his madness he failed to kill the Atreidae and Odysseus. His ardent wish to kill his own comrades inevitably prevents him from returning to the fold of the Achaeans. One could draw some comparison between him and Achilles by claiming that Achilles too caused the death of many of his comrades by not joining the Achaeans on the battlefield. However, Achilles did not attempt to kill any of the Achaeans himself. Ajax's unabated wish to do so does not seem excusable. The quest for honour and fame does not trump one's obligation of loyalty to one's comrades.

## Tecmessa's role and speech

It is unclear whether *Ajax* precedes *Antigone*, or vice versa, but both are considered to be early Sophoclean dramas, first produced in the 440s.[7] Both employ a similar dramatic methodology whereby a secondary character serves as a foil to the protagonist, with the resulting dialogues serving to add depth to the audience's understanding of the main character. Thus as the plot of *Ajax* evolves, Sophocles expands Tecmessa's role from that of a messenger transmitting information about Ajax's actions and mood into a character whose interactions with Ajax are vital to the audience's understanding of him. This methodology may be seen more clearly in *Antigone* and in the much later *Electra*.[8] In the exchanges between Antigone and Ismene, we learn of Antigone's determination to bury her brother and her stubbornness in resolving to carry out her plan, whatever the consequences. Through the interaction between Chrysothemis and Electra we learn of Electra's fathomless resolve to avenge her father even at the price of matricide. In both of these plays, each sister tries unsuccessfully to persuade the other. The case of Ajax and Tecmessa does not exactly parallel the interactions between the two sets of sisters, as there is a difference in status and gender. Furthermore, the efforts at persuasion are all on Tecmessa's side; Ajax at first seems merely to issue orders. Nevertheless, Tecmessa's exchanges with Ajax are essential in revealing his character, which turns out to be somewhat different from audience expectations based on the Homeric epics. Tecmessa is also far more than just a foil to Ajax, being herself sharply individualized.[9]

Tecmessa's descriptions of Ajax's behaviour towards her, noted above, are indicative of a certain complexity in the relationship between them. On the one hand, Ajax is prone to silence her with harsh retorts such as: 'a woman's greatest gift is silence' (293), and it is fear that moves her to tell Ajax the fateful night's events in their entirety (315–16). However, the introductory remark by the Chorus that she is 'Ajax' slave brought to his bed at spear point' for whom 'he cares deeply' (211–12), reveals another side to the relationship, and later on Tecmessa herself admits that he has treated her better in the past (808). In whatever way Ajax's comments strike us nowadays, this kind of attitude toward women's expression may be found in other tragedies as well. Tecmessa herself refers to Ajax's comment regarding the desirability of a woman's silence as being 'the old cliché' (*hymnoumena*, 292).[10] On the other hand, her language describing Ajax's behaviour throughout the night might indicate that she was as surprised by his treatment of her as she was by his lamentations. It is possible that both of these behaviours were out of character. The change in manner may be intended to intimate that something is still profoundly amiss with the hero's state of mind. Indeed, when in lines 394–7 Ajax makes an agonized plea to die, (which he begins with a clear demonstration of his unbalanced mind in lines 394–5: 'Darkness is my only light, and death's the brightest light of all'), Tecmessa responds by exclaiming how changed his behaviour is: 'To hear him speak this, such a brave and noble man – he'd never have spoken like this before' (410–11).

Despite Ajax's harsh treatment of her, Tecmessa persists in trying to calm him. She first addresses Ajax onstage at line 368, where she asks him not to continue his litany about the insult that he has suffered: 'Ajax, please – master, please – *don't speak* like that.' Her address is polite but expressed in a vigorous imperative mode, which reinforces the feeling that she is no ordinary slave. On the other hand, any time she gives him advice, she always prefaces it with the formal address 'master Ajax' (cf. 485, 585). Thus while implicitly giving him counsel, she explicitly acknowledges that Ajax is her superior, as if to compensate for her daring. Ajax's reaction to Tecmessa's pleas is fierce and dismissive: 'Leave me! Go! Go away! *aiai aiai*' (369–70). Ajax is clearly impatient with Tecmessa, but it is possible that his commands reflect awareness of her potential sway over him. This could be the reason he wants her either to be quiet or leave.

It is noteworthy that at this point Tecmessa is not afraid of Ajax, as she had been previously. Instead, she now dares to counter his wishes, remains at his side, and continues pleading with him: 'By all the gods, stop now! Be rational!' (371). Sophoclean protagonists are often urged by their foils to yield and 'think', or 'think right', i.e. be rational.[11] This is what Ismene asks of Antigone (*Ant.* 49) and Chrysothemis of Electra (*El.* 394, 890, 1038, cf. 384). Tecmessa's persistent intervention, even though ignored, allows the playwright to expose Ajax's character, with the same dramaturgical approach to characterization he uses for Antigone and Electra. The audience first learn that Ajax is still obsessed with destroying Odysseus and any others he sees as responsible for having caused his shame. He is devastated both at having suffered a grave injustice, and at having been thwarted in his attempt to avenge and correct this injustice. He shows no remorse for having tried to kill his comrades in arms, being solely concerned with the damage to his own honour, and how others might view him. That he has suffered madness does not, in itself, demoralize him but he regrets that the madness diverted him from his purpose. It is Ajax's own reputation that is most important for him.

Indeed, it is necessary that the audience understand Ajax's state of mind in order to make sense of his subsequent behaviour. His agonized monologue (430–80) explores all avenues open to him for salvaging his lost honour. He considers going home and leaving the Atreidae to their own devices. However, his father, Telamon, had returned home from Troy in full glory, and Ajax cannot face him empty handed, with no prize for valour, and worse still, humiliated. Nor can he attack the Trojans and perish with honour, because this might serve the Atreidae. He sees no value or joy in a life with no hope of honour. In his mind there are only two options for a noble man: to live with honour or die with honour. We ought to remember that for a Homeric hero it was not enough to be sure of his own prowess, bravery and supreme merit: he must also receive public acknowledgement of it. The public denial of Ajax's honour, shown both in losing the armour and in the mockery made of him for slaughtering the flocks, leaves him without the option of remaining alive, since his honour consists in what others think of him. Ajax therefore decides on a quick and noble death at his own hand.

Tecmessa's speech countering Ajax's resolve to commit suicide follows (485–524). Some view her speech as being so emotional that it cannot be analysed using logical points (e.g. Kamerbeek 1963: on 485 sqq.). Others, with whom this paper is in agreement, point out that the speech is 'complex in structure and dense in thought'.[12] The speech attempts to counter Ajax's wish to die by intertwining appeals to his passion for honour with references to the need to adjust to changing circumstances and to the ethical and social values that matter to a Homeric hero: shame, pity and gratitude.

Tecmessa does not counter head-on Ajax's maxim that a noble man must live with honour or die honourably (479–80); indeed, how could she? Instead she offers a different maxim: 'It's the worst thing in the world to suffer a cruel twist of fate' (485–6), which she exemplifies by her own lot: 'I was born free. My father was a powerful man, the richest in all Phrygia. Now thanks to the gods and to your victory in battle I'm a slave' (487–90). She makes two points.

First, she creates a common ground between herself and Ajax by bringing up the idea of the vicissitudes of fortune: she has suffered at the hands of fate as he does. Second, her experience also implies that one needs to adapt. Changes in one's fortune call upon the afflicted person to adjust to new circumstances. She implies that enduring misfortune is not an insurmountable hurdle: it is possible to reconcile oneself to a changed status brought about by bitter blows of a perverse fate and still pursue life. Tecmessa remembers to flatter Ajax's might, of which he is so proud, and to present his actions as in line with the gods' will.

After establishing a common ground of suffering due to hostile fate, Tecmessa seems to purposefully pass over Ajax's account of his lost honour and focuses on the future instead of the past. She counters Ajax's claim that death will bring him honour by vividly describing how in fact his honour will be diminished if he dies now. She cleverly ties her fate to his, claiming that when she and their son Eurysaces are dragged off as slaves, her servitude will detract from Ajax's greatness. In short, what happens to her reflects on Ajax. His enemies would point a finger at her and say: 'Look at her now, Ajax's bed-mate! And he was *once the greatest of the* Greeks! How are the mighty fallen!' (501–2). Tecmessa once more flatters Ajax for his might, but turns his valour on its head by claiming that it would make her downfall into slavery even more poignant. She presents the imagined speaker as more insulting than pitying (cf. Hector in *Il.* 6.459–61), and adds that her servitude will be shameful not only to him but also to his family. The implicit message is that if he worries about seeming a coward to his father by not winning Achilles's armour and thus losing his honour, how does he think he would seem to Telamon when his widow is mocked and dragged off as a slave by his enemies?

Tecmessa introduces Ajax's mother Periboea into her arguments, asking that he consider her, too. By alluding to the importance of a mother, Tecmessa invokes another aspect of her own relationship with Ajax: she is the mother of his child; she and Ajax are a unit as Telamon and Periboea are. That is to say, she, Tecmessa, is part of his family. Once more Tecmessa attempts to divert Ajax's thoughts from the past to the present and future. Instead of concentrating on Telamon's glorious past, she tries to focus Ajax's concern on the *present* state of his parents: they are old now, she says; they need their son for what they will be going through in the future.

She argues that Ajax should feel *shame* (*aidōs*) for thinking of abandoning his father in his painful old age and his mother who keeps praying for his safe return (507–9). The feeling of *shame* (*aidōs*) is a powerful motivational force for a Homeric hero, as is evident in the scene between Hector and Andromache on the Scaean Gates in Book Six of the *Iliad* (405–93), a scene which is universally thought by scholars to be mirrored in the exchange between Ajax and Tecmessa.[13] When the tearful Andromache begs Hector not to return to the battle where he might be killed, leaving her a widow and their son an orphan, Hector answers: 'Woman/Wife (*gynai*), I also think of all these things, but I feel terribly *shamed* (*aideomai*) before the Trojans, and their long-robed wives, if like a coward I hide away from the battle' (441–3). By bringing up the sense of *shame*, Tecmessa avails herself not only of what a Homeric hero sees as a moral obligation that should overcome his personal wishes, but also of a value that the Homeric Ajax was known to urge in moments of crisis. The majority of the spectators would be aware of this.[14]

From *shame* related to the debt owed to one's parents, Tecmessa moves to *pity* and the importance of *gratitude*; both powerful feelings motivating the *Iliadic* heroes to action. Pity would cause one comrade to come to the aid of another on the battlefield, or avenge a fallen companion.[15] As pity for the young, unprotected and downtrodden is an important heroic value, it is natural for Tecmessa to call upon Ajax to have pity for his son Eurysaces who, in case of his father's death, will be taken into the custody of strangers. We should note that she does not explicitly ask Ajax to pity *her*. She says: 'And, master, pity your son, alone and orphaned, no-one to look after him, no family, no friends. Think of the suffering your death would bring him – *and me, too* (*k'amoi*)' (510–12). We get a better idea of her self-effacement if we compare her words with those of Andromache to Hector: 'My dear, your own strength will destroy you, and you have no pity for your infant child, *nor for me, ill-fated, who soon will be your widow*' (*Il.* 6. 407–9, cf. 431–2).

Andromache explicitly puts herself forward and emphasizes her future widowhood immediately after mentioning their son, Astyanax. Tecmessa pleads for herself as an afterthought, as *an extension* of Eurysaces. She assumes that the fate of Eurysaces would certainly be more pressing to Ajax than her own misery. Garvie (1988, 520) comments: 'Tecmessa modestly and humbly subordinates herself to Ajax's parents and his son.' At the same time, Tecmessa also knows that she and Eurysaces are bound; in no place is it implied that Eurysaces is or should be on his own without her. This assumption is supported by the fact that Ajax eventually states that he pities both his son *and* Tecmessa (652–3). In his mind they are conjoined as one.

In a structure close to ring composition, just before her final appeal on the basis of gratitude, Tecmessa returns to her attempts to establish common ground with Ajax, this time through a common sense of abandonment. This feeling of desertion is certainly close to the heart of Ajax, who is excruciatingly aware of his own isolation and rejection (349–50, 466–7, 682–3). Tecmessa dwells on her own isolation and complete dependence on Ajax: 'Where would

I live – how could I *afford* to live – without you? All my security's bound in you' (518–19).[16] Unlike the sailors, who have families in Salamis to whom they can return, she has no place to go: 'I've no-one else to turn to, only you – because *you* wrecked my country' (514–15).

Lastly, Tecmessa brings up the value of reciprocity, or more precisely of *gratitude* (*charis*), a powerful motivational force in the *Iliad*. Asking Ajax to consider what she has done for him, she attributes nobility to the one who honours the value of gratitude, and nicely includes the word 'noble' in her last line, responding to Ajax's use of the word in the last line of his speech (480), but in a reversed argument (in the following translation 'reputation' stands for 'noble').[17]

> So spare a little thought for me. A real man spares some thought for those who've made him happy. Kindness (*charis*) brings out kindness (*charis*) in return, but if you don't give any thought to those who've helped you in the past – well, that's the end of that man's reputation.
>
> 520–4

Gratitude, like pity, motivates a Homeric hero to save his comrades. The spectators versed in Homer would remember that it was Ajax, one of the three members of the embassy to Achilles in Book Nine of the *Iliad*, who based his plea to Achilles on the need to respect the value of gratitude:[18]

> But Achilles has made savage the heroic heart in his chest,
> unmerciful man! Nor does he care for the affection (*philotēs*) of
> his comrades, with which, pitiless man, we have honored him
> by the ships above all others.
>
> 629–32

Achilles, Ajax claims, does not reciprocate the Achaeans' love for him. He does not love them back, and thus he neglects the value of gratitude, which should have prompted him to come back to the battlefield. Ajax's was the shortest of the three ambassadors' speeches, only nineteen lines (9.624–42), in contrast to eighty-two of Odysseus (*Il.* 9. 225–306) and 172 by Phoenix (*Il.* 9.434– 605), but it was Ajax's brief statement that prompted Achilles to stay: 'Ajax, ... you seem to speak *after my own mind*' (*Il.* 9.644–5). No longer will he go back to Phthia as he threatened to do after Briseis had been taken away from him. He will stay at Troy, although he will refrain from battle unless his own ships are attacked.

The obligation of gratitude is Tecmessa's trump card. The audience must have realized that Sophocles makes Tecmessa battle Ajax rhetorically using the same principle Ajax himself called upon Achilles to follow in the *Iliad*. The spectators must respect her knowledge of what might influence Ajax.

In summary, Tecmessa focuses first on the need to adapt to change, and then invokes three important Homeric values: *shame, pity* and *gratitude*. These should lead Ajax to reverse his decision out of consideration for the fates of his elderly parents, of his young and defenceless son, and lastly of Tecmessa herself. Neglecting these values will only pile one dishonour upon another. She couches her plea to Ajax in an implied suggestion of the common ground they share: the lives of both of them have been exposed to a capricious fortune, and both feel abandoned.

Ajax does not reply to Tecmessa. When the Chorus ask him to pity her and approve of her words, he says nothing about pity or her speech, but snaps that she will have his approval if she obeys him by bringing their son before him. However, what follows shows that in fact he was listening carefully to what she had to say.[19] Tecmessa asked him to show regard for his parents by returning alive to Salamis, and to pity their son and herself. Ajax responds to her requests with a twist. He does not seem to reverse his resolve to commit suicide, but uses Eurysaces as an answer to Tecmessa's requests. He gives orders for Teucer to take Eurysaces to Salamis, and 'to show' the boy to his parents. Thus, Ajax not only ensures Eurysaces' safety after his death, but presumably is satisfied that even though his parents won't see their son back alive, they can enjoy their grandson as their son's reflection. Ajax is passing his responsibility to tend for his parents in their old age on to Eurysaces (568–9). It is noteworthy that until Tecmessa mentioned his mother, Ajax was so focused on the disappointment he caused his father by not winning Achilles' arms, that he never mentioned her. Now he mentions her by name. The one person passed over in his reply is Tecmessa. Does taking Eurysaces to Salamis imply that Tecmessa will accompany him? We are not told explicitly. In his speech to Eurysaces, it is clear that Ajax recognizes that at this stage of the child's life he is a source of joy for his mother (558–9). It is indeed unlikely that an infant or a toddler boy would be separated from his mother. Once Ajax is dead, the situation changes for both Eurysaces and Tecmessa. Eurysaces will become the only legitimate heir to the house of Telamon, and it is unlikely that his mother would not also be welcome in their house.[20] Tecmessa's silence regarding Eurysaces' possible future transport to Salamis might indicate that indeed she never fears a separation.

The biggest impact of Tecmessa's speech can be seen in what is called Ajax's *Trugrede* or 'deception speech' (646–83), in which Ajax contemplates his own possible change of heart within the frame of cosmic changes. He begins by admitting that he does feel pity for Tecmessa and Eurysaces.[21] Having dismissed Tecmessa only a few lines earlier (594–5), giving her very little hope of being able to influence him, this speech must have been a surprising reversal. First Ajax announces that he, who has all along refused to yield or to listen to his friends, recognizes the constant flux which typifies the world we live in. All things grow, come to the light of the day, and then pass into darkness. Then he apparently implies that if this is the guiding principle of the world, perhaps Ajax could change too. Ajax's words also indicate that the most unexpected things could happen: 'I was strong once, as strong as toughened iron, *but what she said – this woman – has undone me*' (650–2). It could be inferred from this statement that Ajax has internalized Tecmessa's plea and has decided to try to adapt to his changed fortunes.

The second half of his speech seems completely out of character with the Ajax seen just a few minutes earlier, as he now states that one must yield to the gods and revere the Atreidae, since they are in power. Once more he uses metaphors from the mighty forces of nature. If the bitter cold of winter gives way to summer, if the awful darkness of night moves over to be replaced by day, if powerful storms step aside for calm weather (666–76), then perhaps he, too, must accept his changed fate. All of these references to powerful forces yielding to change indicate that he has at least listened to Tecmessa's words. He concludes his thoughts with one final comment on the notion of change as applied to human affairs: friendship and enmity, neither lasts forever and both can change at any time (678–83). These words gain poignancy in the final scenes of the play.

In all of his self-realizations, Ajax touches on the ideas that Tecmessa brought up in her speech. Just as forces of nature effect changes within the world, man's fate may change too. It is impossible to resist these changes, so to survive one must adapt. Whether or not he is sincere, on which there is vast scholarly disagreement, it is significant that Ajax bases his monumental speech, just before taking his own life, on the themes Tecmessa brought up in her speech.

## Ajax and Tecmessa

Much has been said about Ajax ignoring, abusing or disrespecting Tecmessa.[22] Does he really ignore Tecmessa out of disregard and disdain because she is his captive bed-fellow? There is no question that his replies to her caring comments are harsh, sometimes savagely so, e.g.: 'Do not ask me, do not question me! It is best to show sense' (586); 'You vex me in excess! ...' (589); 'Speak to those who will listen to you!' (591); 'Already you have said too much!' (592); 'You stupid woman! Do you think that you can change me *now*?' (594–5). He insistently pushes her away to stop her attempts at dissuading him from his decision to kill himself. It is however conceivable that these severe repulses do not stem from disdain, but rather from Ajax's awareness that Tecmessa's words have a strong effect on him and might endanger his resolve.

Ajax's various comments and contempt for women's tears: 'And no tears when you're inside. I know how women love to weep' (579–80) are shared by male characters in other tragedies. In Aeschylus' *Seven against Thebes* Eteocles rudely attempts to silence the Chorus of Virgins, who shriek in terror of the attackers of Thebes. He fears their shrill cries might demoralize the defenders (*Se*.182–202). In Euripides' *Orestes*, Orestes and Pylades decide to keep Electra in the dark about their plan to face the assembly lest she immediately shed tears for Orestes and blunt their courage for facing the crowd of hostile citizens (*Or.* 787–9). In both cases the men are aware of the women's probable reactions and advocate their silence to prevent them from influencing events.

If Ajax is behaving similarly to Eteocles and Orestes, his attempts to keep a distance from his consort are not necessarily due to any lack of fondness or respect for her, but simply because what she might say could influence him. He knows his well-being is at the heart of her considerations, but he simply cannot do what she wants. This is why he wants her to leave, keep away, be silent, and stop wearing down his determination. While tacitly acknowledging that Tecmessa, as the mother of his child, may have some influence over him, Ajax's obsession with his honour, now permanently tarnished, cannot allow him to be swayed by anyone. The simplest way to avoid Tecmessa's influence is to stop her from talking. We hear from the Chorus and Tecmessa that Ajax does feel genuine affection for her and that she has received better treatment from him in the past. This is why Tecmessa keeps trying to retrieve the Ajax she once knew. Tecmessa knows exactly what could move him: shame, pity and gratitude. She knows how to urge Ajax to act out of the moral imperative of customary values. However, none of Tecmessa's arguments overrides Ajax's fateful, and in this case fatal, obsession with Homeric ideas of honour and fame.

To insulate himself from Tecmessa's pressure, Ajax barely speaks to her directly and never reciprocates the immediacy and emotionality in her addresses to him. The only time he approves her actions is when she tells him that she hid Eurysaces for fear he might kill the child in his madness: 'I approve your action and the forethought that you showed' (536, Lloyd-Jones 1994). His use of the dramatic aorist (*epēnesa*, 'I approved'), instead of the present tense 'I approve', distances Ajax emotionally from her.[23] Lloyd (1999, 39) states: 'Ajax's tone is stiffly formal, in marked contrast to Tecmessa's more directly emotional language' (e.g. 527–9). The aorist [tense] distances him somewhat from his acknowledgement of the face-threatening obligations incurred by his madness. In short, in his only direct approbation of her, Ajax is still cold and distant. However, he is not insensitive to her feelings. When he tells Eurysaces what he expects of him when he grows up, Ajax does not forget Tecmessa's current happiness with the boy: 'Till then, well, may soft breezes nurture you, enjoy your childhood. *And bring your mother happiness*' (*mētri tēide charmonēn*, 559). Ajax seems much less self-centred in this scene than one usually gives him credit for.[24] Likewise, there is the ring of sincerity in the pity he expresses for Tecmessa and their son in the *Trugrede*, when he admits that: 'I feel such pity for her, left alone, a widow, and my orphan boy surrounded by my enemies' (652–3).

## Ajax's death

Tecmessa must be taken in to some extent by Ajax's words in his *Trugrede*, as she finally agrees to leave his side and enters the tent. She does not hear Ajax's enigmatic final words to the Chorus, which might have caused her some concern: '... and – even if I'm suffering now – maybe you'll discover soon that I'm at peace' (591–2). After Ajax leaves the stage, the Chorus rejoice, taking his words at face value. Their relief however is not long lived. Once the messenger from Teucer arrives, reporting Calchas' words, it finally becomes clear to the men that Ajax is in imminent mortal danger. Their first step is to call for Tecmessa, and her actions confirm the strong character that Sophocles has built for her throughout the play. It is she who takes charge, giving orders to the men and sending them out in search parties, with the collateral effect that the stage is left empty, making way for Ajax's final suicide scene. It is also Tecmessa who finds Ajax's body immediately after his death. She covers his corpse with a cloak and ardently grieves his passing. The scene after Ajax's death is intense with dramatic irony, since nothing that ensues is quite as Tecmessa has predicted: the Atreidae do not grieve for Ajax (924, 963), but are intransigent in their hatred, and Odysseus does not mock Ajax (963, 971). Sophocles does, however, allow Tecmessa two statements that take us back to the very first scene of the play: 'Nothing that is now would have been, without the gods' (950), and '*They* did not kill him, no ... but the gods' (970), assuming that 'Athene ... in all her cruel divinity has laid these sorrows ... to please Odysseus' (952–3, cf. 971). Yet both Tecmessa and the Chorus are wrong in thinking that 'And so Odysseus, 'the man of many sorrows', laughs in his black sunless heart, his laughter echoing and mocking, gloating in our pain ... (957–8). Ironically, when the Atreidae are determined to deny the decent burial Ajax prayed for, it is Odysseus who succeeds in securing it.

Tecmessa does not speak again after finishing her last speech with the words 'He has gone and left me only sorrow now, and tears' (972–3). When

Teucer arrives, he bids Tecmessa to fetch Eurysaces, and from the point of her re-entry with the boy she is played by a silent extra (1168). The dialogue is taken up by Teucer, the Atreidae and Odysseus, and there is no formal lament sung by Tecmessa for Ajax. In contrast to Ismene and Chrysothemis, who leave the stage permanently before the final sections of their plays, Tecmessa apparently remains. It is true that dramatic convention limited speaking characters onstage to three, but her silence might also represent the simple fact that there is no more reason for her to speak. Her role was to try to defend and protect Ajax from himself. Now that he is dead, her role as defender of Ajax has passed to Teucer, who must protect Ajax from his external enemies. As a woman she can claim no role in the fight against Menelaus and Agamemnon.[25] She has already expressed her praise of Ajax and the painful bereavement and sorrow that a lament would have conveyed. It is unlikely that she is disqualified from singing a lament because she is not his official wife. The *Iliadic* example of Briseis (who likewise was originally an enemy of the Achaeans) singing a moving lament for Achilles counters such an assumption (*Il.* 19. 282–302). The lack of a lament might correspond nicely in the eyes of the spectators with the absence of a reply by Ajax to Odysseus in Book Eleven of the *Odyssey*, where Odysseus in his trip to the Otherworld addresses Ajax, but Ajax ignores him (553–64).

## Conclusion

Some scholars claim that Ajax feels love and compassion for Tecmessa. Others argue that there is no evidence for this kind of empathy, that he is arrogant, self-centred and devoid of any feelings for her.[26] Although Ajax was probably always a self-centred character, his natural solipsistic indifference has not prevented him from choosing Tecmessa as his bed-mate and at times showing her affection. What can be interpreted as apathy to her lot and emotional indifference toward her could also be seen as an effort to suppress his feelings for her, so he could carry out his decision to part forever from her and their son. It is noteworthy that while Ajax is more demonstrative toward Eurysaces, he is not effusive in his affection toward him, as a comparison with the scene between Hector and Astyanax in *Iliad* Book Six shows. This is Ajax, a reserved person. That he treats Tecmessa in a callous manner is indisputable, but this manner should not lead us to assume that he has no feelings for anyone but himself.

It is possible that in leaving the precise nature of the relationship between Ajax and Tecmessa open to debate, Sophocles is pursuing a theme which relates to the play in its entirety. There is a yawning abyss between man's blinkered vision and the understanding of the gods. Not all things can be clear to mere mortals. We may be subject to deceit practised on us purposefully, or may simply misread situations. Not only is one's life on earth limited and subject to the constant changes inflicted upon us by the revolving seasons and the passage of time, but one is also limited in one's capacity to see beyond one's own subjective understanding. When a man, even the mightiest man on earth, with a stature beyond that of any other mortal Homeric hero, tries through pride to rise above his station in the hierarchy of beings, he will be beaten back down to his rightful place by the gods. Ajax brought about his own demise, for it was he and not the Atreidae who allowed his pride to lead him astray and eventually to compromise his honour. Tecmessa, also limited by mortal understanding, is not able to save Ajax, however much she may care for him.

In the end, with the limited power that Ajax does retain, he provides some hope of safety for Tecmessa and their son. It is fitting that Ajax, the house of Telamon, and Tecmessa all find some relief through a very human means, a child. Tecmessa's destiny is bound with that of Eurysaces (944). From the moment of Teucer's arrival it is clear to him that Tecmessa takes care of the boy (985-9), and he treats her as an integral part of the family. He includes her in the burial ritual of cutting locks of their hair to put on the corpse (1173-5), and in the battle of words between him and Agamemnon, he declares that *the three* of them stand together (1309). There was no need for Ajax to spell out what was self-evident: she was meant to be taken to Salamis, to the house of Telamon and Periboea, as the mother of their grandson, even if Sophocles leaves it unstated.

## Notes

1 Finglass (2011) 33
2 Finglass (2011) 40. The Brygos kylix is used to illustrate the cover of this book.
3 201-595, 646-83, 787-814, 891-989, 1168-1417 (by an 'extra').
4 The views of Ajax as a hero calling for admiration are changing and various. For a long time Ajax was understood as a protagonist worthy of admiration since he was a Homeric hero who because of his stringent principles could not be assimilated into the values of the democratic polis, where community was of more importance than the individual. Recent scholarship is less forgiving to Sophoclean Ajax than earlier assessments. For summary of views see Finglass (2011) 42-5
5 As Winnington-Ingram has already stated, 1980, 30 n. 57: '... too much need not be made of this distinction.' Kirk Ormand on the other hand presents a long case for the evolution of Tecmessa's status from spear-captive to fully

fledged wife, implying that she is acutely aware of the critical significance of this change in status both for her own future and that of her son.
6 *gynai*, in Greek the word could mean both.
7 Finglass (2011) 7, 10–11.
8 For the Sophoclean methodology of having secondary characters reveal the intricacies of the major figures, partly by allowing the protagonists to explain their motivations, although the lesser roles themselves are not devoid of individual characterization, see Kirkwood (1994) 100–1; Bowra (1952) 79–82, Winnington-Ingram (1980) 232–42.
9 As noted by Easterling (1977) 124.
10 McClure (1999) 19–20: '... both Athenian and non-Athenian literary texts universally praise female silence and verbal submission ...'.
11 Knox (1964) 13, 15–17.
12 Winnington-Ingram (1980) 29; Stanford (1963 on lines 485–524: 'Tecmessa's following speech is a masterpiece of dramatic composition.'
13 There can be no doubt that Sophocles counted upon the intertextual parallels to heighten the emotions of the scene. Tecmessa's situation was of course in some ways different from that of Andromache. Being a captured spear-bride and not a princess, she was even more vulnerable than Andromache, yet the parallel serves to emphasize that both women displayed a loving care of their husbands as well as concern for their own future. For comparison and scholarship on these two scenes see Poe (1987) 45–9; Hesk (2003) 67–9.
14 Stanford (1963) xxxiii with n. 47.
15 For discussion, see Roisman (1984) 11–14; Gruen (1976) 57–77, esp. 61–64.
16 A very close reminder of Andromache's words to Hector asking him to stay inside the city: 'you are to me my father and my lady mother you are my brother and my strong husband' (*Il.* 6.429–30).
17 For further discussion of the value of gratitude in the play, see Minadeo (1987).
18 For discussion, see Roisman (1984) 14–22.
19 Cf. Winnington-Ingram (1980) 31; *pace* Ormand (1996) 43.
20 Winnington-Ingram (1980) 30 n. 57 tentatively suggests that having Eurysaces as a legitimate heir 'implies perhaps a kind of status for his mother'; Ormand (1996) 48–56 develops this idea further, claiming that Tecmessa transitions from the status of a spear-bride to a wife with Ajax's death. For Tecmessa's status as only a slave, see Synodinou (1987).
21 Knox (1961) 11–14 does not believe his speech was intentionally deceptive: he sees it as a soliloquy not intended for an audience. For an excellent summary of views about Ajax's speech, and pertinent bibliography, see Winnington-Ingram (1980) 46 n. 07; see Garvie (1998) on lines 642–92; for how the spectators might have interpreted his speech, Finglass (2011) on lines 646–92.
22 E.g. Synodinou (1987; Ormand (1996) 43, and bibliographies.

23 The translation in English is in the present tense, but the aorist indicates that 'the judgment was already formed while the other person was speaking'; Lloyd (1999) 24.
24 Adams (1957) 25: 'he [Sophocles] makes us see, through the parts of Tecmessa and Eurysaces, that he [Ajax] is a man of deep feeling and strong affection.'
25 Ormand (1996) 37–41, 57–62, suggests that Tecmessa's silence is not an inevitable result of the three-actor convention, but that the playwright toys with this rule and with use of mute extras 'specifically in order to mark and justify Tekmessa's silent presence. In this way a *social* convention—that women in Athens were not to be heard—is reinforced and validated by dramatic convention, even in unconventional circumstances' (38).
26 For some discussion see Poe (1987) 43–4 with note 74; Adams (1957) 32–3.

9

# A Grief Observed: Tecmessa and Her Sadness-Work in Sophocles' *Ajax*

Stephen Esposito

Chorus   There she is! The young bride, captive of his spear, Tecmessa,
         I see her. She's steeped in this cry of **grief** (*oiktos*).
         894–5

Chorus   The pangs of true **pain** (*gennaia dyē*), I know, pierce your heart.
         938

Tecmessa These things would not have reached this state but for the gods.
Chorus   Too heavy indeed is the burden of **grief** (*achthos*) they've contrived.
         950–1[1]

Tonight all the hells of young **grief** have opened again; the mad word, the bitter resentment, the fluttering of the stomach, the nightmare unreality, the wallowed-in tears. For in **grief** nothing 'stays put.' One keeps on emerging from a phase, but it always recurs. Round and round. Everything repeats ... I thought I could describe a state; make a map of sorrow. **Sorrow**, however, turns out to be not a state but a process. It needs not a map but a history ... **Grief** is like a long valley, a winding valley where any bend may reveal a totally new landscape.

C.S. Lewis, *A Grief Observed*, 69–71, 1962

This chapter will study the onset of grief and the process of mourning at one particular point in the post-suicide portion of *Ajax*, namely the so-called *epi-parodos* ('second parodos', 868–78) and third *kommos* (semi-musical dialogue of lamentation between the Chorus and Tecmessa, 879–973). A new examination of these passages, and especially the *kommos*, is timely because a key part of the Greek text that has long been controversial – Tecmessa's two speeches at the end of each strophe and antistrophe (915–24 and 961–73) – has now been restored to more secure footing by P.J. Finglass.[2] My objective is to argue that one of Sophocles' first priorities immediately after Ajax's suicide (865) is to engage his actors and audience in the process of 'working through' the psychological and moral wounds of his death.[3] This cathartic process is important because it provides some sort of 'purification' or 'cleansing relief' for the emotions (*pathēmata*) of the audience (Aristotle *Poetics* 6, 1449$^b$24–8). Such catharsis usually comes about through a process of *witnessing* the tragic action, *recognizing / understanding* (*anagnōrisis*) why that action has been done, and thereby *beginning to make whole again* the emotional world that has been ruptured by that action; in our case that action is Ajax's suicide.[4] In order to establish the context for my argument I'll first set forth the relevant storyline and highlight the portions important for my discussion. In the second section I'll present my interpretation of the third *kommos*.

## 1. Ajax's suicide: A grief observed?

Just before Ajax's suicide, Tecmessa – his spear-won Phrygian slave / concubine / bride / wife / widow / mother of his son (210, 331, 448–50, 654, 894, 940) – comes to realize that she's been *deceived* (*āpatēmenē*, 807) about her husband and cast out from his *ancient kindness / former favour* (*charitos . . . ek-beblēmenē*, 808; cf. 522). Having arrived at this realization, she attempts to forestall *the stroke of inevitable destiny* (*anankaia tychē*, 803) which threatens to destroy Ajax just as it had once threatened to destroy her. The same phrase recurs in the very first line of her powerful reply (485–524) to Ajax's first major speech (430–80) in which he explains his conception of the heroic code and warrior 'nobility' (*eu-geneia*, 480). At 485 Tecmessa uses the phrase *Aias . . . anankaias tychēs* where the word-play on his name – *Aias . . . anank-aias* – obliquely reminds us that she, though once free, is now *his* spear-won slave: 'O master Ajax, there's no greater evil for mortals than *the stroke of inevitable destiny*.'[5] But right now she wonders, where *is* Ajax? She urges his sailors to search for their captain and to summon his half-brother Teucer. They split into two groups and rush from the orchestra in opposite directions (813–14). Such choral exits occur four other times in extant tragedy but nowhere else are they used to isolate a character.[6] Tecmessa rushes off as well.

The emptiness of the theatrical space *and* the silent pause in the action heighten the tension. To this unusual scenario Sophocles adds another anomaly – a change of scene / location, which occurs only once elsewhere in extant tragedy (Aeschylus, *Eumenides* 235–53).[7] The stage-set no longer represents the ground in front of Ajax's hut on the Trojan coast but rather the 'untrodden spot' (*chōron* ... *astibē*, 652) where he said he was headed to dig a hole and 'hide' his sword (657–9). And indeed he was telling the truth, albeit ambiguously – for Ajax's 'untrodden spot' is the very seaside 'thicket' (*napos*, 892) where Tecmessa will soon discover her impaled husband and his 'hidden' sword.

Into this empty space and silent place Ajax enters alone from the main stage-door and calmly delivers his suicide soliloquy (815–65), announcing that, 'with one swift leap that brings no convulsions, no struggle' (833–4), Hector's sword will rip through his ribs. His earlier sense of shame has subsided somewhat.[8] Whether his suicide occurs in the audience's full view or somewhere offstage remains controversial. What can't be doubted, I think, is that even if the suicide didn't *actually* occur onstage, it's a *virtual* onstage act.[9] Ajax's intense descriptive focus on the sword, its fixity, and his leap onto it (815–23, 833–4) as well as the carefully designed solitariness of the theatrical setting – his soliloquy occupies the entire scene, conspicuously framed by the frantic choral exit and re-entry – all this contributes to a sense of tense anticipation, especially if Ajax has entered with his sword.[10] It hasn't been observed before, to the best of my knowledge, that Sophocles places consistent linguistic emphasis on the *public* revelation of Ajax, first as the sick man 'in full view' (*peri-phanē*, 66), then as the madman 'in full view' (*peri-phanōs,* 81), and finally as the man about to die 'in full view' (*peri-phantos*, 229; cf. *prodēlōs*, 1311).[11] Why would Sophocles repeatedly raise this expectation of conspicuous display only to disappoint at the climactic moment? Oliver Taplin, among many others, believes that Ajax kills himself onstage in full view of the audience: 'Aias, on stage by himself, prepares for death, and ends by throwing himself onto his fixed sword. ... It is a plausible guess that the solo death was the core of Sophocles' conception, and that he built the rest of the play round that.'[12]

An onstage suicide would also produce a stunning contrast to the treatment of his predecessor and arch-rival Aeschylus who had Ajax commit suicide *offstage*. The hero had grown frustrated in his attempts to stab himself; finally a goddess appeared and showed him the one spot he had to strike – his armpit. The suicide is reported by a messenger in the only fragment to survive from Aeschylus' (now lost) *Thracian Women* (named after the chorus), the second play of his *Ajax* trilogy: 'And, since his skin would not yield anywhere to the fatal blow, he kept bending his sword, like a man drawing a bow, until some goddess appeared and showed him the place.'[13]

Certainly it would be very much in keeping with Sophocles' many innovative tendencies in this play to deviate radically from his predecessor by showing the suicide *onstage*. Such deviation would be all the more stunning since it is quite likely that Sophocles' unique stagecraft here – the scene-change and frantic choral exit at 815 and re-entry at 865 – seem to be consciously imitating Aeschylus' *Eumenides*, where the Furies exit to pursue Orestes (235), then the scene changes from Delphi to Athens, and the Furies re-enter in disarray (253).[14]

## 2. Tecmessa's reaction: a grief observed

Immediately after the suicide, however it's staged, the tragedy begins again. It commences, as did the prologue, with a second search for the protagonist. But this is a 'mirror scene' *in reverse* – now the mission, initiated by a human female (Tecmessa), is conducted by Ajax's friends, whereas the earlier search, initiated by a divine female (Athena), was conducted by his enemy; and now its target is a dead man, not a living one; and now it aims to prevent an act of violence, not respond to one.[15] This technique of repeated 'search scenes' divides the drama into two different phases of discovery, and simultaneously signals the *causal* connection between the two searches with the first motivating the second – the failure of Ajax's attempted night-time murder of the Greek commanders motivates his suicide and the subsequent second search.[16]

In the 'second parodos' the two half-choruses of sailors re-enter the orchestra in disarray and in staggered fashion from opposite entry ramps (866–78); such stagecraft is unparalleled elsewhere in extant Sophocles. The intense angst of this second beginning – full of exclamatory lamentations (*iō tlēmōn*; *outoi theatos*; *ōmoi teknon*) and conspicuous verbal echoes between strophe and antistrophe (*tis an . . . tis an*, 879 *emelles . . . emelles*, 925; *ōmo-thumon*, 885 ~ *ōmo-phrōn*, 930; *iō moi moi*, 891 ~ *iō moi moi*, 937) – all this emotional upheaval is contained within and framed by a complex, highly-balanced metrical and thematic structure: the transitional astrophic *epi-parodos* (lyric exchange between the leaders of the hemi-choruses: 866–78) is followed by an epirrhematic lyric dialogue of lament (*kommos*: 879–973) between Tecmessa and the Chorus, composed of symmetrical strophic and antistrophic pairs (879–914 = 925–60) in which she speaks her iambic lines while the chorus recites or sings in agitated metres.[17]

The first words of the *epi-parodos* are memorable and thematically significant: *ponos ponōi ponon pherei. pai, pai, pai . . .*, 'Toil heaps toil upon toil. Where, where, where (have we not wandered)?' (866–8). As F.W.

Schneidewin observes, 'The *par-ech-esis* [the *ech*oing likeness of sound] expresses here the *accumulate*d weight of useless toil which they have endured.'[18] *Ponos ponōi ponon* does indeed express the burdensome toil that the choral search parties have just endured. But I suggest that this conspicuous phrase also foreshadows the burdensome toil still to be borne and that it's the job of the play's last 500 lines to bear that burden. Furthermore I suggest that the emphatic *poly-ptoton* of *ponos ponōi ponon*, i.e. the consecutive repetition of *ponos* in three different cases, added to the panting alliteration of *pai pai pai*, may be taken as indicators of the three toils that remain, all of which are presented in this lyric dialogue – namely, the *toil* of finding Ajax (868–914), the *toil* of attaining his proper burial (915–24); and the *toil* of warding off those who would forbid Ajax's burial and subsequently enslave Tecmessa and Eurysaces (944–73).

The last two words of the *epi-parodos* announce that this will be a scene of significant revelation: 'Nowhere along the path does the man ... *reveal / make clear his presence (dēloi phaneis*, 878).' But suddenly Tecmessa, in a highly unusual entry between the choral and dialogue part of the first strophe (891), interrupts the now-unified Chorus with an offstage scream of despair, *iō moi moi* (891: 'Alas me, alas me!'; repeated at 937).[19] Ajax had already screamed *iō moi moi* (333, 336) and Teucer will soon replicate it (974); thus all three actors are linked by the desperate fear and hopelessness which that scream symbolizes.[20] From her hidden vantage point near the stage-door, or perhaps a secondary stage-door, Tecmessa announces that she's discovered Ajax's corpse in 'nearby thicket' (*napos*: 892).[21] The Chorus finally sees her (894–5): 'There she is! The young bride (*nymphē*), captive of his spear, Tecmessa, I see her. She's steeped in this cry of grief (*oiktos*).' The sight of her husband's bloody body stuns Tecmessa. 'I am destroyed, devastated, totally demolished, friends!' (*oichōk', olōla, diapeporthēmai*: 896). The ascending tricolon of perfect tenses gives a more absolute sense of completeness than other tenses would.[22] And the 'three synonymous verbs in asyndeton, each longer than the preceding (2, 3, 6 syllables) mark the intensification of Tecmessa's grief.'[23] Indeed the last of those three verbs (*dia-portheō*) is almost always used for the sacking of cities and so registers Tecmessa's profound sense of devastation: '*Here he lies* (*hode ... keitai*) wrapped around his *hidden / buried* (*kruph-aios*) *sword*' (899). At last the horrific revelation – here lies his impaled body. The sword convicts him, making clear (*dēlon*) that he killed himself (*autos pros autou*, 906). This sword (*phasgonon*, 899, *enchos*, 907), fixed in the earth by Ajax, is 'the quite special centre–piece of the ensuing lamentations. ...'[24] And, as W.B. Stanford observes, 'we must try to imagine the deeply affecting tones of voice which actors would use in pronouncing words like *iō* and *ōmoi*, the effect of their sorrowful postures and gestures and the melancholy accompaniment of the flute [*aulos*].[25] Ajax, as Sophocles' most unexpected master of ambiguity, has done exactly what he said he would do in his 'deception speech', namely 'buried' his sword (*kruph-ō*, 658; *kruph-aios*, 899).

When the Chorus begins to approach the stage area where Tecmessa has discovered the corpse (*pai pai keitai* ...; 'Where, where does Ajax lie ...?' 911–12) she immediately and emphatically stops them: 'He must not be *seen* (*theatos*)! *I will cover him* completely with this enfolding cloak since nobody, at least nobody who is a friend, could bear *to see* him.' (915–17). Just as Ajax's body has become a death-shroud enveloping his sword, so Tecmessa's cloak will become a death-shroud enveloping his corpse. Indeed it has been suggested that her words, '*I will cover him completely with this enfolding cloak*' (*periptychei / pharei kalypsō tōide pampēdēn*, 915–16), signal a significant stage action here: 'for if the cloak is held up in Tecmessa's outspread arms, a temporary curtain is created under cover of which the actor who plays Ajax, being already in the doorway, can make a quick exit. He can now be replaced by an effigy or a mute extra and have ample time to come back on as Teucer.'[26] Such stagecraft could be easily and quickly accomplished and thereby enhance the possibility of an onstage suicide while also avoiding more controversial staging scenarios such as rolling out the *ekkyklema* or having stage-hands bring out a screen. Nevertheless, in whatever way the stagecraft was actually managed, Sophocles has created a stunning thematic juxtaposition here, as Charles Segal notes: 'The scene of the cloak visually concretizes the tragic distance between this rigid warrior and the woman who loves him. He has perished, as he wished, on his firmly fixed sword; all she can do is cover him in her softly enveloping cloak. Both the distance and the closeness between them are infinite; and the stage action catches them both in one of those large paradigmatic gestures characteristic of Greek poetry at its best.'[27] To Segal's acute thematic observation we can add Lewis Campbell's visualization of Sophocles' onstage death scene and Tecmessa's actions: 'The sword-point lifts the garment of Ajax to an apex from which the folds descend. At 906 she has raised the edge of the garment, and is gazing at the mangled form beneath it. At 915, by a revulsion of feeling, she draws it (or perhaps her own veil) over him so as to cover him more completely than before. The point of the sword is hidden by the garment, the blade in the body, the hilt in the ground.'[28]

This visualization gets importantly supplemented a bit later when Teucer tells his attendant to uncover Ajax's corpse: '*Oimoi*. Come, you, lift off the covering (*ek-kalypson*) so that I may see the whole horror.' And when the attendant uncovers the corpse Teucer exclaims: '*O face hard-to-look-at* and full of bitter daring ...' (*dys-theaton omma*, 1004; cf. *theatos*, 915).[29] What becomes immediately clear from the language of the text is that Ajax has fallen on his sword *face-upwards*.³⁰ This visualization flies in the face of a long iconographic tradition of Ajax falling *face-down* on his sword. But it does conspicuously recall the famous red-figure vase of the renowned Brygos Painter, *c*. 490 BCE, some forty to fifty years *before* Sophocles' play (*c*. 450–440 BCE).³¹ The interior of this cup shows Ajax impaled *face-upwards* on his sword and a woman covering his corpse with her cloak. Timothy Dugan writes provocatively about the Brygos cup painting and its relation to Sophocles' play:

> Tecmessa's cover-up is, in itself, an act of defiance and provocation for the slave-wife. Effectively ... she asserts that Ajax will be buried quickly and honourably, his entrails will not be carrion for birds, predatory scavengers or the scorn of Agamemnon, Menelaus, or any of Ajax's detractors. And although the image of the grieving Tecmessa is mournful, the acquiescent, but slyly emancipated, slave-wife is a theatrical prototype for Antigone, Phaedra, and Iphigeneia, as well as antecedent to the Sophocles character 'Tecmessa'.³²

The sight of the impaled bloody corpse overwhelms Tecmessa. 'Alas, what am I going to do? (*oimoi, ti drasō*; 920; cf. 457, 809, 1024) Who of your *friends* will lift you up? Where is Teucer? If he should come, how timely he would arrive to *join in composing* (*syn-kat-harmosai*) his fallen brother here.' (920–22). As J.C. Kamerbeek notes, 'The first thing Tecmessa thinks of is the burial of Ajax. It must be performed by Teucer.'³³ In the antistrophe she laments that the Greek commanders might well subject her and her young son to 'the yoke of necessity' (*douleias zyga*, 944; cf. 496–505). But when the chorus starts mentioning how Atreus' sons and 'much-enduring' (*poly-talas*) Odysseus are now surely mocking Ajax's misfortunes (*ep-hybrizei* ... *gelai* ... *gelōta*, 955–8), at that moment her anger and defiance ignite: 'Well *let them mock* (*gelōntōn*), and *let them revel* (*kapichairontōn*) in this man's miseries! Perhaps now that he's dead, they'll lament his absence in the thick of battle. ... *So let Odysseus insolently abuse* (*hybrizetō*) the bereaved with his taunts!' For all that she is devastated by Ajax's suicide and the pain he has bequeathed her (*anias* ... *goous*, 973), over the course of this lyric dialogue she's begun to work through her grief and find her former toughness, which culminates in the three strong imperatives of 961 and 971. Earlier on she had exhibited a similar determination in her riposte to Ajax (485–524); now she's regained her mettle.

Throughout this complex semi-lyrical antiphonal dirge (*threnōn*, 971) the grieving Tecmessa is demonstrably the driving force: she is the one who discovers her impaled husband, explains his suicide, covers his corpse with her cloak so he can't be viewed, asks where Teucer is, initiates the call for burial rites, confidently claims that Ajax's grandeur deserves to be lamented even by his enemies, predicts the enslavement of herself and her son to her new Greek taskmasters, explains Athena's malevolent role in her husband's demise (as a favour to Odysseus), and boldly defies the insolent mockery of Agamemnon, Menelaos and Odysseus.

All this embodies the process of Tecmessa's sadness-work – not only her final strophe and antistrophe but the preceding back-and-forth exchange between her and the Chorus. This sadness-work is tellingly framed by her first and last verbs in the *kommos*, namely *oichōka* ('I am gone / destroyed,' 896) and *di-oichetai* ('he is completely gone / destroyed,' 973); this verb *oichomai* is often a euphemism for death (as at 743). I reiterate the apt remark of C.S. Lewis with which I began the essay:

> For in **grief** nothing 'stays put.' One keeps on emerging from a phase, but it always recurs. Round and round. Everything repeats ... I thought I could describe a state; make a map of sorrow. Sorrow, however, turns out to be not a state but a process. It needs not a map but a history, ... **Grief** is like a long valley, a winding valley where any bend may reveal a totally new landscape.

So it is for Tecmessa: the *kommos* presents a miniature history of her grief-work. Just as the Chorus begins each strophe and antistrophe with a ten-line unified lyric (879–90 = 925–36) so she concludes each strophe and antistrophe with two eight-line speeches (iambic trimeters) which respond metrically to one another, each resuming and developing a theme highlighted by the chorus (915–24; 961–73). As mentioned at the outset of this essay, these passages have long been controversial. But P.J. Finglass, following Nauck's lead in deleting 918–19 and 966–70, has put the text back on a more secure footing. Using Finglass's text I will translate the two stanzas in sequential order. It is good to see them back-to-back since they form the respective eight-line conclusions of the strophe and antistrophe of the *kommos*.[34]

Lines 915–24 (minus 918–19, which are probably spurious):

915 Mark me – he must not be *seen* (*outoi theatos*)! No, I will cover (*kalypsō*) him
916 completely with this enfolding cloak here (*peri-ptychei pharei tōide*),
917 since none who love him could stomach *to see* (*blepein*) him.
920 Alas, what shall I do (*oimoi, ti drasō*)? Who of your beloved will lift you?

921   Where is Teucer? How timely now would be his coming, if he should come, to join
922   the burial rites and compose the corpse (*syn-kath-armosai*) of his fallen brother here!
923   Alas ill-fated Ajax, from such a height are you now fallen so low –
924   how worthy (*axios*) you are to deserve dirges (*thrēnōn*) even from your enemies!

Lines 961–73 (minus 966–70, which are also probably spurious):

961   So let them [Atreus' sons] mock (*gelōntōn*), and let them revel in this man's ruin!
962   Even though they didn't desire him during his life,
963   perhaps in the stress of battle they'll lament his death.
964   For ignorant fools don't realize the good
965   they hold in their hands till they've thrown it away.
971   So let Odysseus abuse the bereaved (*en kenois*) with his insolent taunts (*hybris*)!
972   Since (*gar*) for those who are bereaved (*autois*) Ajax lives no longer, but for me
973   he's left behind anguish (*anias*) and lamentation (*goous*) by his dying (*di-oichetai*).

It is important to remember that neither Tecmessa nor the Chorus (the play's internal audience) heard Ajax's suicide speech nor saw it, as did we (the external audience). Even if we, the external audience, didn't see the suicide onstage (as some would argue) we certainly saw it virtually. Through Ajax's words (815–65) we come to feel his emotions and hear his reasoning – we get to 'read' his articulate, passionate and fierce 'suicide note'. Tecmessa got none of that; all she gets is the terrifying end result – her husband's spiked corpse. We observe her grief first-hand. We hear her first offstage screams – *io moi moi . . . io tlemon* (891, 893). Through her we almost get to be 'eye-witnesses' to the suicide a second time. But she demands that we not see the corpse – 'Mark me – he must not be seen!' (*outoi theatos*, 915).

As Tecmessa grieves, so we grieve; indeed because she grieves we can grieve. What Sophocles gives us is, in C.S. Lewis' words, 'a grief observed'. This is the cathartic work of tragedy, its gift to us – the unloosening of the rage, the 'working through' of the sorrow and feelings of helplessness, the deep pain of a wife looking upon her husband impaled upon her enemy's sword, a deeply conflicted and flawed man whom she loved and tried desperately to save, and finally her defiance of his enemies. As C.S. Lewis says, 'I thought I could describe a state; make a map of sorrow. Sorrow, however, turns out to be not a state but a process. It needs not a map but a history.' We hear and watch Tecmessa go through this process of devastation and defiance and we go through it with her vicariously.

It has been claimed that 'Tekmessa is unique in tragedy in that she does not lament.' Given our preceding argument I consider this judgement incorrect. Rather Sophocles shows her in the process of doing some serious sadness-work in the eighty or so lines of the *kommos* (since her entry at 891). After the *kommos* Tecmessa exits (973) and then returns at 1168, but she remains completely silent till the end of the play. Kirk Ormand wonders why: 'What would be more natural than for Tekmessa to join in at 1223 [i.e. right after the third stasimon, 1185–1222] with a lament of her own? We have, therefore, every reason to expect some sort of formal lament for Ajax by Tekmessa, and it is little short of astounding that it never happens.'[35] But there is no reason to expect any more lamentation from her. She has expressed her feelings powerfully in the lyric dialogue, much more powerfully than a fuller and more formal lament because of the unpredictable rapid-fire pace of her to-and-fro with the Chorus. Sophocles gives us something of a double-barrelled 'formal' lament in her two eight-line metrically responding stanzas at 915–24 and 961–73. But there is no compelling theatrical or dramatic reason for any more spoken lamentation from Tecmessa.[36] Her *silent* lamentation, as she kneels beside the massive corpse of Ajax at centre-stage, is much more powerful than more words could be. To be sure there's still some serious work to be done to secure Ajax's burial and reclamation of honour. That's why, after the third *kommos*, the plot moves from the private, domestic female arena to the public, political male arena. As Patricia Easterling notes, 'Women have a place in the imaginative place of tragedy, but it is generally a place separate from the political sphere of the men. ...'[37] Tecmessa is silent henceforth because she has had her say; she went toe-to-toe in the ring with Ajax earlier on, and proved to be his toughest, most demanding opponent.[38] She threw some potent punches and Ajax felt their sting (e.g. *ethēlunthēn stoma / pros tēsde tēs gunaikos*, 'I have been softened like a woman in my speech because of this woman here': 651-2). Once he went missing, she became boss: she initiated the search for him, found his corpse, covered and protected it, and expressed concern for Teucer's whereabouts, for his extricating the sword and for his beginning the proper burial rituals. Then she scolded the Greek commanders and Athena's favouritism to Odysseus, and finally, in her last two lines (972–3), expressed the particular devastation caused by his death. At 973 her speaking role is over – she's spoken her 200 lines and fought the good fight – time to pass the baton. Now it's Teucer's turn – now he'll get his 200 lines to fight for Ajax's burial and honour.[39]

At Teucer's bidding Tecmessa departs (989) to fetch and protect Eurysaces from the enemy. After Teucer's 'funeral oration' over Ajax's body (992–1039) and his testy debate with Menelaus (1047–1162) Tecmessa re-enters (1162) *in complete silence* (with attendants); Taplin observes that it's quite unusual for a major character to make a silent entry.[40] Tecmessa neither speaks nor is spoken to; but her silence will speak much more loudly than any words could as she now (1168–84) forms part of a suppliant tableau with Teucer and young Eury-saces, 'Wide-Shield'. The trio huddle around Ajax's corpse and perform a brief but powerful ritual of remembrance and ceremonial burial which creates something like a temporary sacred space for the family in mourning, an inviolable asylum where Ajax's corpse is seemingly 'guarding its guardians'[41] just as much as the suppliants are 'giving power to a lifeless body, a process that will accelerate through the final scene of the play.'[42] As they offer locks of their hair to Ajax, their tender gathering around his massive body will serve as the unmoving pathetic backdrop for the angry debate between Teucer and Agamemnon (1223–1315). For the play's final 250 lines the woman who has by now become Ajax's legitimate wife (*gynē*) sits or kneels at centre-stage beside her husband without saying a word; it may well be that Sophocles 'intended her silent presence to serve as a symbol of passive grief and as a dumb [= silent] protest against the men's self-important language.'[43]

## Notes

1 All translations are my own, usually fairly literal and usually modified from Esposito (2010); I follow the Greek text in Finglass' edition (2011).
2 See Finglass *CQ* (2009a) and (2011) *ad loc.*
3 Cf. Simon (1978) 274: 'the term "working through," particularly in relation to the tragic conception of knowledge through suffering ... connotes a willingness to suffer the consequences of one's choice, and not to short-cut the process of grief and anguish by seeking palliatives ... It is not insight alone that allows for change and growth; the process of gaining the insight is probably at least as important as the insight itself.' On Ajax's process of 'working through' in *Ajax* and on Achilles' process in the *Iliad* see Simon 128 and 72–7. This idea is related to Jonathan Shay's concept of 'griefwork'; he argues 'that healing from trauma depends upon communalization of the trauma – being able safely to tell the story to someone who is listening and who can be trusted to retell it truthfully to others in the community.' Shay (1994) 4.
4 On catharsis see Easterling (1996) 178: 'For Aristotle the cathartic process seems to be a continuous whole: recognition and the painful emotions that it

generates, witnessed with pity and fear by the audience, are not separated off, as in the communal weeping model, into immediate emotional release and (often subsequent) intellectual reflection.'; cf. Segal (1996) 156-7.
5 Compare other puns on Ajax's name at 370, 430-2, 904, 914.
6 Taplin (1977) 375-6 notes the other choral exits: *Eumenides* 225-35; *Alcestis* 746-861; *Helen* 564-674; *Rhesus* 385-515.
7 Change of scene after 814: thus the great majority of scholars, e.g. Campbell (1881); Stanford (1963); Kamerbeek (1963); Gardiner (1979) 12; Seale (1982) 163; Taplin (1983) 151; Taplin ( in Most and Ozbek *Staging Ajax's Suicide*, 2015) 187, 190; Lloyd-Jones (Loeb, 1994) 105; Scott (1996) 84; Hubbard (2003) 164; Finglass (2011) 12 and 376; Liapis (2015) 131-2, 139; Battezatto (2015) 233; Most (2015) 291.
8 Gibert (1995) 132-3.
9 Cf. Seale (1982) 165: 'Even if the final moments of death are concealed in some way by the screen of bushes, the spectators must feel that they have witnessed the act. The text and the dramatic development require a visual, not an imagined climax.'
10 A brief list of scholars who think Ajax's sword is *visible* during his suicide speech: e.g. Taplin in Reverdin and Grange (1983) 151; Taplin (trans. 2015) 77, 312; Taplin ( in Most and Ozbek *Staging Ajax's Suicide*, 2015) 187; Stanford (1963) 166; Seale (1982) 163; Lloyd-Jones (Loeb 1994) 105; Liapis (2015) 141-145, especially on the importance of *deictic* pronouns in Ajax's suicide speech; *contra* Finglass (in Most and Ozbek *Staging Ajax's Suicide*, 2015) 195-206.
11 I first proposed this idea in Esposito (2010) note at 815 and pp. 200-2.
12 Taplin (2015, trans.) 77; cf. 312-13. Other believers in Ajax's *on-stage* suicide include the Scholiast on 864, translated in Arnott (1962) 133 and Pöhlmann (1997) 42; Campbell and Abbott (1876) 48 and 94; Flickinger (1918) 244; Taplin (1978) 86 and 189, n. 5; Garrison (1995) 52; Garvie (1998) 203; Mastronarde (2012); Liapis (2015) 141, 147, 153-4.
13 Aeschylus fragment 83, translated by Sommerstein (2008) 100-1; cf. Mills (1980-1) 130-1; March (1991-3) 4-8; Garvie (1998) 4; Finglass (2011) 33.
14 On Sophocles' *conscious imitation* of Aeschylus here see Scott (1996) 286, n. 199; cf. Taplin (1977) 376, 378-81, 417.
15 Kamerbeek (1953) at 874; Taplin (1977) 379-85, Taplin (1978) 148-9; Burton (1980) 32; Winnington-Ingram (1980) 57; Hubbard (2003) 164; Finglass (2011) 390.
16 Seale (1982) 166; Garrison (1995) 52; Finglass (2011) 390. On the play's 'double plot,' i.e. divine retribution and human quarrel, see Tyler (1974).
17 On the structure of 866-973 see Esposito (2010) *ad loc*.
18 Schneidewin (1853) at 866.
19 On Tecmessa's unusual entry at 891 see Taplin (1977) 385 n. 1.
20 Taplin (1978) 109, 148-9.
21 Liapis (2015) 147-54.
22 Campbell (1881) at 896.

23 Garvie (1998) at 896.
24 Seale (1982) 167.
25 Stanford (1963) 177. See also Alyson Melzer's chapter in this book.
26 Mills (1980–1) 133, following Flickinger (1918) 244, 174; similarly Taplin (1978) 189 n. 5; Taplin (trans. 2015) 314; Liapis (2015) 147–8; contrast Heath and Okell (2007) 373–4; Finglass (2015) 206–8.
27 Segal (1980) 129; cf. Segal (1981) 117: 'Tecmessa's concealing [of Ajax's body] is an act of loving *philia* (cf. 917), whereas Ajax's concealing (658, 899) is an act which rejects *philoi*.'
28 Campbell (1881) at 899; cf. Seale (1982) 167.
29 On the ambiguities of 1004, esp. *dystheaton omma*, see Ferguson (1970) 22; Seale (1982) 169; Golder (1990) 33 n.19. At this point it would appear that Teucer and his attendant begin to extricate the sword from the Ajax 'dummy' in preparation for the upcoming suppliant tableau scene at 1168–84; see Mills (1980–1) 133–4; Taplin (1978) 87: 'the action [by Teucer at 1024 ff.] of drawing the sword from Ajax is the turning-point away from the low ebb of despair.'
30 Line 1004 pretty clearly seems to reveal that Ajax fell *backwards* on his sword, such that his face (*omma*) was looking *upwards*. This was noticed long ago by Thomas Mitchell (1844) *ad loc.*: 'Teucer speaks, intently *gazing on his brother's face* [my italics], which is now uncovered.' Similarly many subsequent scholars; e.g. Kamerbeek (1953), Stanford (1963); Golder (1990) 27; (1992) 356–7; (1999) 18; Lloyd-Jones (1994) 125; Garvie (1998) 93; Esposito (2010) 58; Finglass (2011) 424.
31 The Brygos Painter kylix, dated *c.* 490 BCE (Getty Museum 86.AE.286), appears on the cover of this book and can be seen in an excellent large colour photo in Finglass (*Omnibus* 2011a) 27; cf. Catoni (2015) 22–4 and figures 13a–c; Davies (1971); Taplin (1978) figure 11 and note 11; Segal (1981) 117–8; March (1991–3) 6; Golder (1992) 356–8; Garvie (1998) 3 note 10 and 219; Shapiro (1994) 153–5; Esposito (2010) 58, note on 1004; Finglass (2011 commentary) 40; Dugan (2018) 57–9.
32 Dugan (2018) 58.
33 Kamerbeek (1953) at 920; cf. Campbell (1881) *ad loc.*
34 For the controversial text of Tecmessa's two speeches at 915–24 and 961–73 I use the text of Finglass 2009, reprinted in his 2011 commentary. Battezatto (2015) 240–1 is hesitant about deleting 918–19 but his objection is unpersuasive; Tecmessa's first words in the strophe are *outoi theatos* (915), emphatically indicating the *immediate* horror of the spectacle; there's no need to have two *subsequent* lines of gory detail. Cf. Heath (1987) 198 n. 68. Taplin (trans. 2015) 314 considers 971–3 weak and doubts their authenticity. I have suggested in my text above that they are excellent closing lines (not least because of the conspicuous ring composition of *oichōka*, 'I am gone / destroyed', 896 and *di-oichetai*, 'he is completely gone / destroyed', 973). For a useful discussion of 961–73 see A.C. Pearson (1922). After line 924 Finglass (2011 *ad loc.*) would have Tecmessa depart briefly behind the *skene* to cover

Ajax's body. I don't share that opinion since I believe the corpse-covering occurs at 915–24.
35 Ormand (1996) 40; Foley (2001) 90 n. 164, correctly observes that 'Tecmessa does in fact include most of the standard elements of wifely lament at 937–73, and hence the audience may not expect any further lament from her until Ajax' funeral takes place.' Finglass (2011) 416 also comments on Ormand's argument: 'if Tecmessa's silence was to have this significance, we might have expected attention to be drawn to it in some way.' Cf. Wiersma (1984) 35 who aptly says of Tecmessa: 'Accordingly she is in a position to stand aloof from the subsequent action without suggesting subordination. The poet has no reason to drag Tecmessa into participating in the coming rhetorical tilt (over Ajax' corpse!). Nor could she plausibly take part in Teucer's and Eurysaces' ritual dealings with the dead father and hero (1170ff, 1402 ff.), for the parallel scene 545 ff. was exclusively a matter between Ajax and his little son.'
36 Cf. Heath (1987) 198.
37 Easterling (1987) 25.
38 On Tecmessa's courageous confrontational monologue to Ajax at 485–524 see Easterling (1984) for fine analysis; cf. Sorum (1986) 368: 'Tecmessa's claim is not simply a redefinition of a traditional idea from a woman's perspective. Rather it is a critique of the ethic espoused by Ajax ... when it is removed from its heroic context.'
39 On some interesting parallelisms between Tecmessa's and Teucer's monologues (284–330 and 992–1039) see Hubbard (2003) 163–4.
40 Taplin (1977) 284.
41 Sommerstein (2015) 246; cf. Esposito (2010) note on 1168.
42 Scott (1996) 91–2.
43 Stanford (1963) 205.

10

# Heroic Values and Lesser Mortals

## Carmel McCallum-Barry

In *Ajax* Sophocles examines heroic values through the central character, Ajax, but also through other characters who are not on his magnificent scale. The meaning of 'heroic values' is not easy to define, but pride in one's ancestry (nobility of birth), prowess as a warrior and position as leader of men are recognized as valued attributes that give a man honour and status. These attributes were part of the heroes' portrayal in the Homeric poems and continued to be claimed by the aristocratic élite in democratic Athens, where there were often tensions between these privileged families and the *demos* as a whole. In this volume Laura Swift demonstrates that in his portrait of Ajax Sophocles highlights the negative aspects of these qualities. We can also sense disenchantment with heroic values through his treatment of other 'heroic' characters in the play, in particular Agamemnon, leader of the expedition against Troy, his brother Menelaus and Teucer, half-brother to Ajax. These are the noble heroes, but we should also consider the ordinary fighting men of the Chorus, who sailed to Troy under Ajax's leadership. They have no part in aristocratic claims of status, but as members of the same army their fortunes are affected by the behaviour and fortunes of their leaders.

There are sometimes jarring contrasts between the portrayal of the heroes in *Ajax* and what an audience might expect from their appearances in the *Iliad* and *Odyssey* of Homer. However it is the job of a theatre audience to deal with and think about what the playwright chooses to give them. We are familiar with the necessity to rethink our attitudes when watching a film or television version of our favourite classics – the numerous reworkings of Jane Austen alone testify to the frequent need for a new look at familiar heroines and heroes. All three tragedians in the fifth century BC demonstrate the desire to reconsider traditional views of the great heroes for contemporary society and several factors play a part in their reappraisal. As in *Ajax* the tensions between aristocratic and democratic claims encourage them to query older heroic values and the heroes' relationship to the wider community of which they are part. We must also take into account that the blossoming of Athenian wealth and power in the aftermath of the Persian Wars had given them a different perspective on their place in the Greek world and on their fellow Greeks who had fought together with them to repel the Persians.

The high-souled hero who is intent on a destructive course of action and will not be dissuaded by those who care for him is a frequent theme in Sophocles' tragedies. His tragic heroes and heroines are solitary, isolated figures who choose to put themselves outside of their group, refusing to listen to the advice of friends or loved ones and who stubbornly go to meet their fate alone. Ajax is an exceptional hero, one of the greatest warriors in the Greek army; as great as Achilles, according to Teucer. But his overwhelming pride and concern for his own honour leads him to the most shameful unheroic actions in trying to kill his fellow warriors as they sleep. Several other characters in the play, lesser in comparison with the tragic central figure, are strongly attached to Ajax; these are his brother Teucer and his followers who form the Chorus, together with Tecmessa who plays an important part in helping the audience to understand Ajax's character and values (see Hanna Roisman this volume). Their fortunes are linked with his, and his ruin is theirs.

The opening of *Ajax* is unusual in extant Sophoclean tragedy in that a god's voice is the first to be heard as Athene gloatingly explains to Odysseus how she has maddened Ajax and goaded him into actions that are both terrible and dishonourable for the great warrior. When he regains his mind he is not ashamed that he wished to kill his fellows, only that he did not succeed. Athene herself sums up the magnitude of Ajax's humiliation: although he still has strength as a warrior (witness the slaughter of the animals), his mental state, his ability as a leader of men is no longer strong; the god has destroyed his mind (119). 'So, Odysseus, do you see how powerful we gods are? Did you ever meet a more far-sighted man, a man who could respond to any situation?'

Ajax decides to die as honourably as he can, using Hector's sword as the weapon. In doing so he acts alone and for himself, abandoning those who care for him and depend on his strength for their safety. Tecmessa and the Chorus discover his body first and though Teucer arrives too late to save his brother he intends to give him an honourable burial as a hero. The great man has been brought down by a god, not by other men.

However, Agamemnon and Menelaus deny Ajax's heroic status, ignore his previous contributions as a warrior and are ready to leave his body unburied on the shore as food for birds of prey. Menelaus is first to arrive and immediately forbids Teucer to bury Ajax, asserting that his body can be treated in this way because he is an enemy who tried to kill the army leaders. He insults Ajax, denying that he was a noble hero, and continues with insults to Teucer who counters by insulting Menelaus. It is not the measured argument of courtroom debate, but the arguments and insults repeatedly focus on the Greek words used to judge a man's worth or status in society and also on terms that show approval or condemnation of his behaviour within that society. These occur throughout the play from the beginning and build a complex picture of the difficulties faced when trying to assess a man's 'goodness' in an ethical sense when the customary terms of approval are based on birth. In traditional Greek thinking, a man who is noble and well born is *esthlos* (good) or *eugenēs* (of good birth). Good in a very wide sense is *kalos* which can be applied to actions, thoughts and looks (only noble people can be good looking). Men who are low born do not merit such a varied vocabulary, *kakos* the opposite of *kalos*, covers many meanings including low born, humble in status, bad or wicked (of people, actions and things).

Nobility of birth does not necessarily go hand in hand with right behaviour and the contending parties in *Ajax* all claim that their opponents have acted contrary to accepted standards of proper conduct. In assessing behaviour a key group of words for unacceptable, abhorrent behaviour is connected with *hubris* and its derivatives. Although we need to put aside modern meanings of the word, there are still very many interpretations of what *hubris* meant in the fifth century BC. But to say that it is used of outrageous behaviour, often violent, that results from aggressive self-assertion or pride is hopefully a safe definition. After killing the flocks the deluded Ajax displays outrageous behaviour when he boasts about killing his fellow Greeks and his intention to torture Odysseus (96–110). The Chorus in their opening song say that this is the behaviour of Ajax's enemies ('such arrogance' 153), who mock his misery ('the *hubris* of his enemies' 196). In contrast to the man who commits *hubris* is one who is *sōphrōn*, showing balanced good sense and thoughtfulness, self-control. Athene's last speech to Odysseus in the opening scene of the play is a warning before the action unfolds of the dangers of pride. It is dangerous to boast about being better than the gods or other men because all things change and a man's fortunes can be ruined in a day, as we see. Her closing words (132-3) can give us pointers for the rest of the play, 'Gods love the wise (those who are *sōphrōn*). But we detest wrongdoers (those who are *kakos*).'

In the dispute after Ajax's death over whether or not he will be buried, Menelaus and Agamemnon deny Ajax his noble heroic status and also assert that in his past behaviour he has been guilty of *hubris* towards them. The characterization of the sons of Atreus is not a favourable one and in the case of Menelaus departs drastically from his portrayal in the *Iliad*, where he is a typical heroic warrior, although not in the top rank with Ajax, Diomedes and Agamemnon. He accepts the challenge of Paris to fight in single combat in order to end the war, and is described by Priam as noble looking and regal

(*Iliad* 3.166–70). Later when Hector too proposes to end the war by single combat Menelaus is first to volunteer (*Iliad* 7.94).

However the portrayal of Menelaus in Athenian tragedy is connected with his role as king of Sparta and was often hostile due to the tensions that arose between the two states after the Persian Wars. Sparta was a closed repressive society where children were trained from an early age to serve the state and military service was the prime duty of every male citizen. Athens was an open, enterprising state moving towards a full democracy and the Athenian view of Spartan character and institutions was one of dislike and distrust. Clashes between the two for leadership of the Greek states eventually led to the Peloponnesian War in 431 BC. The political tensions were reflected in fifth-century drama where Menelaus is often portrayed with the characteristics that Athenians thought of as typically Spartan. As Teucer is preparing to bury Ajax's body Menelaus arrives and immediately forbids Teucer to bury his brother. He and Agamemnon have decided on this and he accuses Ajax of disobedience to his commander as if he were just a common soldier, adding that because he tried to kill the Greek chieftains he will be treated as an enemy, and left unburied. 'It's the sign of bad (*kakos*) character when an underling (*dēmotēs*, common citizen) refuses to obey his betters. You can't expect a city to enjoy the rule of law when there's no fear attached' (1071–2).

After this authoritarian statement he declares further that a man who does as he pleases and who does not obey his superiors is committing *hubris* (1081). Throughout his angry and threatening speech Menelaus repeats the need for men to feel fear of those in charge and his accusation that Ajax was insubordinate to his superiors. His militaristic repressive attitude represents what many Athenians in the audience would have expected from a Spartan. He ends by echoing Athene's warning that all things can change: 'The pendulum shifts all the time. Ajax was glorious once. And proud (a man who commits *hubris*). But now my hour has come. Now it is my turn to be proud' (1088–9). So Menelaus is threatening to behave in the same fashion that he has just condemned in Ajax, and in addition warns Teucer that if he does bury Ajax, 'you'll be digging your *own* grave' (1090). The Chorus recognizes what this means and after Menelaus has finished they protest that he should not himself commit *hubris* in dishonouring the dead (1091–2). Teucer's response is more ironic and questions Menelaus's claim to noble status. 'I'll never be surprised again if the lower class commits offences when the so-called upper classes (*eugenēs*) say such offensive things' (1093–5).

The two men continue their argument with an exchange of personal insults, in which Teucer identifies Menelaus with a man who 'triumphed insolently' (behaved with *hubris*, 1151) at the misfortunes of others. Each participant in the argument has accused his opponent of *hubris*, and it seems that they have run out of material as Menelaus storms off, promising to use force to get his way.

Agamemnon enters a little later after a choral interlude. As we see him in the *Iliad* Agamemnon is a touchy, quick tempered man, but ready to apologize when necessary and as leader concerned to do what is best for the army as a whole. The overbearing and bullying aspects of his character are emphasized in *Ajax* as they often were in Greek drama, but the broad outlines of Homer's portrayal are still recognizable. He begins with an attack on the status of both Ajax and Teucer, and is outraged that Teucer should criticize him and Menelaus, especially as Teucer is a slave woman's son. He belittles Ajax's exploits in war, saying that his deeds were nothing out of the ordinary. 'Was he the only man in the Greek army?' he asks (1238).

When Agamemnon turns to focus his attack on Teucer he links the two issues of good birth and good behaviour, 'You're a nobody standing up for a nobody. And now you're claiming that your generals have no jurisdiction over the Greek army or the fleet and that Ajax came here as his own man!' (1231-4). He maintains that Teucer as a slave should not be allowed to speak so freely and that as a barbarian he can't even speak Greek. Theoretically Agamemnon can make these claims because Teucer's mother was not of Greek birth; she was a princess captured by Heracles when he attacked the city of Troy in the generation before the Trojan War. He is also (1259) offended by Teucer's behaviour, 'you're insolent and insubordinate (boldly acting with *hubris*). So, see some sense (be *sōphron*).'

Agamemnon's insults take no account of the portrayal of Teucer as a hero in Homer; his status is seen purely from a fifth-century Athenian point of view. After 450 BC Athenian citizenship was restricted to those whose mother and father were citizens and only they could enjoy the privileges of being Athenian. The advantages are described by Pericles in his oration over the dead after the first year of the Peloponnesian War (Thucydides 2. 37-40). They included the freedom to participate in politics and administration of justice as well as tolerance of their actions in private life: the contrast with life in oligarchic Sparta is obvious. We might also see here some signs of the tension between the democracy and the aristocratic élite, who had often married rich foreign women.

Menelaus, Teucer and Agamemnon use the same language to accuse their opponents of being guilty of *hubris* and not behaving with moderation and sense. No Athenian audience could accept the insistence of the sons of Atreus that Ajax was a common man, of low status, as he clearly was chief of the contingent from Salamis and his father Telamon had been a companion of Heracles. So the insults are not only petty and mean, but irrational nonsense, and serve to accentuate the characterization of Menelaus and Agamemnon as blustering bullies, inferior human beings. Besides using such inaccurate arguments the two kings also appear lesser because of their refusal to allow Ajax to be buried, in contrast to the more generous spirit shown by Odysseus later in the play. Hating one's enemy was approved behaviour and to deny an enemy proper burial could be considered an extension of legitimate revenge. However in the fifth century it must have been a subject of interest and debate because refusal of burial is a common motif in tragedy. It appears also as the central issue in Sophocles' *Antigone*.

Teucer must also be considered a lesser mortal. His response to Menelaus and Agamemnon shows him as a lesser version of Ajax, who surely would never have taken part in these wrangling debates reminiscent of playground boasting and threats. In his hatred of the two kings and of Odysseus he is similar to his brother but in the end he is more willing to be reconciled whereas Ajax considers it more honourable to die. Menelaus and Agamemnon consider him to be inferior on the heroic level because he is an archer, often thought in the fifth century BC to be of lower status in the army than those who fought with shield and spear. However in Homer his position as a hero is not questioned and we find him and Ajax fighting beside each other in the major encounters. In one desperate battle while Achilles is still absent from the fighting, Ajax uses his huge shield to protect Teucer while he carefully takes aim; using this cooperative technique he brought down nine men and was enthusiastically praised by Agamemnon for his deeds: 'Teucer, dear man, son of Telamon, leader of men, that's the way to shoot' (*Iliad* 8.281–2). When Teucer was wounded by Hector in this battle Ajax ran forward to cover and protect him until he could be carried off the field (*Iliad* 8.331–2), just as Teucer now protects his brother's body in death.

Perhaps Sophocles does not emphasize his heroic status here because Ajax is his focus and all are lesser in comparison with him. In their verbal battles none of the heroes comes out of their encounters perfectly: even Teucer is overly partisan and exaggerates Ajax's exploits (see Laura Swift in this volume). Until Odysseus arrives bringing on a tone of balanced reason, all are hot headed and angry, the weapons here being insults about family ancestry and brave exploits.

Least of all the lesser mortals are the men of the Chorus, who have followed Ajax their chief to fight at Troy. They are dependent on him as soldiers on their general and as sailors on their captain. They and Ajax are men of Salamis, an island in the Saronic Gulf offshore from Attica, whose men are traditionally seafarers. When Athens was at her most powerful in the fifth century it was because of her navy: the men who sailed the ships formed the backbone of the democratic assembly, with huge influence on decision making. In the heroic scenario of the Trojan War such men had little or no influence, but Sophocles' audience contained many who could contrast their own life in democratic Athens with that of the common man in heroic times when aristocratic chieftains had control over their lives. In the world of the play these men have no voice and at their first appearance the Chorus demonstrates their dependence on Ajax their leader (137–140):

when fortune smiles
    on you
i too
rejoice
but
when zeus
    batters you
and
when the greeks
insult you
i am frightened
    and
i tremble
    like a quivering dove

The small men need the great heroes to protect them, and they in turn provide support for their leaders; they depend on each other for survival (158–62). They call on Ajax to rouse himself to defend his people and himself, but when Tecmessa enters to explain what has happened to their leader, her news terrifies them. Their reaction is to hide, to board the ships and sail off, afraid that they will share whatever punishment lies in store for him (254–5):

i'm
  afraid
i'll die
  with him
    if i
    stand by him
in a hail
of stones

When Ajax does come out of his tent he speaks to them first (357–61), and asks his faithful crew to help him to kill himself, 'the strong relying on the weak', as the Chorus had said earlier (161), but the dependence of the weak is greater. The Chorus, Tecmessa and Eurysaces need the hero's protection, they cannot allow him to die. Nevertheless they are all helpless against his inflexible will. When they are left on stage at the end of this episode the Chorus sings of the misery that Ajax's decision to die will bring to all who care for him and are dependent on his honourable status. They sing of their yearning for home after the long years at war, and picture the effect his death will have on the others whose honour is linked to his: the grief his mother will feel hearing of Ajax's disgrace and his father's shame.

The reactions of the ordinary men of the Chorus are a simple and immediate response in the moment and reflect the ups and downs that Ajax's erratic behaviour encourages. So they take his 'deception speech' (646–93) at its face value. It raises false hopes in them; they dance and sing for joy. Although they realize the enormity of what he has done they hope that in time he can be reconciled with Agamemnon and Menelaus and that they too will be safe, for their own survival is much in their minds. They join Tecmessa in hunting for Ajax and when she discovers the body she knows that her life is destroyed, and that she and her son will probably be enslaved by Ajax's enemies. The Chorus too know that they are ruined, their hopes of home gone, their lives at risk:

> my general
> i was
>     your shipmate
> and you've
>     killed me

The sailors of the Chorus have no power in the heroic world and are dependent on Ajax for the life they lead. His stubborn hatred of those who voted against him and awarded the arms of Achilles to Odysseus led him to attempt to kill the army leaders and so, with the intervention of Athene, to his madness. In choosing 'honourable' suicide he has deserted and failed the weaker mortals who need him for defence. Without Ajax they have no place or purpose in the army. In their final song before Agamemnon arrives they repeat their earlier laments: the long years of war away from home and all its pleasures, from love and loved ones. There is no pleasure in life now for them and they long to be home in Attica. This is their last extended song: for the remainder of the action they speak in prose metres, confined to comments of one or two lines. Thus the very structure of the play reflects the interdependence of the Chorus and Ajax; after his death and their lament they no longer exercise their traditional singing role.

When Agamemnon enters after their song he concentrates his anger on Teucer, playing down the fighting prowess of Ajax and insulting Teucer, accusing him of outrageous behaviour, implying that he is *kakos* since he is not a free-born Greek (1258-9). He explicitly contrasts the two types of behaviour that have been already debated, saying that Teucer is acting with *hubris* and ordering him to be *sōphron*.

The long-suffering Chorus plead for reasonableness (1264-5), 'I wish you'd both learn self restraint!' (be *sōphrōn*). Teucer ignores them and responds to the criticism of Ajax's deeds in war with an exaggerated version of some episodes of the *Iliad* (see Laura Swift on this and on the portrayal of Odysseus). He then goes on to talk about Agamemnon's own foreign ancestry, particularly his infamous and notorious parents, Atreus and Aithra, and has no need to exaggerate here.

There seems to be no way to stop the wrangling so it is not surprising that the Chorus have changed their attitude to Odysseus and now welcome his arrival, expecting him to resolve the dispute over Ajax's burial. Odysseus' words on entering, 'I could hear Agamemnon and Menelaus squabbling over our hero's corpse' (1318-9), seem to indicate disapproval of the undignified quarrel and recognition of Ajax's honourable status. He sets about calming things down immediately. In reply to Agamemnon's complaints he says it is perfectly reasonable for Teucer to insult Agamemnon if he and Ajax had been insulted, and in this scene he shows sympathy for Ajax in death just as in the prologue he did for Ajax in his madness. Odysseus appeals to Agamemnon as a friend not to act (continue to act?) with hatred and violence to prevent Ajax's burial for then he will be trampling on Justice; although he is careful not to use the word itself he is describing the actions of a man who commits *hubris*.

He insists that even an enemy should not be ill-treated and dishonoured in death as it would not be right (just) and also acknowledges Ajax's honourable status as a great heroic warrior: '... with the exception of Achilles Ajax was the best of all Greeks who came to Troy' (1340-1). These sentiments are important and are repeated in his closing words: 'It's not right (just) to punish a good man (*esthlos*) when he's dead' (1344-5). His insistence on what is right and just would appeal to an Athenian audience, who were very familiar with the law courts as jurors and litigants, and Odysseus as mediator has gained respect and honour for the dead Ajax.

The closing words of a tragedy traditionally belong to the Chorus and here they echo the theme, recurrent throughout the play, of alternation in human life, reminding us that no man can know when his fortunes will change (1418-20).

In *Ajax* Sophocles looks at the old heroic world of Homer from the point of view of fifth-century Athens and in doing so encourages his audience to think about the place of traditional values in a democratic state. Although the old aristocratic families still had wealth and influence, every ordinary (male) citizen had a voice in state decisions and could attain the highest offices in the state. The old ideals based on birth which equated 'good' with 'noble' could no longer hold for every citizen; some adjustments were necessary. In *Ajax* it seems to be the adaptable Odysseus who provides a solution when he persuades Agamemnon to compromise with Ajax after his death.

Standards of traditional noble behaviour are also questioned. The fiery pride of the noble warrior, whether it is Ajax or Agamemnon, has destructive consequences for the wider community. In its place we see references throughout the play to the importance of wise moderation, of being *sōphrōn*. Even those least moderate (Ajax, Menelaus, Agamemnon) ask others to be *sōphrōn*. However only Odysseus and the Chorus show this 'cooperative' virtue in their appeals for reconciliation and compromise, and perhaps could have prompted the audience to re-evaluate the definition of a 'good' man.

11

# Odysseus and Empathy

Brad Levett

At the beginning of the play, the goddess Athena has maddened the hero Ajax into believing that a herd of livestock he is torturing is in fact the leadership of the Greeks, in particular Agamemnon, Menelaus, and Odysseus. Viewing them as responsible for his loss to Odysseus in the awarding of the arms of Achilles, he seeks to strike back at those former military comrades he now views as enemies. Athena, patron god of Odysseus, and angered by Ajax' previous, arrogant refusal of her aid in battle (770–7), invites Odysseus to mock and laugh at his rival in his pathetic and delusional condition (79). Such a response to the misfortunes of one's enemies is entirely in keeping with the heroic code of ethics that governs the behaviour of the characters at Troy, and is continually assumed by various characters in the play to be standard ethical behaviour towards an enemy (e.g. Ajax at 379–82; 454–5; the Chorus at 955–60; 988–9; 1042–3; Tecmessa at 961–2; 969). Yet, despite other characters in the play repeatedly assuming that Odysseus and the other leaders are indeed enjoying and mocking Ajax' downfall, Odysseus declines Athena's offer (121–4):

> And although we're enemies, I pity him. Poor man! Deranged. Demented.
> But I can see myself in him. Yes, I can see us all, all human beings.
> We're nothing but delusions, empty shadows.

This humane response of Odysseus has been rightly noted and emphasized by readers and interpreters, for the play continually reminds us that such an ethical position is, in its literary and social contexts, highly distinctive. In addition to the comments of other characters that highlight Odysseus' feelings of pity rather than any desire to gloat over an enemy, Odysseus can be directly contrasted with Ajax in the so-called deception speech, where Ajax talks of feeling pity for Tecmessa and his son if he should kill himself and thus abandon them (653–4). Of course, Ajax does not ultimately act on this feeling, and thus his inability to help a loved one based on a feeling of pity can be contrasted with Odysseus' decision to help an enemy based on the same emotional reaction. Moreover, Odysseus' response and his ethical choice are highlighted in the play by the simple fact that they are crucial for its resolution, since it is only through Odysseus' intervention with the Atreidae (Agamemnon and Menelaus) that Ajax is buried and further conflict is avoided between the Greek army and the Salaminian troops. Thus, the play specifically draws our attention to the issue of Odysseus' remarkable response and asks us to consider just what it means.

In what follows we will explore three questions regarding Odysseus' ethical choice. First, how is Odysseus able to respond with a level of concern for others, even an enemy, when other characters in the play are often highly focused on issues of self-benefit? Secondly, just why does Odysseus act as he does? That is, what is his motivation to act upon his sense of empathy for Ajax in order to seek that the dead hero receive the burial rites and honours that he deserves for his previous service in the Greek army? Finally, to what extent should the figure of Odysseus in the play and his empathetic concern for a former enemy be understood as a role model for his historical audience?

First, Odysseus is able to have such a response to his enemy because some of his core characteristics as a mythological figure, especially as he is portrayed in the *Odyssey*, are conducive to such a reaction. The links between *Ajax* and the *Iliad* have often been (rightly) emphasized, but the Odysseus of the *Odyssey* is also important for understanding the play since it helps explain his behaviour. Odysseus is known above all else for his cunning intellect, but this intelligence is often closely connected specifically to his ability to understand other individuals. The opening of the *Odyssey* notes that he 'saw the cities of many men and understood their thought' (*Odyssey* 1.3), and time and time again we see his ability to understand others as a cornerstone to this intelligence, whether it be the carefully flattering language he uses to address the princess Nausicaa to calm her and win her over (*Odyssey* 6.149–85), or his clear-eyed recognition of the human weaknesses of his men, such as when they succumb to hunger on the Isle of the Sun and eat the sacred cattle, despite his repeated warnings (*Odyssey* 12.271–388). Moreover, his understanding of human nature includes understanding himself and that most crucial Greek religious ethic, the recognition of his own limitations as a mortal, especially in comparison with the gods. This is clearly seen in the episode when Odysseus, kept captive by the divine nymph Calypso on her island as her partner, declines her offer to make him immortal so he can live with her forever (*Odyssey* 5.203–24). He admits that his mortal wife Penelope cannot compare with a goddess, but nevertheless desires to keep to his human position. Interestingly he specifically links this to his recognition that it is his human lot to suffer in life (*Odyssey* 5.221–4), and indeed the opening of the

*Odysseus and Empathy* 143

poem also emphasized that he was someone who 'suffered many pains on the sea' (*Odyssey* 1.4). Finally, another closely related character trait is his flexibility, his ability to adapt to changing conditions, and hence his description as a man 'of many turns' (*Odyssey* 1.1). Thus, the core characteristics of Odysseus are ones that are ideally suited to feeling empathy due to an ability to understand his fellow man, specifically through a recognition of the inherent nature of humanity as one that involves reversal and suffering. His ability to change his mind and feelings about a former enemy are also understandable as a result of his flexible nature.

Equally important, however, is that the play sets the conditions needed for Odysseus to respond as he does. When Odysseus first reacts to Athena's account of Ajax' madness, he does so with great fear (74–5), and reasonably so, given that an enemy of his is currently in an insane, murderous rage. It is only when Athena promises to hide Odysseus from Ajax' gaze, and then makes good on that promise, that he stops being fearful and is able to respond to Ajax in a sympathetic manner. Being able to watch Ajax in his madness without fear of personal harm seems to be a requirement for Odysseus' response. Later, Aristotle will give a very similar account of our response to tragedy, which he states consists of a combination of pity and fear. At the risk of oversimplifying an old and complicated issue, this means that we recognize the suffering of others from a distance (pity) but also experience a close personal anxiety that this sort of calamity could also happen to us (fear). In short, to feel empathy for another involves being able to identity with them without going so far as to get lost in the negative emotion itself. So long as Odysseus is simply fearing for his own safety, he cannot think empathetically of others. Yet once he is removed from immediate harm and the self-involved need for self-preservation, while still remaining able to understand that disastrous reversals of fortune can also befall him since such pitfalls are simply part of the human condition, he is then able to feel empathy for Ajax. Indeed, while Athena at first simply offered to Odysseus the opportunity to gloat over his fallen enemy, as a typical gesture in the ethical system of competition and reputation, she may well be setting the scene in order to allow Odysseus to respond as he does. While not emphasizing pity (and indeed, given that she is currently punishing Ajax for his arrogant claim that he did not need Athena's aid in battle, we would not expect her to), she does note that humans must respect the gods and recognize the frailty of human fortunes (118–20, 127–33). Thus, while she makes a point about a basic religious truth for the Greeks, she does so by creating the conditions for Odysseus to be both linked to and distanced from his former enemy. His witnessing of the raw power of the gods to manipulate a mortal reminds him of his own human frailty, while Athena's protection in turn allows him to play the spectator safely and feel for another rather than being lost in issues of self-preservation. Athena in effect teaches Odysseus a lesson that he learns to the fullest extent because he recognizes its truth in an emotionally and ethically engaged fashion.

Yet if Odysseus is the type, and finds himself in the proper conditions, to be able to feel sympathy for a former mortal enemy, why does he act upon this emotional response with the decision to convince his superiors to allow for Ajax' burial? Feeling sympathy for someone does not necessitate that we act in support on the basis of that feeling. As noted, Ajax fails ultimately to act on his pity for his family, whom he has a much greater ethical obligation to aid compared to the largely absent obligation for Odysseus to help his former rival. At the end of their debate, near the play's finale, Agamemnon suggests that Odysseus is simply acting out of personal interest, just like everyone does (1364–7):

**Agamemnon** So you want me to allow the burial?
**Odysseus** I do. You see, one day I'll need to be buried, too.
**Agamemnon** So in the end it's just about each man looking out for himself?
**Odysseus** Who else should I rather look out for?

As can be seen, Odysseus does not disabuse Agamemnon of this interpretation, perhaps simply for the practical reason that it wouldn't help to convince him, and indeed it is only really the appeal to their bond of friendship that leads Agamemnon to allow the burial (1331–2, 1371–2). Yet the comment should be seen as designed to make an audience question its validity. First, the explicit point that Odysseus' wish to allow Ajax to be buried in order to ensure his own later burial seems a bit far-fetched; Odysseus is defending a general principle that it is just to properly bury with honours those who were good men in life (or at least mostly so), but this is not of course some guarantee that he will specifically be treated properly upon his death due to his own adherence to the principle.

More importantly, the comments here raise for an audience the general question of what benefit Odysseus receives from his act of kindness to Ajax' memory. And it does so precisely because it brings to mind the simple point that the play does not indicate that there is in fact *any* direct benefit for his actions. As previously noted, the opportunity to mock an opponent by itself entailed, by the heroic code of competition, an elevation of status for the victorious individual who could thus proclaim himself greater than his opponent. Indeed, the original cause of the conflict, the competition for Achilles' arms, was precisely about status and position within the army.

Odysseus not only gives up this advantage, but even risks incurring some amount of disadvantage in his decision to aid Ajax. While it can be granted that he seems more than capable of getting around his superior officer and friend Agamemnon, his decision to defend the honour of an individual who just tried to torture and murder Agamemnon is not exactly an obvious means for improving his relationship with his commander. Odysseus' actions of course win him the respect and support of Teucer (1381–5), but given the relatively weak position of Teucer at the moment it is not clear whether this is much of an advantage. Odysseus' actions do not even win him the support of Ajax, seemingly, as Teucer specifically turns down Odysseus' offer to help with the burial on the basis of the assumption that the dead man would be offended by it (1393–5), an assumption that recalls the famous scene in the *Odyssey* when, in the underworld, the shade of Ajax still refuses to have anything to do with Odysseus and turns away in silence when Odysseus asks to speak with him (*Odyssey* 11.541–64).

It is, I think, instructive to perform the thought experiment of considering what reasons Odysseus could have given to support his advice to bury Ajax' body. An obvious justification would have been that the Greeks considered it a religious obligation to bury all corpses. Odysseus suggests this when he says that Agamemnon, by denying Ajax a burial, 'would be destroying the laws of the gods' (1343–4). He then, however, specifies that it is wrong to harm a good man when he is dead (1344–5). While the issue is a complicated one, it is not at all clear that the religious injunction that the dead must be buried is limited to those who were good men. At a bare minimum, dead bodies 'belonged' to Hades, the god of the underworld, regardless of any assessment of ethical considerations. So too, as one specific example, Antigone's defence of the burial of her brother Polyneices in *Antigone* does not depend on any assessment of whether he was a good or bad man in his life, and the play essentially validates her in this viewpoint. It is, rather, Odysseus' view that Ajax, having been a great warrior on the Greek side previously in the war, deserves a proper burial due to that fact, despite the human fallibility that overtook him at the end of his life. Importantly, his assessment of the dead hero's life as a whole, as he says, allows him to place more weight on his military accomplishments than on his hatred ('His excellence wins me over more than his hatred', 1357). But this qualification added to the more straightforward rule that the dead must be buried in fact makes it easier for Agamemnon to resist the religious argument: since Ajax attempted to torture and kill him, it is easy enough for Agamemnon to deny that Ajax was in fact a 'good' man in his view (1354). Were Odysseus to emphasize the basic religious need for burial of bodies, regardless of any assessment of the dead man's life, his position would in fact be stronger. Thus, the underemphasizing of an obvious religious reason to bury the body of Ajax in turn emphasizes that he is acting simply on the basis of his personal ethical beliefs. Without being unduly romantic or idealized in our understanding of the character, Odysseus seems to act as he does simply and only because of ethical concerns for what he considers to be the right thing to do, and in doing so he employs a sense of what is right which is not dependent on estimations of benefit or advantage. 'Pity based on the common fate of all living creatures has been put into action as positive help that transcends the boundaries of personal feuds' (Blundell 1989: 103).

It is worth looking briefly at a later play by Sophocles, *Philoctetes*, as it shares some important similarities in this regard, though here the characterization of Odysseus is very different, and it is Neoptolemus, the son of Achilles, who experiences empathy for another. In this play Neoptolemus comes with Odysseus to the island of Lemnos to capture the abandoned hero Philoctetes, because it has been prophesized that Troy will not fall to the Greeks without the aid of Philoctetes and the bow of Heracles which Philoctetes now possesses. Philoctetes was abandoned alone on the island years ago by Odysseus and the Atreidae because he had (and still has at the time of the play) a festering wound on his leg which was disrupting the religious rites of the Greeks due to its stench and Philoctetes' cries of pain. Philoctetes is now deeply embittered with the Greeks in general, and so Odysseus persuades the young man Neoptolemus to use deception to obtain Philoctetes' bow, since he will not be willing come to Troy to aid the Greeks. Neoptolemus is hesitant to use deception to obtain his goals, since he says it is not part of his nature to use trickery, but he is convinced to put this objection aside for the sake of the benefit he will eventually gain from acquiring the bow. In the course of the play Neoptolemus gains Philoctetes' trust, but when the older hero is seized by a terrible attack of his festering wound, Neoptolemus comes to feel pity for Philoctetes, and indeed as a result to question his ethical behaviour up to this point. He eventually gives back the bow which he had obtained when Philoctetes had his attack, and even agrees to abandon the Greek war effort at Troy in order to bring Philoctetes back to Greece. This will dash Neoptolemus' desire for glory in battle as well as potentially bring the wrath of the Greek army against him for betrayal, but he nevertheless resolves to act on the basis of his ethical beliefs. In addition to a number of similarities that can be seen here with Odysseus' behaviour in *Ajax*, note in particular that in both plays it is the visual presentation of another human being's suffering that leads the agent in question to feel for his fellow man, and to act on the basis of a personal ethical system as a result of this emotional reaction. Thus, while Sophocles does not present it as an argument that can be logically defended (more on this below), the two similar scenes do suggest that the playwright held it to be true that experiencing in a personal and direct fashion the plight of others could be a powerful force for ethical behaviour. The recognition of the shared humanity of another individual in both cases leads a person toward ethical behaviour not motivated by personal benefit.

At this point we can turn to the final question of whether Odysseus' behaviour in *Ajax* should or can be taken as something for an audience to emulate. From what we have discussed so far, it might well seem that such behaviour, the ability to feel empathy for an enemy and to act as a consequence for the benefit of this enemy, is presented as beyond the scope of the average spectator. It has been noted that the basic character of Odysseus was one that made him ideally suited to understanding the plight of others, and that the play specifically emphasizes his exceptional nature. Indeed, we can add to our previous points the basic fact that no-one else in the play is able to feel for or forgive an enemy. Ajax dies cursing the Atreidae (835–8), Agamemnon leaves the stage insisting that he will always consider Ajax an enemy (1373–4), and Teucer, like his brother, also curses Agamemnon and Menelaus (1389–92). Teucer accepts Odysseus as a friend when once he would have considered him an enemy for his rivalry with his brother, but of course this change of viewpoint only comes about due to the remarkable choice of Odysseus to help get permission to bury Ajax' body (Teucer ironically says that Odysseus 'deceived' [1382] him in this regard, playing upon Odysseus' reputation for trickery). Thus, it could simply be the case that Odysseus is exceptional in his ethical behaviour. Moreover, at least as we have explained the matter thus far, no real logical explanation is given for why or how Odysseus is able to act upon his emotional and ethical response to Ajax' plight, which might only increase our feeling that his behaviour is idiosyncratic.

However, I think all of this can be explained by giving proper emphasis to the metatheatrical nature of Odysseus' response to Ajax. Scholars have noted that metatheatricality, understood as a drama drawing attention to itself as a fictive performance ('a play within a play') permeates the scene. By making Ajax unable to see Odysseus, and indeed by Odysseus' amazed response to this ability which only emphasizes the point, Athena makes Odysseus a literal spectator to the scene being played out before him. Whereas before he feared for himself, as someone personally engaged in the events occurring, now he can safely view Ajax and his condition from a removed and safe position, just as any audience is, in this sense, 'protected' from terrible events presented upon the stage by the knowledge that it is in fact a performance and that they are not personally engaged in the events themselves. The scene also repeatedly employs verbs of seeing to emphasize this aspect of spectating. Thus, if the audience recognizes that Athena is in effect putting on a small tragedy for Odysseus to watch, then they can align this with the activity they are currently engaged in themselves, and so identify with Odysseus, in the sense of sharing a role if not in the sense of sharing the same set of personal characteristics. It was suggested above, since Athena ends with a very direct and deliberate meaning for Odysseus to take away from what he has witnessed, namely the familiar injunction to understand the limitations of being a human and in turn to respect the superior power of the gods, that she precisely set this scene in order for Odysseus to learn from it. Thus, given that Odysseus is to learn this lesson by occupying the same position of spectator that the historical audience occupied, it can be inferred that this audience is also meant to learn something from the scene. And what they learn is exactly to feel empathy through the depiction of the suffering of fellow humans, perhaps even enemies, when they undergo extreme changes of fortune for the worse, and to make ethical choices on the basis of such experiences.

Now, such an emotional response, of course, is not guaranteed: any individual spectator, then or now, for a plurality of different reasons, might be left cold to the depiction of Ajax' dementia. Moreover, we should be careful to specify that the play does not 'teach' the audience in any literal, explicit fashion. Since in Athenian tragedy the poet does not address his audience directly, he cannot teach in such a directly didactic fashion. Yet, like Aristotle specifically, the Greeks did generally think of themselves as learning from their poets, although this could sometimes be understood in something of a heavy-handed and literal fashion (e.g., the rhapsode Ion, in Plato's *Ion*, claiming that he knew how to be a good general because he knew his Homer, and Homer understood what was required to be a good general). However, as long as we keep these caveats in mind, the scene can be understood to suggest to its audience how to respond to tragic drama more generally. In so far as any individual responds with empathy to Ajax' dementia, whether spontaneously or led by the example of Odysseus' own response (and of course it may well not be possible to strictly separate the two), she or he can see themselves in the same position as Odysseus and so understand that we can take meaning from such emotional responses, just as Odysseus does not simply feel pity for Ajax' condition, but recognizes that the inherent frailty of human fortune is such that even one horrendous decision should not be allowed to wipe out a lifetime of achievement. Indeed, it is worth re-emphasizing that Odysseus seems to learn more than Athena intended, in so far as her purpose can be understood to be limited to showing the need to respect the gods, whereas Odysseus learned in addition to feel empathy for an enemy despite the fact that he fell into ruin precisely *because* he did not properly respect the gods, for this can only further stress the point that we can learn ethical behaviour from our emotional response to tragedy. Odysseus' ability, in one sense, to see beyond even his patron god Athena shows that the potential for learning from a tragedy is such that it can go beyond any deliberate lesson originally intended by the play's composer.

We can also suggest that this identification of role as spectator between audience and Odysseus also goes some way to explain the missing reason for why Odysseus can act on his sense of empathy for Ajax. As noted there is no real explicit reason for this ability, but if we accept that it stems from Odysseus' emotional response to the terrible suffering of a fellow human being, and if the audience, to whatever extent, follows Odysseus in this reaction, this very feeling of empathy becomes, in a loose but I think not unsatisfying sense, at least part of the reason why Odysseus is driven to act on the basis of his feeling of empathy. We can suggest that it is the very strength of the emotional response, which the audience is intended to share, that serves as a form of moral compulsion to adapt one's behaviour.

Thus, while Odysseus is certainly an idealized figure in the play, and his behaviour exceptional in numerous ways, the metatheatrical representation of his ability to learn from his emotional response to terrible events affecting a fellow mortal suggests that he is still accessible to an audience as a role model. Again in line with Aristotle's understanding, he is greater than us but still recognizably human, allowing for an audience to see themselves in him despite important differences, just as he is able to see himself in the downfall of Ajax. Because Odysseus can be understood to stand in the place of the spectator of tragedy in his scene with Ajax, he serves to at least suggest how an audience can react and learn from their reactions to tragic drama. Thus, he can serve not only as an exemplar for the specific point of the value and need to have a sense of a shared humanity, but also as a general guideline for our experience and reaction to tragic drama more generally.

## Suggestions for further reading

For a well-regarded recent general study of the play, including insightful observations on the issues discussed here, see Hesk 2003. On the large issue of Aristotle's understanding of tragedy, with reference to a number of important points specifically related to *Ajax* (Chapter 6), such as its metatheatricality (pp. 185–92) and its similarity to Aristotelian notions of empathy (e.g. p. 124), see recently Munteanu 2012, as well as the seminal work of Konstan 2006, chapters 6 and 10 on fear and pity respectively. For the shortcomings of Ajax' ethical stance towards his family, see Blundell 1989, pp. 72–81, and pp. 95–105 for the ethical virtues of Odysseus. For an old, but still valuable, study that emphasizes a (somewhat romantic) view of Sophocles as a 'humanist', see Whitman 1951.

12

# Post-Traumatic Stress Disorder and the Performance Reception of Sophocles' *Ajax*

Emma Cole

Did Ajax commit suicide because he was suffering from Post-Traumatic Stress Disorder (PTSD)? Although it is impossible to answer this question definitively, theatre practitioners throughout the twenty-first century have found great success in interpreting Sophocles' *Ajax* through the lens of PTSD. Such productions often have explicit social impact aims, seeking either to provide a form of performative therapy for people experiencing PTSD or to educate civilians about the challenges facing returning combatants. In this chapter I introduce the debates surrounding the presence of combat trauma in antiquity and detail three productions of *Ajax* that invite audiences to read the eponymous character as suffering from PTSD, namely Outside the Wire's 'Theater of War' project (2009–present), Timberlake Wertenbaker's *Our Ajax* (2013), and Aquila Theatre's *Ajax* receptions (2009–present). I explore how all three receptions attempt to redress combat trauma by contributing to the de-stigmatization of PTSD within the home, wider society and the military, and argue that irrespective of the play's function in antiquity, today *Ajax* exemplifies the potential therapeutic power of tragedy to mediate traumatic experience.

## Combat trauma in antiquity

The idea that ancient combatants may have suffered from various forms of combat trauma, including PTSD, Traumatic Brain Injury and/or Combat Stress Injury, can be traced back to the work of American psychiatrist Jonathan Shay. While treating Vietnam veterans suffering from severe, chronic PTSD, Shay became struck by the similarities between the symptoms of his patients and the depictions of warriors in Homeric epic. He went on to argue in his monographs *Achilles in Vietnam* (Shay 1994) and *Odysseus in America* (Shay 2002) that Achilles is a prototype warrior suffering from what we now call PTSD, and Odysseus that of a traumatized veteran struggling to reintegrate into civilian life following deployment. By exemplifying the transhistorical nature of these issues Shay believed he could pave the way towards the de-stigmatization of combat trauma in public discourse and find ancient precedents that modern psychiatry can adopt in treating PTSD.

Shay suggests that there are two primary triggers that cause PTSD in war: a betrayal of 'what's right' by a commander, and the onset of what he calls the 'berserk state' (Shay 1994, xiii). He cites an example of the former trigger as Agamemnon's decision to take Achilles' war prize, Briseis, for himself and argues that the latter trigger is represented by the notion of an *aristeia*, or the idea that a soldier 'has nothing to lose and everything to gain from reckless frenzy' (Shay 1994, 79–80). He argues that 'once a person has entered the berserk state, he or she is changed *forever*', meaning that unless treated, any soldier that survives the berserk state will have symptoms of PTSD. Sophocles' *Ajax* includes examples that can be considered as Shay's two triggers of PTSD: the awarding of Achilles' armour to Odysseus over Ajax, which provides the immediate context for the tragedy, can be thought of as the betrayal trigger, while Ajax's slaughter of cattle in the opening of the play under the belief that they were fellow Argive soldiers can be theorized as an example of him 'going berserk'.

The step from diagnosing characters in literary texts with symptoms of combat trauma to asserting the presence of PTSD in antiquity more generally is controversial. The so-called 'universalist' position relies upon a transhistorical understanding of experience, where the same mental illnesses can be found throughout time and retrospectively diagnosed. In contrast, several ancient historians have presented convincing evidence indicating that although it is hypothetically possible for ancient combatants to suffer from combat trauma and to diagnose mental health illnesses retrospectively, the sociomilitary environment required to produce PTSD did not then exist. For example, there is a lack of consensus about the percentage of ancient combatants who had first-hand experience of battle in comparison to modern veterans, with David Konstan (2014, 8) arguing that they 'fought almost continually in vicious hand-to-hand engagements', while Everett Wheeler (1991) and Louis Rawlings (2007) suggest that the Greeks in fact rarely fought pitched battles, meaning that out of all the veterans it is likely that only a small portion actually fought in hand-to-hand combat. Aislinn Melchior further notes that clinical studies specifically link both Traumatic Brain Injury and the hyper-vigilance required from modern soldiers serving in Afghanistan and Iraq to PTSD, neither of which were factors in ancient hand-to-hand combat (Melchior 2011, 218–19), while finally Jason Crowley argues that the psychological, social and technical environment in which the Athenian hoplite was placed profoundly protected the combatants from PTSD and Combat Stress Injury (Crowley 2014, 116).

Those invested in the idea that combat trauma existed in antiquity further complicate the debate by commonly supporting the idea that not only did it exist, but that forms of therapeutic treatment for the disorder did too. Shay, for example, argues that the ancient theatre provided a fully realized narrative which communalized trauma and provided therapy for those suffering from combat stress and needing assistance in reintegrating into civilian life, positing that:

> Athenian theater was created and performed by combat veterans for an audience of combat veterans; they did this to enable returning soldiers to function together in a *democratic* polity [...] the ancient Athenians reintegrated their returning warriors through recurring participation in the rituals of theatre.
>
> Shay 1995

Furthermore, Peter Meineck suggests that 'theater may have always been intended to address the experiences of fighting men' (Meineck 2009, 177), while Bryan Doerries argues that *Ajax* specifically is written in a code that civilians need military audiences to translate for them (Doerries 2012). Viewing the communal, ritualized City Dionysia as a reintegration ritual for returning combatants encourages one to prioritize interpretations of the staged tragedies which focus on the psychological experiences of active and returning warriors. For *Ajax* such an interpretation directs one's focus to the first half of the play, and in particular Ajax's frenzied slaughter of the cattle and post-combat suicidal behaviour, over other readings of the play such as those explored elsewhere in this volume, including transitioning concepts of heroism (Swift and McCallum-Barry) and the impact of warfare upon the family unit (Roisman). Given the content of *Ajax* it is unsurprising that the tragedy has become the vehicle from classical antiquity par excellence for exploring PTSD onstage, but one should not forget that there are other potential interpretations of the play.

Although viewing the City Dionysia as a reintegration ritual for returning combatants only considers selective evidence as to the purpose and the potential audience demographic of the ancient theatre, it is true that there was an association between theatre and warfare in fifth-century Athens. Beyond the subject matter of many extant dramatic texts the connection is manifest in the parade of war orphans who were brought up at state expense and given their first armour at the City Dionysia, the fact that the chorus was likely made up of *ephebes* (young men undergoing military training), and the first-hand experience of many of the actors, playwrights, and audience members, including Sophocles himself, of military service. Furthermore, there is persuasive evidence linking theatre with therapy; beyond generic connections between poetry and healing Robin Mitchell-Boyask notes that the later placement of a statue of Asclepius, the god of healing, on the southeastern slope of the Acropolis may associate drama with the healing process (Mitchell-Boyask 2008, 105–21), and the most famous Greek theatre today is at the healing sanctuary at Epidaurus. Although there are tantalizing connections between theatre, warfare and therapy in fifth-century Greece, there is ultimately a lack of conclusive evidence indicating the presence of combat trauma in antiquity, and it is far from a given that the ancient theatre was intended as a form of performative therapy for returning soldiers; if the theatre did hold this function, it is likely that it was also doing other things for other audience members concurrently. The lack of clarity, however, does not negate the possibility of interpreting *Ajax* through the lens of PTSD in modern theatre and nor does it invalidate the suggestion that the play may provide a form of performative therapy in the modern world.

## Outside the Wire's 'Theater of War' project

Theatre director Bryan Doerries and psychiatrist Phyllis Kaufman co-founded Theater of War productions in 2009. Today Doerries is the sole Artistic Director and runs three different public health and social impact courses, titled The Ajax and Philoctetes Program, the Ajax Program, and the Female Warrior Program. All three contain staged readings of Sophocles' *Ajax* and are conceived to be about and for military personnel, veterans, their families and caregivers. Doerries' aim for the project is 'to destigmatize psychological injury by placing it in an ancient warrior context' (Doerries 2018). Each programme runs for approximately two hours and features a reading of select Sophoclean scenes, translated by Doerries specifically for a military audience and read by professional, often high-profile actors. The readings take place around a table in diverse settings, including professional theatre auditoria, military bases, schools and hospitals. The actors wear everyday clothes and the house lights are left on, creating an informal atmosphere. Following the readings, a 'town-hall-style' chaired discussion ensues featuring a panel typically containing: an active duty soldier; a veteran; a spouse or other family member of a veteran; and a mental health professional and/or a member of the military chaplaincy. Across all three programmes, which respectively focus on the tragic hero and the 'seen and unseen wounds of war', the impact of combat trauma upon service members and their families, and the post-deployment circumstances of female combatants, a range of scenes from *Ajax* are read, usually including the opening section of Sophocles' play, Tecmessa's attempt to talk Ajax around from his intent on suicide, and Ajax's final monologue before his death. The panel then leads a discussion about how the themes raised in these scenes speak to their own experiences before inviting the audience to reflect upon and share their own understanding of the themes of *Ajax*.

Doerries and his team do not use the phrase combat trauma or PTSD in the publicity for the three Theater of War programmes, preferring instead to describe Ajax as 'a fierce warrior who slips into a depression' (Doerries 2018). However, the invitation for audiences to connect their own experiences to those of the characters in *Ajax* makes interpreting the character through the lens of PTSD almost inevitable. It is a fact that current veterans are experiencing extreme difficulties reintegrating into civilian life; in 2010, twenty-two US veterans committed suicide every day, and it is now estimated that between 20–30 per cent of the over two million American soldiers deployed to Iraq and Afghanistan since 9/11 will return with either PTSD or Traumatic Brain Injury (Higgins 2013). Meanwhile, in the UK, in 2012 more British soldiers committed suicide than died in combat. The statistic represents a 40 per cent increase on 2011 and is, in reality, much higher, as the Ministry of Defence statistics do not include veteran suicides, and deaths through overdose or car accident – even when intentional – are not classified by the coroner as suicide. Given this data it is likely that a high percentage of the Theater of War audiences either know someone who is, or are themselves personally, suffering from combat-induced PTSD, and quotations from attendees in which they link their illnesses to the character of *Ajax* are regularly used in the publicity and press for the project. In his 2012 Pop Tech keynote, for example, Doerries shared a paradigmatic quotation from a soldier who stated that 'knowing that PTSD is from BC makes me feel less alone in the world' (Doerries 2012a).

By any standard measure the Theater of War programme is a success. It has run more than 300 times in the US, Europe and Japan, for a total audience of over 80,000 service members, veterans and their families (Doerries 2018). It has won international acclaim, and in 2017 Doerries was named the New York City's Public Artist in Residence and funded from the Stavros Niarchos Foundation to run sixty further Theater of War events across the city between 2017 and 2019. Previously, the project received $3.7 million from the Pentagon to continue its work; the funding evinces the therapeutic value of the project, as the Pentagon does not have an arts supporting brief but one that focuses on the clinical care, prevention and research of psychological health. Within academia, however, the project has been somewhat more controversial due to the underlying implication that Ajax himself suffered from a form of combat trauma. Furthermore, while Laura Lodewyck and Sara Monoson (2015, 652) defend the project for democratizing Greek drama in terms of audience, interpretation, format and focus, Helen Morales (2016) notes that the reluctance of Theater of War to make a partisan statement about the US government, foreign policy, and warfare means the project is ultimately 'untrue to the spirit of Greek tragedy'. As a work of performance reception there are undoubtedly limitations to the social impact of Theater of War and the potential beneficiaries of the project's performative therapy. Nevertheless, the Theater of War demonstrates how *Ajax* can play a role in public discourse about the psychological impact of war and for this reason is a crucial chapter in the reception history of *Ajax*.

## Timberlake Wertenbaker's *Our Ajax*

Timberlake Wertenbaker's *Our Ajax* premiered at London's Southwark Playhouse in November 2013 in a production directed by David Mercatali. *Our Ajax* was a straight commercial production rather than, like Doerries' programme, a social impact project. The Southwark Playhouse was configured as a thrust stage and the predominantly civilian, regular-theatre-going audience entered the space through gates topped with barbed wire. The *mise-en-scène* included a stage floor covered with sand and a set dominated by a large tent against the far upstage wall of the stage. The design implied that the action was taking place on a UK army base in a desert location, reminiscent of then-current British deployments to Iraq and Afghanistan. The actors, who included Joe Dixon as Ajax, were costumed in military fatigues and the dialogue was modern and militaristic, filled with acronyms and references to automatic weaponry. Although the dialogue was rewritten as entirely contemporary and certain sections, such as the choral odes, bore no linguistic resemblance to Sophocles' text, Wertenbaker preserved the overall structure and story of *Ajax* and even retained characters that can be deemed dramaturgically challenging in contemporary theatre such as the goddess Athena and the mute Eurysaces. Except for Wertenbaker's removal of Agamemnon, and Mercatali's decision to cast the chorus of combatants with just five actors (four male and one female), the overall narrative remained close to Sophocles' text.

PTSD was crucial to the interpretation of *Ajax* contained in Wertenbaker's reception. The project started out as a 'literal' translation of Sophocles' play that Wertenbaker wrote in collaboration with classicist Margaret Williamson

(Wertenbaker 2013, 5). Wertenbaker, however, ultimately decided that she did not want to write a translation but rather a new play about a soldier who had 'cracked'; she stated that during the writing process:

> A new play was superimposing itself on the literal: contemporary, based on current wars, set in a British army base. The war in Afghanistan was dragging on and there were a lot of headlines about the casualties – and suicides. *Ajax* became *Our Ajax*.
>
> Wertenbaker 2013, 5

As part of the adaptation, which she described as 'inspired by Sophocles' *Ajax*' (Wertenbaker 2013, 7), Wertenbaker interviewed staff, combatants and veterans from both military academies and the organization, Veterans in Prison. The comments that the cast and creatives made about *Our Ajax* in publicity for the production reinforced the significance of PTSD to their understanding of the material; Mercatali noted that thinking about the text through the lens of PTSD remained crucial throughout the rehearsal process, in which veterans from Iraq and Afghanistan visited the cast and 'The soldiers would constantly talk about PTSD' (Mercatali 2014), while Dixon, for example, stated in an interview with Phosile Mashinkila that 'although post traumatic stress disorder is a term we use today to explain some of the casualties of conflict, if you look at descriptions of soldiers from ancient texts through to Shakespeare, clearly warriors across the millennia have had the same symptoms' (Mashinkila 2013). The content of the play itself also made the interpretation clear, with Wertenbaker's Ajax claiming that his mind has 'gone AWOL / thrown this illness on me / this cloak of martial fury' (Wertenbaker 2013, 36) while her equivalent of the chorus leader, the Company Sergeant Major, states that 'Ajax the bravest of them all / but now brooding, alone, eating himself up / gone Elvis – CR-PTSD'd' (Combat Related-PTSD) (Wertenbaker 2013, 45). Due to the billing of *Our Ajax* as an adaptation, rather than a translation, and the title change from *Ajax* to *Our Ajax* the PTSD dimension was implicitly foregrounded as anachronistic and there was no direct implication (aside from Dixon's comment) that Sophocles' equivalent necessarily suffered from combat trauma.

Unlike Doerries' project *Our Ajax* received mixed critical success, with the narrative fidelity sitting, for some audience members, uncomfortably with the modern setting. Wertenbaker, for example, persisted with the device of a messenger speech to announce the prophecy of Ajax's death, but had the character's speech delivered via text messages which the chorus read aloud. She also retained a choric function for the group of soldiers by having them sing and dance to contemporary music on the radio. Comments regarding 'anachronistic oddities' (Billington 2013) and the script failing to coalesce 'the text's dual loyalties' (Marlowe 2013) were frequent in the production reviews. Although of less commercial success than my prior example *Our Ajax* nevertheless effectively used classical tragedy to exemplify the effect of combat trauma upon modern-day soldiers and as an explicitly anachronistic adaptation makes a less problematic association between combat trauma and antiquity than can be seen in other receptions.

## Aquila Theatre's *Ajax* receptions

Aquila Theatre's work with Sophocles' *Ajax* bridges the Theater of War programme and *Our Ajax*. The company have been experimenting with receptions of *Ajax* over the past decade and have incorporated the tragedy into a variety of different formats depending upon target audience and funder. The first instalment, titled *Ancient Greeks/Modern Lives*, featured staged readings from Aeschylus' *Agamemnon*, Sophocles' *Ajax*, Euripides' *Heracles*, and Book 23 of the *Odyssey* (Meineck 2012, 12). A later version, titled *Homecoming: The Return of the Warrior*, included staged readings of Sophocles' *Ajax* and *Philoctetes*. Both readings were staged by actors associated with Aquila Theatre. The most recent iteration was titled *The Warrior Chorus* and consisted of four 'thematic units', one of which, titled *The Dilemma of War*, revolved around Sophocles' *Ajax*. In contrast to the previous examples *The Warrior Chorus* was staged by veterans with the assistance of scholars. Despite the different titles and combinations of ancient texts all receptions were the brainchild of NYU classicist Peter Meineck and his company Aquila Theatre, and operated as part of the company's public humanities programme funded through the National Endowment for the Humanities. The programme seeks to bring theatrical events, readings, and lectures into underserved cultural institutions (Aquila Theatre 2018).

Like in Theater of War the two initial *Ajax* receptions consisted of a staged reading followed by a post-show discussion. The commonality is likely not entirely incidental as Aquila actors performed as readers in an early Theater of War showcase (Lodewyck and Monoson 2015, 661). However, in contrast to Doerries' work the Aquila Theatre readings were rehearsed and Meineck served as director. Whereas Doerries' actors arrived on the day of performance and read the extracts 'cold', Meineck's ensemble presented a more 'polished' reading which, although staged without props or costumes, was closer to a professional theatre production and thus recognizable in format to the main target audience of the theatre-going public; Lodewyck and Monoson note that Aquila 'specifically seek out audiences who might not be aware of the challenges facing active duty and veteran military personnel and to alert the civic community to the concerns of these fellow citizens' (Lodewyck and Monoson 2015, 662). Although one-quarter of the programmes were oriented towards veterans, the primary focus of the *Ancient Greeks/Modern Lives* and *Homecoming* programmes was on educating civilians about the impact of modern warfare, rather than de-stigmatizing mental health within the army.

In addition to having a broad, civilian-based target audience more akin to Wertenbaker's *Our Ajax* than Doerries' Theater of War, the *Ajax* extract that Meineck's ensemble focused upon directed the audience's attention not to the injured warrior but 'on the reality of his wife Tecmessa's vulnerable situation as well as her personal strengths' (Lodewyck and Monoson 2015, 660). The actors read Tecmessa's description of Ajax's massacre of the cattle and the aftermath of his crime [201–330]; the distancing of Ajax from the audience encouraged spectators to focus on Tecmessa's interpretation of Ajax's actions, rather than the behaviour itself. In other words, the reception did not go as far as implying that Ajax was suffering from combat trauma, but if anything invited the audience to consider how Tecmessa might perceive his actions as a form of PTSD. Despite this more tangential association between *Ajax* and combat trauma, Meineck is on record making strong claims about the relevance of PTSD to his understanding of Greek tragedy. Although he is more cautious than both Shay and Doerries in his claims about the therapeutic role of tragedy for veterans in antiquity, possibly due to his status as an academic rather than an entrepreneur, Meineck does claim that 'The effects of combat trauma are well described in the dramatic literature of the Ancient Greeks' and 'What is now known as Post Traumatic Stress Disorder (PTSD) or combat trauma was certainly familiar to the ancient Greeks' (Meineck 2012, 7, 11). These arguments, however, are not foregrounded in the Aquila *Ajax* receptions, and although Meineck does serve as a panellist on some post-show discussions he maintains that the chosen scene prompts discussion not necessarily about combat trauma but about 'the specific challenges facing military wives and civilians impacted by war both in war zones and back at home, but also by active duty female service members' (Lodewyck and Monoson 2015, 660). Aquila's *Ajax* receptions therefore exemplify the debates surrounding the pertinence of PTSD to classical tragedy in a more subtle, academically uncontroversial manner. The receptions notably also extend the range of beneficiaries of the tragedy's modern performative therapy, and demonstrate how not only modern soldiers, but also spouses and civilians, might benefit from exposure to Sophocles' *Ajax*.

## Conclusion

As three paradigmatic examples Bryan Doerries' *Theater of War*, Timberlake Wertenbaker's *Our Ajax*, and Aquila Theatre's *Ajax* receptions demonstrate the diverse ways in which contemporary performance receptions incorporate research and reflect current debates about the relevance of PTSD to antiquity. Each reception has its own strengths: Doerries' project staged *Ajax* to assist in de-stigmatizing mental illness within the army; Wertenbaker's *Our Ajax* used current research into PTSD to create an entirely new play; and Aquila Theatre demonstrated how not just soldiers and veterans can benefit from *Ajax's* performative therapy, but also spouses and civilians. It is in targeting these final demographics that the greatest possibilities remain for future receptions. Notably, not a single one of the three examples substantially engaged with the second half of Sophocles' diptych; although Wertenbaker included a discussion about the fate of Ajax's corpse, the 40 per cent of Sophocles' tragedy that takes place after Ajax's suicide was reduced to around 20 per cent in the adapted script, meaning the focus was still placed squarely on the tragic hero. As Peter Burian has argued it is 'the polyphony of distinct and distinctive voices in the play [*Ajax*] that permit us – indeed require us – to consider a variety of perspectives beyond those of the hero' (Burian 2012, 69). Seizing the opportunity to explore how *Ajax* might assist suffering family members of a deceased veteran or educating families and caregivers as to how they can support those seemingly beyond help through engagement with the second half of the diptych may be useful in bridging the gaps in understanding between 'military' and 'non-military' people brought about by the increasing social marginalization of the army, and remains an enticing possibility for future receptions.

Despite the strengths of each reception there remains a degree of controversy around the practice of interpreting *Ajax* through the lens of PTSD given the uncertainty regarding the presence of combat trauma in antiquity. It is easy to wash our hands of the debates surrounding PTSD: for classicists to get tied up in debates over the veracity of the illness in antiquity or to restrict themselves to descriptions of the use of the classics in social impact settings, for medical experts to concentrate on the specificities of the illness and its diagnosis in contemporary psychiatry, and for all to withhold empathy due to a lack of sympathy towards the war which caused the injury. Yet if we critically engage with the types of receptions covered in this chapter, and work towards expanding how tragedies like *Ajax* can play a role in public discourses about the impact of war, we may more fully harness the therapeutic power of tragedy to mediate traumatic experience. Irrespective of *Ajax's* role in antiquity, today Sophocles' tragedy is a powerful tool for spreading awareness and prompting discussion about, and possibly even treating, PTSD.

# Sophocles' *Ajax*

translated by David Stuttard

# Dramatis Personae

*In order of appearance*

**Athene**       Greek goddess not only of wisdom and skill but also of fighting in battle. She favours the Greeks in the Trojan war, and especially Odysseus.
**Odysseus**     Greek general distinguished for his quick mind and silver tongue.
**Ajax**         Greek general once considered second only to Achilles in bravery.
**Chorus**       soldiers who have sailed with Ajax to Troy from Salamis.
**Tecmessa**     once an Asiatic princess, now Ajax's slave who has acquired wifely status.
**Eurysaces**    (*silent character*) Ajax and Tecmessa's young son.
**Messenger**    a member of the Greek army.
**Teucer**       Ajax's half-brother born to a slave woman.
**Menelaus**     Greek general, king of Sparta, husband of the flighty Helen.
**Agamemnon**    Greek general, king of Argos, brother of Menelaus, commander-in-chief of the Greek army at Troy.
**Silent attendants**

*Ajax* was probably written for performance at the Theatre of Dionysus in Athens, around or slightly after the year 440 BC.

Unusually in extant tragedy, the action, which begins at dawn, is apparently set in two different locations. Lines 1–814 take place in front of Ajax's tent in the Greek army encampment at Troy, while for the remainder of the play the scene shifts to a secluded copse near the seashore.

No stage directions are given in the original text. All those contained in the translation are extrapolated from the context. Certain conventions are presupposed: in the first part of the play, the *skene* (stage building) represents Ajax's tent, with the entrances and exits of Ajax and Tecmessa being made through its central door, and the two *eisodoi* (passageways) on either side of the *skene* probably being used by Athene and Odysseus respectively; in the second part, the *skene* probably represents the grove, with one of the *eisodoi* imagined as leading to Ajax's tent, and the other to the rest of the Greek encampment. In the first production the *ekkuklema*, a low trolley that slid in and out through the *skene* doors, may have been used to remove the actor playing Ajax before he fell on his sword and subsequently to reveal his corpse, now represented by a dummy. However, the precise staging of this scene remains a mystery.

Within the translation that follows, choral passages or passages using verse forms other than iambic trimeters are usually identified by both a change of layout and the use of lowercase lettering throughout, including for proper names. Line numbers refer to those in standard Greek texts.

*Outside Ajax's tent. Daybreak. A blood-trail leads to the tent. Enter* Odysseus, *a blazing torch in his hand. He is casting round, following the trail. As he nears the tent, an eerie voice is heard.*

**Athene**  Son of Laertes – Odysseus! Every time I see you, you're looking for a way to trap your enemies. Yes! I can see you there beside the tents, beside Ajax's ships, far out on the army's wing where he's been billeted.

I've been watching you track him, sniffing his fresh scent to find out if he's in his lair or if he's gone. You're like some Spartan hunting dog that can detect the slightest trace! And now your path has brought you here – here to your quarry. He's only just gone to ground, his forehead drenched with sweat, and both hands sticky, syrupy with blood.  10

No need to look inside! But speak! Tell me the reason for this urgent search. And then learn, too. From me. You see, I know what's happening.

**Odysseus**  Athene! I can't see you, but I know it's you. I love you more than any other god. I can hear your voice! It excites my soul to action! It's like the high-pitched trumpet call that wakens sluggish sentries from sleep.

You're right! You've interpreted the situation perfectly – why I've been tracking him, my enemy, the 'great shield-bearer', Ajax. It's him I'm after, no-- one else. It's his tracks I've been following for so long.  20

What he did last night – this night – it's all so strange, so unbelievable – if he did actually do it. You see... we don't know anything for certain: everything's unclear. I wanted to find out myself, so I volunteered for duty.

You see... the cattle that we'd rounded up in raids – we found them just now, freshly slaughtered, butchered, and their herdsmen dead beside them. And everyone says he did it! A sentry told me how he'd seen him running fast across the plain, his sword still dripping blood.  30

So I followed his tracks. One moment I could see them well; the next I'd lose them and I couldn't make them out. So, you've come at the right moment. You've kept me straight before and you'll keep me straight in the future!

**Athene**  Odysseus, I know. I've been here some time. I've been watching you and your quarry with great interest.

**Odysseus**  So, am I on the right track?

**Athene**  You are. He's guilty.

**Odysseus**  Why did he do it? It's so senseless!  40

**Athene**  He's jealous and angry about Achilles' armour.

**Odysseus**  So why the cattle raid?

**Athene**  He thought he was spilling *your* blood.

**Odysseus**  You mean he meant to kill the Greeks?

**Athene**  And if I'd not intervened, he'd have succeeded.

**Odysseus**  What was he thinking? How could he hope to manage *that*?

**Athene**  By night. Covertly. On his own.

**Odysseus**  Did he get near us? Did he find us?

**Athene**  He came right up to the tents of your two generals.

**Odysseus**  So, if he did want to kill us, what stopped him?           50

**Athene**  Me! *I* stopped him. I blurred his vision. I made him see things differently. I made him vent his anger on the sheep and cattle, rounded up in raids, but not yet allocated, and on the herdsmen guarding them. He threw himself among them, slicing at them, smashing spines, and killing everything around him.

These two? He thinks he's killed the sons of Atreus – and over here another and another of the generals – and he attacks them all. Lurching, lunging, sick, deluded! I kept on goading him! I kept on driving him towards the jaws  60
of ruin.

And when he'd had enough of his great exploits, he lashed together any sheep and cattle that were still alive and drove them home – like they were *men* he'd taken captive, not horned beasts! And now that he's got them trussed up in his tent, he's torturing them. I'll let you see how mad he is, so you can tell the Greeks exactly what you've seen. No, stay! Don't be afraid. He'll not hurt you. I'll turn his eyes and stop him seeing you.           70

(*to* Ajax *inside the tent*) You! Ajax! Take a break from tying up prisoners and come outside! Now! Ajax, that's an order! Outside! Now!

**Odysseus**  What are you doing, Athene? Don't call him out!

**Athene**  Be quiet! Or do you want me to call you a coward?

**Odysseus**  No, by the gods, no! Let him stay inside.

**Athene**  Why shouldn't he come out? He's still only a man!

**Odysseus**  And still my enemy.

**Athene**  And isn't it the loveliest of things to mock our enemies?

**Odysseus**  I'd much rather he stayed inside!   80

**Athene**  Are you frightened of him now he's mad?

**Odysseus**  If he was sane, I'd face him any day.

**Athene**  He won't see you – not even if you're standing next to him.

**Odysseus**  How? Have his eyes gone? Can't he see?

**Athene**  His vision's perfect, but I'll blind him.

**Odysseus**  A god can do anything.

**Athene**  Quiet now. Don't move!

**Odysseus**  All right, I'll stay – although I'd much rather not be here!

**Athene**  You! Ajax! You! I'm ordering you out a second time! Why are you disrespecting your war-ally?   90

*Ajax appears at the entrance to his tent drenched in blood.*

**Ajax**  Athene! Daughter of Zeus! You stood by me! I'll decorate you with gold medals in recognition of my victory!

**Athene**  Well said! Now, tell me! You've soaked your sword nicely in Greek blood?

**Ajax**  Indeed I have! I won't deny it.

**Athene**  And the sons of Atreus – you thrashed them, too?

**Ajax**  They'll not dishonour me again.

**Athene**  You mean they're dead.

**Ajax**  Yes, dead. Just let them try to take away my armour now!   100

**Athene**  Just so! And Laertes' son – Odysseus? What did you do with him? Or did he run away?

**Ajax**  Oh yes, that damned fox – you want to know where he is now?

**Athene**  I do – your greatest enemy.

**Ajax**  He's inside, tied up. Oh, it's the best! But I don't want him to die quite yet.

**Athene**  So, what *do* you want to do with him? What more can he give you?

**Ajax**  I'll tie him to my tent post.

**Athene**  And torture the poor man?

**Ajax**  Before he dies, I'm going to whip him raw.  110

**Athene**  (*sarcastically*) Oh, poor Odysseus! Don't bully him!

**Ajax**  Athene, any other order and I'll obey you. But this will be his punishment: no other.

**Athene**  If it gives you so much pleasure, go to it. See your plan through to the end!

**Ajax**  I'll get to work, then! And here's my directive for *you*: always be my ally, like you are today!

*Exit* Ajax *back into his tent.*

**Athene**  So, Odysseus, do you see how powerful we gods are? Did you ever meet a more far-sighted man, a man who could respond to any  120
situation?

**Odysseus**  No. No-one. And although we're enemies, I pity him. Poor man! Deranged. Demented. But I can see myself in him. Yes, I can see us all, all human beings. We're nothing but delusions, empty shadows.

**Athene**  So look at him and learn never to brag about being better than the gods, or boast because you're stronger than another man – or wealthier. It  130
only needs one day to crush a man's achievements. Or promote them. Gods love the wise. But we detest wrongdoers.

*Exit* Odysseus *the way he has come. Enter* Chorus *of Ajax's warriors.*

**Chorus**  ajax
    son of telamon
    who rule deep-bedded salamis
    out in the roiling sea

  when fortune smiles
    on you
  i too
    rejoice

but
when zeus
    batters you
and
when the greeks
    insult you
i am frightened
   and
i tremble                                                140
    like a quivering dove
        its feathers
            ruffling
        and terror
            dancing in its eyes

last night
there came
a babble
    of black news
        confused
        dishonourable

how
you'd crossed
    the plain of troy
        when horses
        are put out to pasture
and
killed
    the cattle of the greeks
        their spoils of war
        all rounded up
        not yet assigned
and your sword
    flashed
        as you killed them.

odysseus
is whispering
this story
    moulding it

adorning it
   implanting it
      into the ears
      of all he meets
   and they
      so readily
   believe him

he is so easy
   to believe
and anyone
   who hears him
      smiles
      and laughs
      and mocks
         your misery

such arrogance

great men
   make such an easy target
they're impossible
   to miss

no-one would listen
   to such accusations
made
   of me

petty envies
   cling
to great men

and yet
   without them
how could we
   average men
protect
   our cities

the best thing's
to work in harmony
   the weak

                depending on
                        the strong
        the strong
                relying on
                        the weak

but you can't teach
    such philosophy
        to fools
                the sort of men
                who're clamouring against you
and we can't protect you
        from their accusations
                when you're not with us
                king

they chatter
    like great flocks of birds
when you're not there
    to see them

yet
when you come
        abrupt
            unheralded
they cower
in terror
    at the vulture's gaze
and wordless
    they fall
        silent

was it artemis
    the child
        of zeus
    the goddess
        of the bulls
who goaded you
    against the army's
        herds of oxen

            such devastating
                news

           i feel such
                shame
    maybe you failed
        to offer her
        sufficient
        thanks for victory
    or broke
        a promise
    failed to give her
        some prize of honour
                when you brought
                a deer down
                in the hunt
    or did the bronze clad
        war god
        ares
    harbour
        malice
        for a gift
                unpaid
    and lead you
        through the maze
                of night
    to your dishonour

    ajax
        with a clear mind
    you'd never
        have behaved
                like that
    and slaughtered
        cattle

    perhaps the gods
    have sent this sickness

    zeus and apollo
        let what the greeks
                are saying
        not prove to be
                true

       if the great kings
          lay such charges
                against you
    poisons
                whispered in the dark
                      by them
                      or by odysseus
                            that bastard spawn
                            of sisyphus
    don't stay                                                          190
    here
       downcast
    here
       inside
             your tent
          beside
             the sea
    and earn
       bad reputation

    no

    stand

    you've stood aside
       from fighting
       for too long
    and now the flames
       of ruin
             of your ruin
    fill the skies

    the mocking laughter
       of your enemies
       is limitless

    it flaps
    and blusters
       through the windy woods
             reverberating
             echoing
                   from one throat
                   to the next

                    and my despair                                      200
                        engulfs me

*Enter* Tecmessa *from Ajax's tent. She addresses the* Chorus.

**Tecmessa**   you sailed
                    here
                    with my ajax

               you come
                    from salamis
               like him

               though your homeland
               and his father
                    telamon
               are far away now

               and everyone
                    who cares for them
               is plunged
                    in misery

               and ajax
                    mighty ajax
                    in
                    his terrifying
                         majesty
                         his raw unfettered
                              strength
               is sprawled
                    in sickness
               and the chill
                    winds
               lash and
               scourge him

**Chorus**     what happened
                    in the night

               what misadventure

               tell me                                                  210
                    tecmessa

        tecmessa
you may be
   trojan
ajax' slave
   brought
     to his bed
       at spear point
but he cares
   for you
   deeply

and you know
   what happened

tell me

**Tecmessa**   i don't know
      how i can

it's so
   unspeakable

a great weight
   heavy
     as the weight of death
is pressing
   down
     on him

a madness
fell
   on ajax
in the night
   on famous
   ajax
and undid him

you'd see it
   if you looked inside
the mess
   of slaughter

        and nobody responsible       220
        but him

            the blood
                polluting everything

            his sacrifice

Chorus      all that you've said
                his fury
                and his passion
            all that you've said
                it must be faced
                yet it's unbearable

            and even now
            the rumours
                race
                through
                the greek army

            exaggerations
                grow

            i'm afraid
                of what is still
                    to be revealed
                of what is still
                    to come

            his death
                will come
            and all
                will hear
                of how
                he butchered                                                230
                    all the herds
                    and all the herdsmen
                    and their horses
                how
                    he hacked
                and how
                    he stabbed
                and how
                    his sword grew blacker
                    as he killed them

**Tecmessa**   and then he came
  here
  here to us
 herding them
   like captives

  here
 inside the tent
  he slaughtered
  some
    where they were standing
  others
    he smashed their ribs
  and
    tore apart with his bare hands

there were two rams
 white hoofed
 and strutting

 he beheaded one
 tore out
   its tongue
  threw it
   away

and then                240
 he tied
 the other
   on its hind legs
 to the tent post
and he took
 a long thong
   from his horses' tack
and beat it
  with this double lash
   so hard
    the air throbbed
and he shouted
 language
 so obscene
 so cruel
  that no man

>                   only a demon
>             could have taught him

**Chorus**  it's time
>             to shroud our heads
>         and shrink
>             ashamed
>             into the shadows
>
>         it's time
>             to find our ships
>         and bend
>             over the beating oars
>         and set
>             our ship to speed
>             far out
>             across the sea
>
>         the sons of atreus
>         are levelling
>         such threats
>         against us
>
>         i'm
>             afraid
>         i'll die
>             with him
>                 if i
>                     stand by him
>         in a hail
>         of stones
>
>         he's all alone
>             now
>
>         fate
>             monstrous
>         fate
>         has taken him

**Tecmessa**  It's over now. His fury's done. He's calm – like the calm after an ice storm, once the lightning's gone. But now he's plunged into a new despair. It's a painful thing to stare misfortune in the face, and know that nobody's responsible but you.

**Chorus**  But, maybe, if it's over, everything will be alright. A trouble past's a trouble lessened.

**Tecmessa**  What would you rather do, if you had the choice: enjoy life at the cost of your friends' happiness, or share your friends' unhappiness?

**Chorus**  It's worse when everyone's unhappy!

**Tecmessa**  Which is why it's worse, now he's recovered.

**Chorus**  What do you mean? I don't understand.

**Tecmessa**  When he was mad, Ajax was perfectly happy with his fantasies, but it worried us to see him, because we were sane. But now it's over, and he's returned to his old self, he's mortified – and we're still just as worried as we were. So now both parties are unhappy, not just one. Agreed?

**Chorus**  Yes. Yes, I see. And more – I'm worried that a god's behind it. I mean, if now it's over, he's no better than he was when he was ill!

**Tecmessa**  Well, that's how it is.

**Chorus**  How did it all start? We'd like to know. We're just as worried as you are.

**Tecmessa**  I'll tell you. What he's done affects us all.

It was at midnight when the lamps had been put out... He snatched his sword like he was going out on some non-existent mission. I argued with him. I said: 'What are you doing, Ajax? You've had no orders; there's been no messenger; you've heard no trumpet-calls! The army's fast asleep!'

He scarcely deigned to answer me, just kept repeating the old cliché that a woman's greatest gift is silence. I heard him, so I stopped. And out he ran. Alone. What happened next, I don't know. But he came back with his captives, bulls and sheep and sheep-dogs. He decapitated some, slit others' throats, or broke their spines. And the others – all tied up – he tortured them like he was torturing men, though they were only animals.

In the end he left me, went blundering outside, and started talking to some shadow, mocking the sons of Atreus and Odysseus, laughing hysterically as he remembered what he'd done to them.

And when he finished, he came crashing back inside the tent. And somehow slowly, slowly he regained his sanity. And when he looked around and saw the... horror everywhere, he clenched his fists and beat his head and groaned.

And so he sat there, ruined, in the ruin of the corpses of the beasts he'd killed. He sat and tore his hair and raked his nails deep through his scalp. And for a long time – such a time! – he didn't say a word. And then those dreadful threats, what he'd do to me if I didn't tell him everything. He kept on asking what had happened. And I was... absolutely terrified, but I told him everything I could, as much as I could understand it.

And he groaned so agonizingly, so desperately – I've never heard him groan like that before. He'd always said that crying was for cowards, and when  320
he grieved it was in silence, not like a woman, no – no, like the rumbling of a bull.

Now he's just sitting there. He's inconsolable. He won't eat or drink. He's just slumped where he fell, surrounded by the carcasses of all the beasts he killed. He's planning something terrible. I can tell. Somehow I can tell from how he's muttering and sobbing...

You – you're his friends – go in to him. That's what I came to ask you. Help him if you can. Men like him can be won over by their friends.  330

**Chorus**  Tecmessa – your news – it's terrible. That he's suffering like that...

**Ajax**  *(from within the tent) iō moi moi!*

**Tecmessa**  I think there's worse to come. Did you hear Ajax bellowing?

**Ajax**  *(from within the tent) iō moi moi!*

**Chorus**  I think that it's his illness – unless it's realizing what he did when he *was* ill that's upsetting him.

**Ajax**  *(from within the tent) iō!* My son! My son!

**Tecmessa**  Poor Ajax. He's calling for Eurysaces. What does he want? Where  340
*are* you?

**Ajax**  *(from within the tent)* Teucer! Where's Teucer! Will he never come back from his cattle-raid? And all the while I'm ruined!

**Chorus**  He seems rational enough. Open up the tent. Maybe seeing us will return him to his senses.

**Tecmessa**  I've opened it. Now you can see the full extent of what he's done. Now you can see him as he really is.

*Enter* Ajax *from the tent.*

**Ajax**    *iō*

    my friends

    you sailed
      with me

    and
    only you
      friends
    have stayed                                 350
      loyal and true

    look at me now

    a tidal wave
    is surging round me
    and
    the spray
      that drenches
        as the waves break
    is the spray
      of blood

**Chorus**    (*to* Tecmessa) all
    that you said
    just now
    was true

    he's clearly
    lost
      his mind

**Ajax**    *iō*
    you
      were my crewmen

    you
      sailed us
        here
      across the wide sea
        sweeping the waters
        with your oars

    you

|  |  |  |
|---|---|---|
|  | are the only people | |
|  | i can turn to now | 360 |
|  | for comfort | |

        kill me

        now

**Chorus**    no more ill-omened
           words

        don't add
           trouble
        to more
           trouble

        don't pile
           grief
        on
           grief

**Ajax**      can't you see
        me
        mighty ajax
           who was once
           so stalwart
                and
           so steadfast
                and
           so fearless
           in the front line

        can't you see
        how
        i've turned
           my mighty aim
           on animals
           tame animals

        i am
           a laughing stock
           a thing of shame

**Tecmessa**  ajax
           please

|        | master
|        |     please
|        |         don't speak
|        |             like that
| **Ajax** | leave me
|        | go
|        |
|        | go away
|        |
|        | *aiai*                                                      370
|        | *aiai*
| **Chorus** | by all the gods
|        |
|        | stop now
|        |
|        | be rational
| **Ajax** | such cruel fate
|        |     to let
|        |         those enemies
|        |             those demons
|        |                 whose one wish is
|        |                     to crush me
|        |         get away
|        | while all the time
|        |     instead
|        |         i was attacking
|        |             goats and
|        |                 wide-horned cattle
|        |         drenching
|        |             my world
|        |                 in rivers of their blood
| **Chorus** | why torture yourself
|        | with what you've done
|        |
|        | what's done
|        | is done
|        |
|        | nothing can
|        | change it
| **Ajax** | *iō*
|        | odysseus

                he watches
                    everything
                he caused                                              380
                    my suffering
                the filthy parasite

                how
                    he'll be laughing
                now
                and
                    gloating
                        at my ruin

Chorus          it's the gods
                    who choose
                who laughs
                    or cries

Ajax            if only
                    i could
                    see him
                    now
                despite
                    my
                    shame

                *iō moi moi*

Chorus          be careful
                    what you say

                can't you see
                    how bad things are
                    for you

Ajax            zeus
                    my great ancestor

                if only
                    i could kill him now
                        odysseus
                        the parasite
                        the worm
                            with silken tongue
                        my enemy

          and kill 390
               the two kings too
          so then
          when it's all done
               i could die too

**Tecmessa**   then pray
             that i should die
             with you

          why should i
             live
          when you are
             dead

**Ajax**     iō

          darkness
             is my only light

          and death's
             the brightest light
             of all

          come
          take me
          take me
             home to you

          i am no longer
             worthy
          to ask help
             from gods
             or from my fellow men 400

          no

          but athene
             child of zeus
             the goddess warrior
          has ruined me

          where can
             anyone escape
          where can

          i find rest

          my friends
          if all that i have ever done
              lies dead
              with these dead cattle
          if this demented
              cattle-hunt's
              my only glory
          the army
              every man of them
          should rightly kill me

**Tecmessa**    to hear him                                    410
                    speak like this

              such a brave
                  and noble man

              he'd never have
                  spoken like this
                  before

**Ajax**        iō

          you
              sea-lanes
              slicing through the boiling waves
          you
              sea-caves
              on the rocky cliffs
          and
              pastures
              sloping to the water's edge
          you've kept me
          here at troy
              so long
              too long

          no longer now
              at least not
              while i live

          hear me

>           if you
>           understand
> 
>     and you
>           scamander
>           with your streams
>                 so close
>                 so kind to all the greeks                    420
>     you
>           will not see me
>           in this life again
>     a man who
>           it's no empty boast
>           to say
>           was once unequalled
>           in the army
>                 of the greeks
>                 who sailed to troy
>     but now
>           dishonoured
>           broken

**Chorus**  Your situation's desperate. I don't know if I should let you speak or stop you.

**Ajax**  *aiai*! Who could have known my name would suit my agony so  430 perfectly? Aiai! Aiax! My very name's a lamentation stretching out for ever. I'm looking ruin in the face.

My father fought at Troy, but *he* came home crowned with every military honour, saluted as the greatest of the Greeks. And then it was my turn, his son, to come to Troy – no less a man than he was, with a war record to match. But *my* prize is dishonour, death at the hands of fellow  440 Greeks.

One thing I think I know: if Achilles had been still alive to judge the contest for the armour and award it as a prize for bravery, no-one would have taken it but me. But as it was, my bravery meant nothing to the sons of Atreus, so they gave my armour to a shameless cheat.

Well, if my vision and my fuddled mind had not deceived me, they'd not have cheated anyone again. But as it was, the gorgon-eyed goddess, the stony child  450 of Zeus, Athene . . .

I'd almost got them! I was just about to smash them, when she made me sick, mad, made me slaughter beasts!

Things didn't go to plan. And now the sons of Atreus have got away. They're laughing at me. If gods intervene, even cowards can escape a better man.

So, what now? It's obvious the gods hate me. The Greek army hates me too – and Troy, yes, and the plain of Troy!

Should I desert my post? Should I turn my back on the sons of Atreus and sail 460 back home? How could I look my father in the eye? How could he bear to look at *me*, stripped of my honour, when he was held in such *high* honour and esteem? It's not an option.

So, should I single-handedly attack the walls of Troy, one man against so many, go out fighting in a blaze of glory? No, that would only bring more kudos to the sons of Atreus. I can't do *that*.

No, I must find some way, some exploit that will prove to my old father that 470 I'm worthy of his name.

Only a coward wants long life, when everything's against him. But where's the satisfaction in a daily grind of one step forward, one step back along the road to death? Life fed on empty hopes is worthless. But a hero has two options: to live in glory or die in glory. And that to me is everything. 480

**Chorus** Ajax, no-one could find fault with what you've said – or your determination. But pause a moment. Let your friends speak. Don't close your mind.

**Tecmessa** Ajax. Master. It's the worst thing in the world to suffer a cruel twist of fate. I was born free. My father was a powerful man, the richest in all Phrygia. Now thanks to the gods and to your victory in battle I'm a slave. 490

But now, because you took me to your bed, what's good for you is good for me. So I'm begging you – by Zeus who protects our home, and by the bed we share – don't make me have to suffer insults from your enemies! Don't let some stranger get his hands on me!

If you die, I'll be a widow. And before the day's done I'll be taken and dragged off by force – me and your son – for the Greeks to fight over and see who'll be our master. And one of them is sure to taunt me and insult me: 'Look at her 500 now, Ajax's bed-mate! And he was once the greatest of the Greeks! How are the mighty fallen!' That's what he'll say, and that will be my fate, and that's the shame they'll heap on you and all your family.

No, pity your father, left all alone in pitiful old age! Pity your mother, too! She's old now, but she's always praying to the gods to let you live and come back home to her. And, master, pity your son, alone and orphaned, no-one to look after him, no family, no friends. Think of the suffering your death would bring him – and me, too. 510

I've no-one else to turn to, only you – because *you* wrecked my country. And then the next disaster: my mother and my father dead and buried. Where would I live – how could I *afford* to live – without you? All my security's bound up in you. So spare a little thought for me. A real man spares some thought for those who've made him happy. Kindness brings out kindness in return, but if you don't give any thought to those who've helped you in the past – well, that's the end of that man's reputation. 520

**Chorus**  Ajax, if you could feel some sympathy for her – as I do – you'd approve of what she said.

**Ajax**  She'd earn my approval if showed some steel and did as she was told.

**Tecmessa**  Ajax, my love, I'll do anything you say.

**Ajax**  Then bring my son here! Now! So I can see him.  530

**Tecmessa**  I sent him away. I was frightened.

**Ajax**  Why? Because of my… misfortune?

**Tecmessa**  Yes. I was afraid the poor boy might… get in your way… and die.

**Ajax**  Yes, whatever demon was possessing me would have liked *that*!

**Tecmessa**  But I protected him. I kept him away.

**Ajax**  Well done! Well thought through!

**Tecmessa**  So what do you want me to do now?

**Ajax**  Let me see him. Let me speak to him.

**Tecmessa**  He's not far away. Your attendants are looking after him.

**Ajax**  Then why the delay? Why's he not here?  540

**Tecmessa**  *(calling offstage)* Eurysaces! Your father wants you! Who's looking after him? Hold his hand. Help him walk. Bring him out here.

**Ajax**  Is he coming? Is he obeying you?

**Tecmessa**  Yes, look! One of your attendants is bringing him out now.

*Enter* attendant, *bringing with him the young* Eurysaces.

**Ajax**   Lift him up! Lift him up here! If I really *am* his father, he won't be frightened of fresh blood. No! We must break him in early, teach him to imitate his father's rough and ready ways, make him like me.

(*to* Eurysaces) My boy! Be just like me in every way – just be more fortunate. 550
If you managed that you'd be a lucky man.

I envy you right now. You've no idea of all the harm I've caused. Yes – it's the happiest time of life, this, before you know what's going on, before you learn the true meaning of happiness and sadness. But when you're old enough, make sure you show your father's enemies whose son you are! Till then, well, may soft breezes nurture you, enjoy your childhood. And bring your mother happiness.

I guarantee that not one Greek will dare dishonour you, after I'm gone. 560
I'm leaving Teucer to look out for you, my watchman and your constant guardian – even if he's not here now, even if he *is* out hunting enemy.

(*to* Chorus) And you, men – comrades! – I'm assigning this duty to you all. Pass on this order to Teucer: to take him home and give him to my parents, Telamon and Eriboea, to comfort them in their old age, as long as they might 570
live. And don't let any bureaucrat or – or Odysseus, my nemesis – organize a contest for my armour!

(*to* Eurysaces) I want you to have my shield, Eurysaces! I named you after it. It's made from seven skins sown up so tight that no spear can pierce through it. *You* have it. Hold it by its strong grip. Use it well. My other armour will be buried in my grave with me.

(*to* Tecmessa) Now, take him! Quickly! Take my son inside and close the door. And no tears when you're inside. I know how women love to weep. And 580
close the door! Now! Now!! A clever doctor knows that there are some diseases only the knife will cure.

**Chorus**   It frightens me to hear you. And you're being so hasty. I don't like to hear you saying such bitter things

**Tecmessa**   Ajax. Master. What's on your mind?

**Ajax**   No questions, no examination, only self-control – that's best.

**Tecmessa**   I'm desperate! I'm begging you by your son, by all the gods – don't turn your back on us!

**Ajax**  Don't make this harder than it is! I owe the gods nothing! Can't you 590
see that?

**Tecmessa**  Don't take the gods in vain!

**Ajax**  I'm not listening.

**Tecmessa**  Why?

**Ajax**  You've said too much already.

**Tecmessa**  Because I'm frightened, master!

**Ajax**  Quick! Close the doors!

**Tecmessa**  By all the gods, I'm begging you: relent!

**Ajax**  You stupid woman! Do you think that you can change me *now*?

*Exeunt* Tecmessa *and* Eurysaces.

**Chorus**  salamis
    sea-washed and
      blessed
  famous
  renowned
    for ever

  quite unlike                                                                600
    me

me
i've been
  billeted
a lifetime
  here

month after month
on ida's plain
worn down by
  time
my only certainty
  a squalid death
and
  anonymity

and now

         a new plague
ajax                                              610
*omoi moi*
    crouching
        in the tent
            he shares with
                the gods' madness

salamis
    you sent him
        out to fight
    so strong
        before
    unbowed
        in battle

now
    all alone
he sits
    and broods

and all
    his friends
can do
    is worry

his strength
his bravery
all's
    turned
    to dust

alone
    and friendless                                620
fallen to
    the mean
    ungrateful
    sons of atreus

when his mother
    so old
    so frail
hears of
    his madness

>             she'll beat
>                 her breast
>             and tear
>                 her hair
>             and howl
>                 in her raw grief                                630
>                     no ritual grief
>                     for linus now
>                     no liquid lamentation
>                     like a nightingale
>
>             death is the
>                 best thing
>             for
>                 a man
>                 who's lost his mind
>             for
>                 him
>
>             he was the noblest
>                 of all
>                     the greeks
>                 in all
>                     their suffering
>
>             but now
>                 his mind's gone                                 640
>             and he's lost
>                 the way of reason
>
>             and his poor father
>                 still knows nothing
>                 of his madness
>                     cursed
>                     like no other
>                     in his family

*Enter* Ajax *carrying his sword, with* Tecmessa.

**Ajax**   Time stretches to eternity. It brings all things into the light and buries them again in darkness. All is inevitable. Nothing can resist – not even the most binding oath or the most steadfast will.

I was strong once, as strong as toughened iron, but what she said – this 650
woman – has undone me. I feel such pity for her, left alone, a widow, and my
orphan boy surrounded by my enemies.

But me: I'm going to the rock-pools and the meadows by the shore to purify
myself and so escape Athene's heavy anger. And then I'll go to some secluded
place. And there I'll bury this sword of mine, my nemesis, deep in the earth
where no-one will ever see it, but Night and Hades will keep it safe below. 660
Hector was my harshest enemy, and, ever since he gave this sword to me, I've
been dishonoured by the Greeks. It's true what they say: a gift's not a gift if an
enemy gives it, and no good will come of it.

So. In future I'll know to obey the gods and I'll learn to respect the sons of
Atreus. They give the orders, and we must obey. How not? Even the most
awesome, awe-inspiring things obey the laws. Yes! Winter, knee-deep in snow, 670
gives way to the fertility of summer. And all-encircling night is scattered,
when day with its white horses flares into light. Storm winds die down. The
seas grow calm. And even sleep, which conquers everything, allows his
captive to go free, and doesn't keep him chained for ever. So why should I not
discover a new understanding?

In fact I have. I've learned just recently that an enemy should be treated as an
enemy only in the knowledge that one day he might become a friend, while 680
I'd want to help a friend but understand that even friendship doesn't last
forever. For most people, friendship's an unsafe harbour.

But as for all of this, all will be well. (*to* Tecmessa) Tecmessa, go inside and
pray to the gods that all my heart's desires will be fulfilled.

(*to* Chorus) And you! Comrades! Respect my wishes, just like her. And if
Teucer comes, tell him to do right by me, and treat you well, too! I'm going 690
where my journey takes me. So, do as I ask you, and – even if I'm suffering
now – maybe you'll discover soon that I'm at peace.

*Exit* Ajax.

**Chorus**  i'm shaking
    with relief

  i'm flying
    with happiness
  *io io* pan
    pan

o pan
  pan
      you can walk
      on water
come
  from the barren
  snow-deep ridges
  of cyllene

lord
  of the dance
come
dance with me
  dance steps
     from nysia
     and cnossos
possess me                                               700
  and
inspire me

all i want
  to do now
  is to dance

and lord apollo
  delian
  god
  i know
  so well
come over
  the icarian sea
and join with me
  my friend
  forever

ares
  the war god
has dissolved
  the black pain
blinding me

*io io* now
  zeus

the white light
  dawns
and prosperous
days
  for our fast                                          710
    sea-going ships
now ajax
has put all
  his suffering
behind him
and performed
the sacrifices
  due to gods
paying them
the honour
  the great laws
    demand

eternal time
  makes all things
    end

so i say
  nothing
    is impossible
now ajax
has seen
  the error of
    his anger
and
  his quarrel
    with the sons of atreus
it's more than
  i could hope for

*Enter* Messenger *from the direction of the Greek camp.*

**Messenger**   Friends! I want to tell you the news first! Teucer's back! He's   720
back just now from the Mysian mountains. But when he got to the command
headquarters, all the Greeks began to jeer at him. They saw him coming, and
they crowded round him in a circle, and jostled him with insults, called him

brother of a madman, of a traitor to the army, said they were going to stone him, knock him about, and kill him. Things got so wound up that swords were drawn and brawling and, well, men would have got hurt, but then the senior officers arrived and imposed some order. 730

But where's Ajax? I need to let him know. I need to report everything to my superiors.

**Chorus**  He's not in. He left just now. He's changed his mind; he's changed his plan.

**Messenger**  *iou, iou!* They sent me here too late, or else I've been too slow.

**Chorus**  What do you mean? What's wrong? 740

**Messenger**  Teucer said that Ajax mustn't leave his tent until he gets here.

**Chorus**  But I've just told you – he's not here. And with the best plan too: to end his anger with the gods.

**Messenger**  You don't know what you're saying – if Calchas really can foresee the future.

**Chorus**  Why? What does Calchas know about all this? What do *you* know?

**Messenger**  Here's what I heard – and I was *there*. Calchas was at headquarters where the council was in session, but he left the sons of Atreus 750 and stood apart a little, and he took Teucer's right hand – kindly – and he prophesied. He summoned all his skill and prophesied, and said not to let Ajax leave his tent today – only today – if he wanted to see him alive tomorrow, because today the anger of Athene could still strike him down. Those were the prophet's words. And he said that, when a man forgets he is a man and 760 aims too high, and grows too self-important for his good, the gods make everything go wrong; they knock him down; he falls.

When Ajax set out from home, he stupidly ignored his father's good advice. He'd told him: 'Son, seek victory in battle, but seek it only with the help of god.' But Ajax was boastful and unthinking and he said: 'Father, even a coward can win with the gods' help. But I mean to win glory even with*out* their help.' That was his boast. 770

And then, another time, in battle, when Athene was encouraging him to turn and kill the enemy, he talked back to her – quite blasphemous it was, something that he never should have said: 'Lady, go stand with the other Greeks. The line won't break when *I'm* here.' It was words like those that provoked Athene's anger. Oh yes, too self-important.

But if he survives the day, maybe with the gods' help we can save him. At least that's what the prophet said. Teucer just sat there and then suddenly he sent 780 me here to you with orders to place him under guard. But if we've failed, if Calchas really does know... Ajax is a dead man.

**Chorus**  (*calling inside the tent*) Tecmessa! (*to self*) Poor Tecmessa... (*calling inside the tent*) Come outside and hear the news. We're on the razor's edge.

*Enter* Tecmessa *with* Eurysaces

**Tecmessa**  Why are you disturbing me? I'd only just begun to settle.

**Chorus**  Listen to this man. He's come with news about Ajax – worrying 790 news.

**Tecmessa**  *oimoi!* What is it, man? Is it all over?

**Messenger**  I don't know anything about your situation, but I've little hope for Ajax if he's gone outside.

**Tecmessa**  He *is* outside. What you're saying – it's tearing me apart!

**Messenger**  Teucer's orders were for him to stay inside the tent and not go out alone.

**Tecmessa**  But where *is* Teucer? Why's he saying this?

**Messenger**  He's just got back. He's worried that if Ajax goes outside he'll die.

**Tecmessa**  *oimoi talaina!* Who told him this? 800

**Messenger**  Calchas the prophet – he said today's the day that will bring life or death for Ajax.

**Tecmessa**  (*to* Chorus) Friends, save me from this fate! Go quickly! You – bring Teucer to me quickly And you – work your way westwards round the bay. And you – work your way east. Find where he's gone! It's a disaster! I can see now that he's tricked me and broken every trust we had. (*to Eurysaces*) Oh, baby, what am I going to do? Not waste time here! No! As long as I have 810 strength, I'll follow him. We must go now! And quickly! No time to waste if we're to save a man who's eager for his death!

**Chorus**  I'm ready to go now! I'm not just words! I'll follow him as quickly as I can.

All *exeunt in several directions. The scene changes to the seashore near Troy.* Ajax *enters alone. He draws his sword and buries the hilt in the sand.*

**Ajax**   The executioner stands ready, razor-sharp, where it will do most harm. And I've still time to work out the connections: this was my gift from Hector, my enemy, the man I hated most, my greatest enemy. And now it's planted in the soil of Troy, another enemy – its blade filed lovingly until it's   820 razor-sharp. And last, I've planted it and made it firm, the kindest friend to bring the quickest death. Yes, we have all we need.

So, Zeus, as ritual demands, my first prayer is to you. It's nothing special, just a little thing: to send a messenger to Teucer with news of my... disaster, so he can be the first to lift me when I've fallen on my sword and my sword's still wet with blood. I don't want my enemies to find me, and throw my body out like carrion for dogs and birds. These, Zeus, are my prayers to you.   830

Next, Hermes, god who leads souls to the underworld, lay me to rest softly – no hard death throes, just one quick gasp – when I drive the blade between my ribs.

And you, kind Virgin Goddesses – you're always watching over the affairs of men, pacing the earth – you, dreaded Furies of revenge – I pray you: see how I've been destroyed by the two sons of Atreus. Swoop down on them! Tear them apart as they've seen me torn apart [dead at my own hands – let them   840 die, too, at the hands of their own family]! Come, Furies fast to vengeance! Glut your fill on them! And spare no-one from all the army!

And you, Helios, sun god – you drive your chariot across the sky – when you see my homeland, draw in your golden reins and give the news of my disgrace to my old father and my poor sad mother, too. And tell them how I died. Poor mother! When she hears the news her howls of grief will echo through the city.   850

But what's the point in self-indulgent tears? There's only one thing left to do, and it's best to do it quickly.

Death! Death!! Come here, now! Look at me... No – we'll have time enough to talk when I'm with you in your kingdom.

But, daylight, bright light of today, and Helios – the charioteer – this is the last time I shall ever speak to you, the last time, and forever. Daylight; and Salamis, my sacred homeland, land of my fathers; glorious Athens where my cousins   860 live; the springs and rivers and the plain of Troy: I have just this to say to you: You made me who I am. And now I take my leave. These are Ajax's last words to you. From now I shall speak only with the dead.

*Ajax falls on his sword. A pause. Enter* Chorus *from two sides. At first they see neither each other nor the body.*

| | |
|---|---|
| **Chorus 1** | trouble |
| | trouble |
| |   and more |
| | trouble |
| | i've looked |
| |   everywhere |
| | and have i |
| |   found him |
| | no                                           870 |
| | but |
| |   listen |
| | i can hear |
| |   something |
| **Chorus 2** | it's us |
| |   your shipmates |
| **Chorus 1** | any news |
| **Chorus 2** | we've covered |
| |   all the ground |
| | west |
| |   of the ships |
| **Chorus 1** | and anything |
| **Chorus 2** | a lot of trouble |
| |   to find |
| |     nothing |
| **Chorus 1** | the same here |
| |   on the eastern side |
| | no sign of him |
| **Chorus** | i wish |
| | someone |
| |   would come and |
| |     tell us |
| |     where he is |
| | some fisherman                   880 |
| |   returning from |

a night of
    dragging nets
or some goddess
    from olympus
or some sea-nymph
    from the choppy
    bosporus
someone who's
    seen him
someone who
    could tell me
    where he's gone

he's so
    pig-headed

we've tracked him
long and hard

both east
and west

we've taken
trouble
but
no luck at all

he's gone and                                          890
i can't find him

*Enter* Tecmessa, *unseen by the* Chorus. *She sees the body and cries out.*

**Tecmessa**   *io moi moi*!

**Chorus**   who was that
                crying there
             by the scrub-land

**Tecmessa**   *io*
                it's over

**Chorus**   look

             tecmessa

             she's distraught

**Tecmessa**  friends
>it's all over

>nothing left
>>now

**Chorus**  what's wrong

**Tecmessa**  look

>ajax
>>warm still
>>just dead
>
>his sword firm
>>in the ground
>
>and him
>>impaled on it.

**Chorus**  *omoi*                                                                       900

>>my hopes of home
>
>*omoi*
>>my general
>
>i was
>>your shipmate
>
>and you've
>>killed me

>tecmessa
>>you
>>>poor woman

**Tecmessa**  he's done
>>what
>
>he has done

>all i can do
>>is grieve for him

**Chorus**  how
>>did he die
>
>who
>>killed him

**Tecmessa**  he killed
>>himself

          no question

          the sword
              embedded
              in the ground

          him
              fallen
              on it

          all the evidence
              you need

**Chorus**    *omoi*
              was i so blind
          to let him
              bleed to death
          alone                                            910
              abandoned

          i didn't see
              the signs
          i didn't
              think

          i let him
              down

          iron-willed and
          named for sorrow

          where's ajax
              now

**Tecmessa**    No-one will look on him. No. I'll cover him. I'll wrap him in his war cloak. No-one who loves him could bear to see the black blood pouring from his nostrils and his self-inflicted wound. *oimoi!* What am I going to do? What friend will raise you up for burial? Where's Teucer? I wish he'd come here now!   920
I wish he'd raise his brother's corpse, lay out his body! Poor Ajax, you were such a noble man. Look at you now. Even your enemies would weep for you.

**Chorus**    poor ajax

          you were bound
              in time
          to suffer
              for your iron will

>    to suffer
>       endless troubles
>
>    those things                                          930
>    you said
>       about the sons
>       of atreus
>    those threats
>    those menaces
>       and all night long
>
>    so hard
>       to hear them
>
>    yes
>    that was the beginning
>    of these troubles:
>       the contest
>          for the hero's armour
>       to choose
>          the best greek fighter

**Tecmessa**  *io moi moi*

**Chorus**    i know

              your grief

              it goes straight
                to your heart

**Tecmessa**  *io moi moi*

**Chorus**    weep                                          940

                for him
            weep

            there's nothing wrong
                with that

            you loved him
              so much
            and now
              he's gone

**Tecmessa**  you can only
      guess
      how bitterly
        i miss him

**Chorus**  i know

**Tecmessa**  eurysaces
      we'll both
      be slaves now
      and our masters
        will show
        no mercy

**Chorus**  *omoi*

      what the sons of atreus
        might do to you ...

      their cruelty ...

      and when we're
        grieving ...

      it's unimaginable

      i pray
        god
      stops them

**Tecmessa**  it was a god                                    950

      made all this happen

**Chorus**  a tragedy

      too difficult
      to bear

**Tecmessa**  athene
      child of zeus
      is merciless

      she did
        all this
      to please

**Chorus**    while he

    odysseus
        odysseus
            *the man of many sorrows*
        gloats
            in his dark heart
        laughs
            like a madman
        at our suffering

    *feu feu*

    and
        when they hear                                             960
    the sons of atreus
    will join him

**Tecmessa**   Well, let them laugh. Let them enjoy his suffering. They didn't respect him when he was alive, but maybe now he's dead they'll miss him when it's time for fighting. Men like them – crooks – can't see the good that's there in front of them. They only know its value when they lose it. Now he's dead their pleasure's nothing in comparison to my pain. And yet for him it is a blessing. All that he wanted was to die. Now he's achieved his ambition, so why should they gloat over him? *They* didn't kill him. No, it was the gods. So   970 let Odysseus enjoy his empty boasts. Ajax is no longer here for them. He's gone. And all he's left me are my tears.

Teucer *is heard approaching offstage.*

**Teucer**   *io moi moi!*

**Chorus**   Quiet! I think I can hear Teucer crying out in grief.

*Enter* Teucer.

**Teucer**   My brother, oh my dearest brother Ajax! Is it true, the rumour?

**Chorus**   It's true, Teucer. Ajax is dead.

**Teucer**   *omoi!* Such a heavy blow!                         980

**Chorus**   And in such circumstances ...

**Teucer**   Such tragedy ...

**Chorus**   ... all that we can do is mourn.

**Teucer**  It happened all so quickly.

**Chorus**  Yes, too quickly, Teucer.

**Teucer**  Poor man. What of his son, Eurysaces. Is he still here at Troy?

**Chorus**  He's on his own beside the tents.

**Teucer**  Well bring him here as quickly as you can. We don't want any of his enemies to seize him like a lion cub when its mother is not near. Go now! Go quickly! It's human nature to mock men when they're dead.

*Exit* Tecmessa.

**Chorus**  Teucer, before he died, Ajax left the child for you to care for. And you're caring for him now. 990

**Teucer**  This is the saddest thing I've ever seen, and the road that brought me here's the most heart-breaking. I loved you, Ajax. When I heard what had happened I looked for you. I tried to find you. A nasty rumour, like it had a god behind it, raced through the Greek army that you were dead, that you were gone. Even far away I heard it and it broke my heart. But now that I can 1000 you see you, I'm... I'm overwhelmed. *oimoi*.

(*to* Chorus) Come on. Uncover him. I need to see the full extent of what he suffered.

Chorus *helps* Teucer *uncover the body.*

**Teucer**  Your face! It's hard even to look at you! So cruel! So determined! What a crop of suffering you left me when you died. Where can I go now? Who'd want to know me now, when I failed you in your hour of need? Is Telamon – our father – really going to welcome me with open arms when I come home without you? Really? He doesn't even smile when things go well! 1010 *He* won't hold back. He'll lash me with insults. I be 'the slave girl's bastard, who betrayed you out of cowardice and spinelessness' – you, Ajax – though I loved you more than anyone! Or he'll accuse me of deliberately betraying you – to benefit from your death – to inherit your power and property. That's what he'll say. He's such an irritable, spiteful old man, never happier than when he's picking a fight over nothing. And in the end he'll throw me out, and he'll tell everyone that I'm a slave – not free at all. So much for home! But *here* – at Troy 1020 – I have so many enemies, and so few on my side. And all because you died!

*oimoi!* So what am I to do? Should I disentangle your poor broken body from the sword-blade, from your executioner, where you choked out your life? That sword belonged to Hector, and now at last I think he's risen from the dead to kill you, too. See how the two men's fates are intertwined! Hector was tied to the chariot rail with the battle-belt that Ajax gave him – dragged round till he was shredded raw, until his spirit left him. And Ajax died by falling on this sword, his gift from Hector. Surely it was an Erinys, a fury of revenge, who forged this sword! Surely Death himself, cruel craftsman, made the battle-belt!

I think that what has happened here – I think that everything that happens is part of the gods' plan for men. It's my personal opinion. You don't need to accept it ...

**Chorus**  No time for any more! You can think about burying him and what to say later. But for now – the enemy's approaching, no doubt to laugh at our misfortunes and to kick us when we're down, like the coward that he is.

**Teucer**  Who is it? Someone from the army?

**Chorus**  Menelaus, thanks to whom we sailed here in the first place.

**Teucer**  Yes I see him. Now he's here there's no mistaking him.

*Enter* Menelaus

**Menelaus**  You! Orders! Don't touch the corpse. Just leave it where it is.

**Teucer**  What kind of useless order's that?

**Menelaus**  It's my decision. Agamemnon's, too. The supreme commander.

**Teucer**  And do you want to tell me why?

**Menelaus**  Because we brought him out here in the hope he'd be a friend, an ally for the Greeks. But, put to the test, he proved a worse enemy than the Trojans. He plotted to annihilate the army. He crept out at night to kill us. And if some god hadn't intervened to stop him, *we*'d be suffering his fate. It would be *us* lying dead, dishonoured. And he'd still be alive. But as it was, this god diverted his mad anger onto our sheep and cattle.

And that's why no-one's going to bury him, no matter how strong they might be. No. We're going to throw him out on some toxic bit of sand and leave him for seabirds to peck at. So keep a lid on any anger. We might not have managed to control him while he was alive, but now he's dead, he's in our hands, whether you like it or not. He's completely under our jurisdiction. He never *would* obey me when he was alive.

It's the sign of bad character when an underling refuses to obey his betters. You can't expect a city to enjoy the rule of law when there's no fear attached. And equally an army can't be run efficiently without the restraining influence of fear and humiliation. A man might have the most formidable physique, but he needs to know that the slightest thing might bring him down. Believe me, fear and humiliation make for security. But where selfishness and doing just what you like's the order of the day, you know that – though you might enjoy good headwinds for a little while – your city's heading for the rocks; it's going to sink. Fear has its place. Let's not forget that pleasurable pursuits have painful consequences. The pendulum shifts all the time. Ajax was glorious once. And proud. But now my hour has come. And so I order you: don't bury him. Because if you do, you'll be digging your *own* grave. 1080 1090

**Chorus**   Menelaus, you're a man of sound judgement, but don't dishonour the dead.

**Teucer**   Well, men! I'll never be surprised again if the lower class commit offences when the so-called upper classes say such offensive things.

Let's start at the beginning. You say you brought him out here as an ally for the Greeks. But actually he sailed here of his own free will. So who gave *you* the right to give him orders? And who gave you the right to boss about the men *he* brought from Greece? You came here as *Sparta*'s king. You're not *our* general. You've no more right to give *him* orders than he had to give orders to you. You sailed here as an officer for others to command, not as the supreme commander, and you never had a mandate to give Ajax orders. 1100

Give orders to *your* men. Give them a dressing down with those sanctimonious words of yours. I'm going to bury him properly, whatever you and your brother say. Your words don't frighten me. He didn't join this expedition to bring back your wife like all your little lackeys. No. He came to keep the oath he'd sworn. He didn't come for you. He had no time for nobodies like you. 1110

So, off you go. Bring heralds next time. And your commanding officer. I don't care what you say. You're all wind, and you always will be.

**Chorus**   These words – they're not appropriate for this situation. Insults, even if they're justified, go deep.

**Menelaus**   This bowman has ideas above his station. 1120

**Teucer**   There's no shame in being a bowman!

**Menelaus**   Just think how you'd posture if you had a shield!

**Teucer**   I don't need a shield. Even with you fully armed I'd take you any day!

**Menelaus**  You're trying to convince yourself that you're some kind of hero.

**Teucer**  With justice on his side a man can hold his head up high.

**Menelaus**  So it's justice not to punish my murderer?

**Teucer**  Your murderer? Well, here's a miracle! A resurrection from the dead! You're *still alive*!

**Menelaus**  He tried to kill me. A god saved me.

**Teucer**  Well, if the gods saved you, don't turn your back on them now.

**Menelaus**  I'd never dream of breaking the gods' laws.    1130

**Teucer**  But you're here to stop a body from being buried.

**Menelaus**  He was my enemy. It would not be right.

**Teucer**  When did Ajax ever threaten *you* in battle?

**Menelaus**  He hated me. I hated him. Even you must understand.

**Teucer**  He hated you because you were caught vote-rigging to rob him.

**Menelaus**  It was the jury who decided, not me.

**Teucer**  It's so easy to dress up a crime and call it Justice.

**Menelaus**  This outburst of yours. It needs punishing.

**Teucer**  Whatever punishment you have in mind is nothing compared to what I'll give you in return!

**Menelaus**  He won't be buried. That's an order.    1140

**Teucer**  And here's my response: I'm going to bury him.

**Menelaus**  I saw a man once – liked the sound of his own voice. He got his sailors to set out in stormy weather. But when storm-waves came, you could get nothing from him. Not a squeak. He covered his head with his coat and let his crewmen walk all over him. *You* are that man; *you* are that loudmouth; and maybe from a tiny little cloud a great storm wind will gather that will blow out all your blustering.

**Teucer**  I saw a fool once, arrogant – liked to see his neighbours suffer. A    1150
man came to him – he looked a lot like me; he shared my nature. And he stared him down and said: 'Sir, don't abuse the dead. For if you do, then rest assured you'll suffer for it.' He gave the fool this warning face to face. I can see that fool now, right there in front of me, and I think that he's none other... than you. There. Was that too hard a riddle?

**Menelaus**  I'm going. Yes. How humiliating if word got out that I tried to win you round by argument when I could crush you by force!  1160

**Teucer**  Off you go, then. It's much more humiliating for me to have to listen to a blustering fool like you.

*Exit* Menelaus

**Chorus**  there will be
>    trouble

>    teucer
>>    quickly
>>    as you can
>    dig him
>>    a grave
>    set up
>    his tomb
>>    as a memorial
>>    for men
>>    for ever

*Enter* Tecmessa *with* Eurysaces

**Teucer**  Look! They've come at the right time – Tecmessa and Eurysaces – to lay poor Ajax in his grave.  1170

(*to* Eurysaces) Come here, Eurysaces! Stand next to him, and take your father's hand in supplication. Kneel down beside him like a suppliant, and take these locks of hair: mine, and your mother's, and your own, the third. These are your offerings of supplication. Now:

(*praying*) If any man at all in all the army tries to drag you off his body, may he die in shame, may he lie unburied on the earth, and may he and all his family shrivel to their roots, cut down as I cut off this lock of hair from my own head.

(*to* Eurysaces) Take it, Eurysaces, and guard it well. And don't let anyone  1180
move you! Stay there, and hug him close.

(*to* Chorus) And you! Don't just stand there like women! No! Be men. Guard him till I get back. I'm going to dig his grave now, and no-one will stop me.

*Exit* Teucer.

**Chorus**  when will it
>    ever end

so many years
   away from home
unending fighting
   constant trauma
here on the plains                                                1190
   of troy
a constant cause
   of shame
to all
   of greece

whoever it was
   suggested
that the greeks
   ally in war –
i wish he'd
   died first
gone to hades
   found his allies
   there

his troubles
   have sparked off
so many
   other troubles

one man
   has decimated
all humanity

and all the pleasures
that he stole from me:
        garlands
        deep wine cups                              1200
        the sweet throbbing
            of the flute
        uninterrupted
            sleep
        and love affairs
*omoi*
        no chance
        of love affairs

instead
i lie here
   all forgotten
and the
   cold dew
   trickles through
   my hair
chillingly
reminding me
that i'm at troy

till now
   when night terrors
   came
   and spears
   were thrown
my shield
was always with me:
      ajax
      the brave
      the passionate

but now
he has been
sacrificed
   to a malignant fate
what pleasure's
   left for me
what pleasure's
   left in life

i wish i was
   in greece again
standing
   on the headland
   by the trees

where waves are washing
   round the rocks
   below the cliffs
   at sounion

for then
i could come

home
to sacred Athens

*Enter* Teucer

**Teucer**  I got here as quickly as I can. I've just seen Agamemnon, our 'supreme commander'. He's on his way here now. He'll have some words for us, no doubt, some clumsy argument.

*Enter* Agamemnon

**Agamemnon**  So, I hear you've been threatening me, insulting me – and here you are, still free. You're nothing but a slave-whore's runt. Imagine if your mother had been upper class, how you'd have strutted and pontificated then! 1230 You're a nobody standing up for a nobody. And now you're claiming that your generals have no jurisdiction over the Greek army or the fleet and that Ajax came here as his own man! These are serious complaints to hear from a slave like you.

What sort of man was he anyway, this Ajax that you're making such a fuss about? Yes, he attacked, and yes he stood his ground, but I was there, too, every time. Was he the only man in the Greek army?

It was a big mistake for us Greeks to arrange a contest for Achilles' armour, if 1240 Teucer's going to make it out to everyone we cheated, if you and your men won't accept the majority decision. He was defeated! But you – you're always sniping at us, trying to stab us in the back because you've been defeated. Follow your logic and there'd be no law and order – if we made the winners stand aside and promoted losers instead! It can't be allowed!  1250

In times of trouble it's not brawn and muscle that you need but brains. Brains win out every time. An ox is a big animal, but it just needs a little prod to keep him on the straight and narrow. And I can see you need a taste of the same medicine if you don't start thinking straight.

Ajax is dead. He's nothing but a ghost now. But you – you're insolent and insubordinate and letting your tongue run away with you. So, see some sense. Remember where you came from. Bring me someone else – a freeborn 1260 man – to plead your case instead of you. I really can't make out a word you say. I never learnt Barbarian.

**Chorus**  I wish you'd both learn self-restraint! That's my best advice.

**Teucer**  *Feu!* So that's how quickly men forget their gratitude towards the dead –that's how quickly they betray their memory – if this man can't even pay the smallest tribute to your memory, Ajax, even though you risked your life for him so often on the battlefield. But all that's over now, and it can be forgotten.

(*to* Agamemnon) You said a lot just now, and none of it too clever. Have you forgotten the day when you were trapped in your stockade, when it was nearly over, when our luck had turned against us, and he stood his ground, one man alone, and saved you, when the flames were licking the ships' decks, and Hector was leaping high over the trench and would have boarded us? Who stopped him then? Wasn't it Ajax? The man you said that 'where he went you were there every time'? Well, did he do his duty then or not?

And then there was another time when he faced Hector all alone in single combat. He'd had no orders then. No, he was picked by lot. He'd quite deliberately placed his token in the middle of the helmet – and it was no dull lump of clay, but a token that was sure to be the first one picked. It was Ajax did all this! Ajax. And I was standing at his side – the slave with the barbarian mother.

How can you even say these things? Don't you know that Pelops – your own grandfather – was a Phrygian 'barbarian'? Or that your father, Atreus, served his brother a barbaric feast – his brother's children? Your mother was a Cretan whore – when your father found her sleeping with a stranger, he rowed her out to sea to feed the fishes. And with a background like that you think that you can shame my family?

I am the son of Telamon. He won the prize for being the best man in the army. And what *was* his prize? My mother, a princess, the daughter of Laomedon. Heracles gave her to my father as a prize picked from Troy's booty. So both my parents are high born. I'm high born, too.

Ajax endured so much. He's lying here dead. And I could never shame my flesh and blood, by letting you dispose of him without a burial – even if you can shame yourself by issuing the order.

Understand this: if you do try to dispose of him, you'll be disposing of three corpses: his, and mine, and yours. I'd rather die in plain sight, protecting him, than fighting for your wife – or did I mean your brother's? So, look to yourself, not me! If you offer me the slightest provocation, you'll wish you'd stayed the coward and not tried out your bravery on me.

*Enter* Odysseus

**Chorus**  Odysseus! Sir! You've come just in time – that is, if you don't want to enflame the crisis but to mediate.

**Odysseus**   Gentlemen! What's going on? Even from some distance I could hear Agamemnon and Menelaus squabbling over our hero's corpse.

**Agamemnon**   Indeed, Odysseus. Sir. We were being insulted by this man here.   1320

**Odysseus**   What did he say? I can pardon insults if they've been provoked.

**Agamemnon**   It was *me* insulted *him*. But he provoked me.

**Odysseus**   And what did he do to upset you?

**Agamemnon**   He refuses to leave the corpse unburied. He says he'll disobey my orders and bury it.

**Odysseus**   May I speak frankly to you as a friend, and still retain your friendship?

**Agamemnon**   Of course. I'd be a fool not to listen to you. I count you as my   1330
closest friend here.

**Odysseus**   Then listen to me now. In the name of all the gods, do not allow this man to be disposed of so ... ruthlessly without a burial. Don't let your rage and hatred take you over so much that you trample Justice. Ever since I beat him and won Achilles' armour, Ajax was my worst enemy in all the army. Yes, we hated one another, but even so I don't want to pay him back by dishonouring him now. So I'm not going to deny that – with the exception of Achilles – Ajax was the best of all Greeks who came to Troy. It would not be   1340
right if you dishonoured him. And anyway, it's the gods' laws you'd be desecrating, not Ajax. It's not right to punish a good man when he'd dead, even if you do hate him.

**Agamemnon**   So you'd take his side, not mine, Odysseus?

**Odysseus**   Yes. I hated him when it was right for me to hate him.

**Agamemnon**   But don't you want to crush him now he's dead?

**Odysseus**   Agamemnon, where's the pleasure in a squalid victory like that?

**Agamemnon**   You know how hard it is for kings to show respect.   1350

**Odysseus**   But they can still respect their friends who give them good advice.

**Agamemnon**   A good man should obey those in authority.

**Odysseus**   Enough! You can give in to friends and still keep your authority.

**Agamemnon**   Remember what he was like before you shower him with respect!

**Odysseus**  He was my enemy. But more than that, he was a noble man.

**Agamemnon**  What do you want to do then? Honour your enemy's corpse?

**Odysseus**  His bravery counts for more than our hatred.

**Agamemnon**  There's a word for men like you: inconstant.

**Odysseus**  I think you'll find that most men can be friends one day and enemies the next.

**Agamemnon**  And do you really value such friendships?  1360

**Odysseus**  I don't value inflexibility.

**Agamemnon**  So today you want to make us look like cowards?

**Odysseus**  No. Like men of Justice in the eyes of Greece.

**Agamemnon**  So you want me to allow the burial?

**Odysseus**  I do. You see, one day I'll need to be buried, too.

**Agamemnon**  So in the end it's just about each man looking out for himself?

**Odysseus**  Who else should I rather look out for?

**Agamemnon**  You must take responsibility for this, not me.

**Odysseus**  However you arrange it, you'll come out of this well.

**Agamemnon**  You have my permission. And you know I'd grant permission  1370 even for a more significant request. But alive or dead, Ajax will be my enemy. Do with him what you will.

*Exit* Agamemnon.

**Chorus**  You've just proved what a clever man you are, Odysseus. Anyone who says otherwise is a fool!

**Odysseus**  And now a word to Teucer: I was your staunchest enemy; I'm now prepared to be your staunchest friend. And I'd like to join with you in burying Ajax, perform the rites with you, and leave no duty left undone which mankind owes the noble, glorious dead.  1380

**Teucer**  Odysseus, *you*'re a noble man. I've nothing but praise for what you said just now. I did not expect this of you. You were his greatest enemy in all the Greek army, yet only you stood by him. You were the only man alive who wouldn't let his corpse be desecrated – not like our general and his mad brother, who wanted to dishonour him, to dispose of his body disgracefully, without burial.

So may Zeus, the father, most revered of gods, and the Erinys, the fury who remembers everything, and Justice which brings all things to their end, destroy them both, and pay back pain with pain, because they wanted to dispose of him dishonourably, disgracefully. 1390

But you, Odysseus, the venerable Laertes' son, I hesitate to let you bury him with me, in case I offend the dead. But join us in all the other rites, and if you wish to bring anyone else from the army with you, we'll make him welcome. I shall make all the other arrangements. But I want you to know: you're a good man, and a good friend.

**Odysseus**   I would have liked to be there. But if you'd rather that I'm not, I must respect your decision and go. 1400

*Exit* Odysseus.

**Teucer**   enough now

>   the time's
>      already
>   been too long

>   no more
>      delay

>   you
>   dig
>      his grave

>   and you
>   set up
>      tall tripods
>      with their cauldrons
>         for the holy water
>   and set
>      the fires

>   the time
>      has come

>   another unit
>   go
>      to his tent
>      and
>   fetch

>           his armour
>
>   eurysaces
>   he was
>       your father
>
>   you've little
>       strength
>   but hold him
>       in your hands
>   and help
>       me lift him
>
>   he's still
>       warm
>
>   dark power's still
>       in him
>
>   and now
>   let all
>       who ever claimed him
>       as a friend
>   come quick
>   and pay
>       the honours
>       owed to
>       good
>       and noble men
>
>   for there has never been
>   in all the world
>   a better man
>   than ajax

**Chorus**   man learns much

>       through experience
>
>   but we've not
>   experienced
>       the future
>   and no-one
>   can foretell
>       what it might hold

# Bibliography

Adams, S.M., *Sophocles the Playwright*, Toronto, 1957.
Alexiou, M., *The Ritual Lament in Greek Tradition*, 2nd edition, Lanham, MD, 2002.
Aquila Theatre, 'Applied Theatre', Aquila Theatre, 2018. https://www.aquilatheatre.com/innovative-public-programming/ [accessed 26 July 2018].
Arnott, P., 'The Suicide of Ajax', Appendix II in *Greek Scenic Conventions in the Fifth Century B.C*, Oxford, 131–3, 1962.
Battezatto, L., 'Ajax on the Ground', in Most and Ozbek, Pisa, 223–43, 2015.
Billington, M., 'Our Ajax – Review', *London Theatre Record*, xxxiii: 23, 1063, 2013.
Blundell, M.W., *Helping Friends and Harming Enemies: A Study in Sophocles and Greek Ethics*, Cambridge, 1989.
Bowra, C.M., *Sophoclean Tragedy*, Oxford, 1952.
Bradshaw, D.J., 'The Ajax Myth and the Polis: Old Values and New', in Pozzi and Wickersham (eds), *Myth and Polis*, Ithaca and London, 99–125, 1991.
Burian, P., 'Polyphonic Ajax', in K. Ormand (ed.), *A Companion to Sophocles*, Malden, MA and West Sussex, 69–83, 2012.
Burian, P., 'Supplication and Hero Cult in Sophocles' *Ajax*', *Greek, Roman and Byzantine Studies* 13, 151–6, 1972.
Burton, R.W.B., *The Chorus in Sophocles' Tragedies*, Oxford, 1980.
Campbell, L. (ed.), *Sophocles: The Plays and Fragments, II, Ajax, Electra, Trachiniae, Philoctetes, Fragments*, Oxford, 1881.
Campbell, L. and E. Abbott, *Sophocles in Single Plays: Ajax*, Oxford, 1876.
Carson, A., 'Screaming in Translation: the *Electra* of Sophocles', in A. Carson (ed. and trans.), *Electra*, Oxford, 41–8, 2001.
Catoni, M., 'The Iconographic Tradition of the Suicide of Ajax: Some Questions', in Most and Ozbek, Pisa, 15–30, 2015.
Christodoulou, G.A., *Ta archaia scholia eis Aianta tou Sophokleous*, Athens, 1977.
Clinton, K., *The Sacred Officials of the Eleusinian Mysteries*, Philadelphia: Transactions of the American Philological Society 64, 3, 1974.
Corradi, M.T., 'Lo scudo in Grecia', *Rivista di Cultura Classica e Medioevale* 53, 87–97, 2011.
Crowley, J., 'Beyond the Universal Soldier: Combat Trauma in Classical Antiquity', in P. Meineck and D. Konstan (eds), *Combat Trauma and the Ancient Greeks*, New York, 2014.
Davies, M.I., 'Ajax and Tecmessa: A Cup by the Brygos Painter in the Bareiss Collection', *Antike Kunst* 14, 60–70, 1971.
Davis, M., *The Epic Cycle*, Bristol, 1989.
Doerries, B., 'Overview', *Outside the Wire*, 2018. http://theaterofwar.com/projects/theater-of-war/overview [accessed 23 July 2018].

Doerries, B., 'Pop Tech Keynote', *Trend Hunter Keynote Trends*, 25 May, 2012a. https://www.trendhunter.com/keynote/theater-of-war-keynote [accessed 23 July 2018].
Doerries, B., 'Theater of War', *National Endowment for the Arts Magazine*, 2012 http://arts.gov/content/theater-war$hash.95zgk4aKdpuf [accessed 20 July 2018].
Dué, C., *The Captive Woman's Lament in Greek Tragedy*, Austin, TX, 2006.
Dugan, T., *The Many Lives of Ajax: The Trojan War Hero from Antiquity to Modern Times*, Jefferson, North Carolina, 2018.
Dutta, S. (ed., comm. and trans.), *Sophocles Ajax*, Cambridge, 2001.
Easterling, P.E., 'Character in Sophocles', *Greece and Rome* 24, 121–9, 1977.
Easterling, P.E., 'The Tragic Homer', *Bulletin of the Institute of Classical Studies* 31, 1–8, 1984.
Easterling, P.E., 'Weeping, Witnessing, and the Tragic Audience: Response to Segal', in M.S. Silk (ed.), *Tragedy and the Tragic: Greek Theatre and Beyond*, 173–81, Oxford, 1996.
Easterling, P.E., 'Women in Tragic Space', *Bulletin of the Institute of Classical Studies* 34, 15–26, 1987.
Esposito, S., 'The Changing Roles of the Sophoclean Chorus', *Arion* 3rd series, 4, 85–114, 1996.
Esposito, S. (ed.), *Odysseus at Troy: Ajax, Hecuba, and Trojan Women*, translations with commentary by Stephen Esposito, Robin Mitchell-Boyask and Diskin Clay respectively, Focus: Newburyport, MA, 2010.
Faber, M.D., *Suicide and Greek Tragedy*, New York, 1970.
Falkner, T., 'Scholars versus Actors: Text and Performance in the Greek Tragic Scholia', in P. Easterling and E. Hall (eds) *Greek and Roman Actors*, Cambridge, 342–61, 2002.
Ferguson, J., 'Ambiguity in Ajax', *Dioniso* 44, 12–29, 1970.
Finglass, P.J., 'Interpolation and Responsion in Sophocles' *Ajax*', *Classical Quarterly* 59.2, 335–52, 2009a.
Finglass, P.J., 'Second Thoughts on the Sword', in Most and Ozbek, 193–210, Pisa, 2015.
Finglass, P.J. (ed. and comm.), *Sophocles: Ajax*, Cambridge, 2011.
Finglass, P.J., 'Sophocles' *Ajax* and the Vase-Painters', *Omnibus* 62, 25–7, 2011a.
Finglass, P.J., 'Unveiling Tecmessa', *Mnemosyne* 62, 272–82, 2009.
Flickinger, R.C., *The Greek Theater and Its Drama*, Chicago, 1918.
Foley, H., *Female Acts in Greek Tragedy*, Princeton, 2001.
Foley, H., 'The Contradictions of Tragic Marriage', chapter 2 in *Female Acts in Greek Tragedy*, 57–105, Princeton and Oxford, 2001a.
Garland, R.S.J., 'Suicide in Greek Tragedy', in H. Roisman (ed.), *The Encyclopedia of Greek Tragedy*, vol. 3, Malden, MA, and Oxford, 1377–9, 2014.
Gardiner, C., 'The Staging of the Death of Ajax', *Classical Journal* 75, 10–14, 1979.
Gardiner, C., *The Sophoclean Chorus: A Study of Character and Function*, Iowa, 1987.

Garrison, E.P., *Groaning Tears: Ethical and Dramatic Aspects of Suicide in Greek Tragedy*, Leiden, New York, Köln, 1995.
Garrison, E.P., 'Suicide in Greek Tragedy', *Journal of Psychology and Judaism* 24.1, 77-97, 2000.
Garvie, A.F., *Sophocles* Ajax, Warminster, 1998.
Garvie, A.F., 'The death of Ajax', in Most and Ozbek, Pisa, 31-46, 2015.
Gibert, J., *Change of Mind in Greek Tragedy*, Göttingen, 1995.
Golder, H. and R. Pevear, (ed. and trans.), *Sophocles: Aias, the Greek Tragedy in New Translations*, Oxford, 1999.
Golder, H., 'Sophocles' *Ajax*: beyond the shadow of time', *Arion* 3rd series, 1, 9-34, 1990.
Golder, H., 'Visual Meaning in Greek Drama: Sophocles' *Ajax* and the Art of Dying', in Fernando Poyatos (ed.) *Advances in Nonverbal Communication*, 323-60, Amsterdam and Philadelphia, 1992.
Gruen, P., 'Battle Revenge in Homer's *Iliad*: A Contribution to the Understanding of Narrative Patterns in the Early Greek Epic' (Diss.), 1976.
Gurd, S.A., *Dissonance: Auditory Aesthetics in Ancient Greece*, New York, 2016.
Heath, M. and E. Okell, 'Sophocles' *Ajax*: Expect the Unexpected', *Classical Quarterly*, 57, 363-80, 2007.
Heath, M., *The Poetics of Greek Tragedy*, London, 1987.
Heiden, B., 'Emotion, acting, and the Athenian ethos', in A. Sommerstein, S. Halliwell, J. Henderson, B. Zimmerman (eds), *Tragedy, Comedy and the Polis: Papers form the Greek Drama Conference Nottingham, 18-20 July 1990*, Bari, 145-66, 1993.
Henrichs, A., 'The Tomb of Aias and the Prospect of Hero Cult in Sophokles', *Classical Antiquity* 12, 165-80, 1993.
Hesk, J., *Sophocles: Ajax*, London, 2003.
Higgins, C., 'The Odyssey: A Soldier's Road Home', *The Guardian*, 30 November 2013. https://www.theguardian.com/books/2013/nov/30/odyssey-soldier-afghanistan-military-homer [accessed 23 July 2018].
Holmes, B., *The Symptom and the Subject: the Emergence of the Physical Body in Ancient Greece*, Princeton, 2010.
Hubbard, T., 'The Architecture of Sophocles' *Ajax*', *Hermes* 131, 158-71, 2003.
Jebb, R.C. (ed., comm. and trans.), *Sophocles: The Plays and Fragments, Part VII, The Ajax*, Cambridge, 1896.
Kamerbeek, J.C., *The Plays of Sophocles: Commentaries, Part I. The Ajax*, Leiden, 1953.
Kamerbeek, J.C., *The Plays of Sophocles. Part I. The Ajax*, English translation by H. Schreuder, Revised by A. Parker, 2nd edition, Leiden, 1963.
Kearns, E., *The Heroes of Attica*, London, 1989.
Kirkwood, G.M., *A Study of Sophoclean Drama: with a new preface and enlarged bibliographical note*, Ithaca, 1994.
Knox, B.M.W., 'The Ajax of Sophocles', *Harvard Studies in Classical Philology* 65, 1-37, 1961.

Knox, B. M.W., *The Heroic Temper: Studies in Sophoclean Tragedy*, Berkeley, CA, 1964.
Konstan, D., 'Combat Trauma: The Missing Diagnosis in Ancient Greece?', in P. Meineck and D. Konstan (eds), *Combat Trauma and the Ancient Greeks*. New York, 2014.
Konstan, D., *The Emotions of the Ancient Greeks: Studies in Aristotle and Classical Literature*, Toronto, 2006.
Lardinois, A., 'The Polysemy of Gnomic Expressions and Ajax' Deception Speech in Sophocles and the Greek Language', in I. De Jong and A. Rijksbaron (eds), *Aspects of Diction, Syntax, and Pragmatics*, Leiden and Boston, 213–23, 2006.
Ley, G., 'A Scenic Plot of Sophocles' *Ajax* and *Philoctetes*', *Eranos* 86, 85–115, 1988.
Liapis, V., 'Genre, Space and Stagecraft in *Ajax*', in Most and Ozbek, 121–58, Pisa, 2015.
Lloyd-Jones, H. (ed. and trans.), *Sophocles: Ajax, Electra, Oedipus Tyrannus*, Cambridge and London, 1994.
Lloyd, M.A., 'The Tragic Aorist', *Classical Quarterly*, 49, 24–45, 1999.
Lodewyck, L. and S. Monoson, 'Performing for Soldiers: Twenty-First-Century Experiments in Greek Theater in the U.S.A.', in K. Bosher, F. Macintosh, J. McConnell, and P. Rankine (eds), *The Oxford Handbook of Greek Drama in the Americas*, Oxford, 2015.
Loraux, N., *The Mourning Voice: An Essay on Greek Tragedy* [trans. from the French by E. Trapnell Rawlings], Ithaca, 2002.
March, J., 'Sophocles' *Ajax*: The Death and Burial of a Hero', *Bulletin of the Institute of Classical Studies*, 1–36, 1991–3.
Marlowe, S., 'Our Ajax', *London Theatre Record*, xxxiii: 23: 1064, 2013.
Marshall, C.W., 'Sophocles *Didaskalos*', in K. Ormand (ed.), *A Companion to Sophocles*, Malden, MA, 187–203, 2012.
Mashinkila, P., 'Feature: Spotlight on Joe Dixon', *A Younger Theatre*, 12 November 2013. http://www.ayoungertheatre.com/feature-spotlight-on-joe-dixon-southwark-playhouse-our-ajax-timberlake-wertenbaker/ [accessed 25 July 2018].
Mastronarde, D., Review of Finglass' commentary on *Ajax* in *Bryn Mawr Classical Review*, 2012.
Mauduit, C. (2015), 'Scénario pour un suicide', in Most and Ozbek, 47–74, Pisa, 2015.
McClure, L., *Spoken like a Woman: Speech and Gender in Athenian Drama*, Princeton, NJ, 1999.
Meineck, P., 'Combat Trauma and the Tragic Stage: "Restoration" by Cultural Catharsis', *Intertexts*, 16: 1: 7–24, 2012.
Meineck, P., '"These are the Men whose minds the dead have ravaged": "Theatre of War/The Philoctetes Project"', *Arion*, 17: 1, 173–92, 2009.
Melchior, A., 'Caesar in Vietnam: Did Roman Soldiers Suffer from Post-Traumatic Stress Disorder?', *Greece & Rome*, 58: 2: 209–23, 2011.

Mercatali, D., 'David Mercatali', *Practitioners' Voices in Classical Reception Studies*, 5, 2014. http://www.open.ac.uk/arts/research/pvcrs/2014/mercatali [accessed 25 July 2018].
Mills, S.P., 'The Death of Ajax', *Classical Journal* 76.2, 129–35, 1980–1.
Minadeo, R.W., 'Sophocles' Ajax and *kakia*', *Eranos* 85, 19–23, 1987.
Mitchell-Boyask, R., *Plague and the Athenian Imagination: Drama, History, and the Cult of Asclepius*, Cambridge, 2008.
Mitchell, T., *The Ajax of Sophocles with Notes Critical and Explanatory*, Oxford, 1844.
Moore, J. (ed. and trans.), *Sophocles Ajax*, Chicago, 1957.
Morales, H., 'Timeless Classics', *The Times Literary Supplement*, 31 August 2016. https://www.the-tls.co.uk/articles/public/timeless-classics/ [accessed 23 July 2017].
Most, G.W., 'The Stage Action in the Second Half of Sophocles' *Ajax*: A Tentative Reconstruction', in Most and Ozbek, 289–96, Pisa, 2015.
Most, G.W. and L. Ozbek, (eds), *Staging Ajax's Suicide*, Pisa, 2015.
Mueller, M., *Objects as Actors: Props and the Poetics of Performance in Greek Tragedy*, Chicago and London, 2016.
Munteanu, D., *Tragic Pathos: Pity and Fear in Greek Philosophy and Tragedy*, Cambridge, 2012.
Nielsen, R.M., 'Sophocles Ajax: A matter of judgement', *Antichthon* 12, 18–27, 1978.
Nooter, S., *The Mortal Voice in the Tragedies of Aeschylus*, Cambridge, 2017.
Nooter, S., *When Heroes Sing: Sophocles and the Shifting Soundscape of Tragedy*, Cambridge, 2012.
Ormand, K., *Exchange and the Maiden: Marriage in Sophoclean Tragedy*, Austin, TX, 1999.
Ormand, K., 'Silent by Convention? Sophocles' Tekmessa', *American Journal of Philology* 117, 37–64, 1996.
Parker, R., 'Religion and the Athenian Empire', in P. Low (ed.) *The Athenian Empire*, Edinburgh, 146–58, 2008.
Pearson, A.C., 'Sophocles, *Ajax*, 961–973', *Classical Quarterly* 16, 124–36, 1922.
Perdicoyianni-Paléologue, H., 'The Interjections in Greek Tragedy', *Quaderni Urbinati di Cultura Classica* 70(1), 49–88, 2002.
Poe, J.P., *Genre and Meaning in Sophocles' Ajax*, Frankfurt am Main, 1987.
Pöhlmann, E., 'Stage and Action in Sophocles' *Ajax*', in Jerzy Axer and Woldemar Görler (eds), *Scaenica Saravi-Varsoviensia: Beitrage zum Antiken Theater und zu seinem Nachleben*, 27–44, Warsaw, 1997.
Pozzi, D.C. and J.M. Wickersham, (eds), *Myth and Polis*, Ithaca and London, 1991.
Rawlings, L., *The Ancient Greeks at War*, Manchester, 2007.
Rehm, R., *The Play of Space: Spatial Transformation in Greek Tragedy*, Princeton, 2002.
Reinhardt, K., *Sophocles*, translated by H. Harvey and D. Harvey with an introduction by H. Lloyd-Jones, Oxford, 1979.

Reverdin, O. and B. Grange, (eds), *Sophocle, Sept Exposés suivis de discussions*, Vandoeuvres and Geneva, 1983.
Roisman, H.M., *Loyalty in Early Greek Epic and Tragedy*, Königstein, 1984.
Scarry, E., *The Body in Pain: The Making and Unmaking of the World*, Oxford, 1985.
Schein, S., 'Sophocles and Homer', in K. Ormand (ed.) *A Companion to Sophocles*, Malden, MA, 424–49, 2012.
Schneidewin, F.W., *The Ajax of Sophocles*, trans. R.B. Paul, London, 1851.
Scott, W.C., *Musical Design in Sophoclean Theater*, Hanover, NH, 1996.
Seaford, R., 'Aeschylus and the Unity of Opposites', *Journal of Hellenic Studies* 123: 141–63, 2003.
Seaford, R., *Cosmology and the Polis*, Cambridge, 2012.
Seaford, R., *Money and the Early Greek Mind*, Cambridge University Press, 2004.
Seaford, R., 'Mysteries and Politics in *Bacchae*', in D.A. Stuttard (ed.), *Looking at Bacchae*, London, 2016.
Seaford, R., *Reciprocity and Ritual*, Oxford, 1994a.
Seaford, R., 'Sophokles and the Mysteries', *Hermes* 122: 275–88, 1994b.
Seaford, R., 'The Fluttering Soul', in U. Dill and C. Walde (eds), *Antike Mythen. Medien, Transformationen und Konstructionen*, 406–14, Berlin and New York, 2009.
Seaford, R., 'The Politics of the Mystic Chorus', in J. Billings, F. Budelmann and F. Macintosh (eds), *Choruses Ancient and Modern*, 261–79, Oxford, 2013.
Seale, D., *Vision and Stagecraft in Sophocles*, Chicago and London, 1982.
Segal, C., 'Catharsis, Audience, and Closure in Greek Tragedy', in M.S. Silk (ed.), *Tragedy and the Tragic: Greek Theatre and Beyond*, 149–72, Oxford, 1996.
Segal, C., *Tragedy and Civilization: An interpretation of Sophocles*, Cambridge, MA and London, 1981.
Segal, C., 'Visual Symbolism and Visual Effects in Sophocles', *Classical World* 74, 125–42, 1980–1; repr. in *Interpreting Greek Tragedy: Myth, Poetry, Text*, 113–36, Ithaca and London, 1986.
Shapiro, H.A., *Myth into Art: Poet and Painter in Classical Greece*, London and New York, 1994.
Shay, J., *Achilles in Vietnam: Combat Trauma and the Undoing of Character*, New York, 1994.
Shay, J., *Odysseus in America: Combat Trauma and the Trials of Homecoming*, London and New York, 2002.
Shay, J., 'The birth of tragedy – out of the needs of democracy', *Didaskalia* 2: 2, 1995. http://www.didaskalia.net/issues/vol2no2/shay.html# [accessed 20 July 2018].
Simon, B., *Mind and Madness in Ancient Greece: The Classical Roots of Modern Psychiatry*, New York and London, 1978.
Sommerstein, A. (ed.), *Aeschylus: Fragments* vol. 3, Cambridge, MA, 2008.
Sommerstein, A., 'Corpses as Tragic Heroes', in Most and Ozbek, 245–60, Pisa, 2015.
Sorum, C., 'Sophocles' *Ajax* in Context', *Classical World*, 79, 361–77, 1986.

Stanford, W.B., *Greek Tragedy and the Emotions: An Introductory Study*, London, 1983.
Stanford, W.B., *Sophocles. Ajax*, edited with Introduction, Revised Text, Commentary, Appendixes, Indexes and Bibliography, Salem, NH, 1985 (reprint of 1963/1979).
Storr, F. (ed. and trans.), *Sophocles, Volume II, Ajax*, London, 1913.
Suter, A., 'Male Lament in Greek Tragedy', in A. Suter (ed.) *Lament: Studies in the Ancient Mediterranean and Beyond*, Oxford, 156–80, 2008.
Svenbro, J., 'Le Mythe d'Ajax: Entre *Aietos* et *AIAI*', *Europe* 82(904–905), 154–73, 2004.
Synodinou, K., 'Tecmessa in the *Ajax* of Sophocles', in *Antike und Abendland* 33, 99–107, 1987.
Taplin, O., *Greek Tragedy in Action*, London, 1978.
Taplin, O., 'Lyric Dialogue and Dramatic Construction in Later Sophocles', *Dioniso*, 55, 115–22, 1984–5.
Taplin, O. (ed. and trans.), *Sophocles, Four Tragedies: Oedipus the King, Aias, Philoctetes, Oedipus at Colonus*, Oxford, 2015.
Taplin, O. in *Sophocle, Sept Exposés suivis de discussions*, J. de Romilly (ed.), Vandoeuvres and Geneva, 151, 1983.
Taplin, O., 'Stage Directions Leading Towards the Tomb of Aias', in Most and Ozbek, 181–92, Pisa, 2015.
Taplin, O., *The Stagecraft of Aeschylus*, Oxford, 1977.
Tipton, J. (ed. and trans.), *Sophocles' Ajax*, Chicago, 2008.
Trapp, R.L., 'Ajax in The *Iliad*', *Classical Journal* 56, 271–5, 1961.
Tyler, J., 'Sophocles' *Ajax* and Sophoclean Plot Construction', *American Journal of Philology*, 95, 24–42, 1974.
Walton, J.M., *Found in Translation: Greek Drama in English*, Cambridge, 2006.
Weiss, N., 'Noise, Music, Speech: The Representation of Lament in Greek Tragedy', *American Journal of Philology* 138(2), 243–66, 2017.
Wertenbaker, T., *Our Ajax*, London, 2013.
Wheeler, E. L., 'The general as hoplite', in V.D. Hanson (ed.), *Hoplites: The Classical Greek Battle Experience*, London and New York, 1991.
Whitman, C., *Sophocles: A Study of Heroic Humanism*, Cambridge MA, 1951.
Wiersma, S., 'Women in Sophocles', *Mnemosyne* 37, 25–55, 1984.
Williams, D., 'Ajax, Odysseus and the Arms of Achilles', *Antike Kunst* 23, 137–45, 1980.
Winnington-Ingram, R.P., *Sophocles: An Interpretation*, Cambridge [Eng.] and New York, 1980.
Wyles, R., *Costume in Greek Tragedy*, London, 2011.
Zanetto, G., 'How to kill oneself like an Ajax', in Most and Ozbek, Pisa, 273–86, 2015.

# Index

Achilles 2–3, 15–16, 18, 21–2, 24–6, 30–3, 35, 38, 40–1, 44, 77, 90, 98, 101–2, 107–8, 112, 132, 136, 139, 146, 151–2
Actors of Dionysus ix
Aeacus 1–2
Aegina 1
Aeschines 86
Aeschylus 4–5, 92, 97, 119
  *Agamemnon* 89, 158
  *Award for Arms* 97
  *Eumenides* 83, 119–20
  *Libation Bearers* 67
  *Seven Against Thebes* 110
  *Suppliant Women* 60
  *Thracian Women* 77–8, 97, 119
  *Women of Salamis* 97
*Aethiopis* 4, 16, 78
Afghanistan 152, 155–7
Agamemnon 2, 10, 25–6, 30–4, 37–8, 43–4, 48–9, 61, 81–2, 84, 89, 94, 97–8, 112–13, 123–4, 127, 131–6, 138–42, 144–5, 147, 152, 156
Aias *see* Ajax
Ajax
  Athenian hero 4–5, 29, 40–1, 50, 93
  attacks cattle 3, 17, 33–4, 36, 45, 47, 56, 78–9, 82, 90, 94, 98–100, 102, 104, 132–3, 141, 152–3, 159
  battle belt 2, 16, 22, 24
  bulwark of Greeks 7, 43
  burial 3, 7–8, 26, 37–40, 62, 83–4, 86, 94, 111, 121, 123, 126–7, 132–4, 136, 139, 142, 144–5, 147, 160
  contest for Achilles' armour 2–3, 16–17, 19–21, 26, 35, 44, 48–9, 61–2, 78–9, 86, 97, 105, 108, 138, 141, 144, 152
  deception speech 37, 47, 56, 58–9, 73, 81–2, 91–2, 94–5, 108–9, 122, 141
  isolation 19, 21, 46–7, 49–50, 71, 73–5, 86, 89–93, 106, 118, 132
  'Lesser' *see* 'Lesser' Ajax
  madness 2, 8, 12, 17, 19, 26, 32, 36, 63, 68–9, 73, 78–9, 81, 98–9, 101–2, 104, 110, 119, 132, 138–9, 141, 143, 148, 152, 157
  mother *see* Periboea
  mystic speech *see* Ajax, deception speech
  rescues Achilles' body 2, 16–17, 44
  shield 2, 18, 20–2, 43–50, 62, 80, 94, 127, 136
  suicide 3, 10–11, 16–7, 19–21, 25–6, 30, 34, 44–5, 48–9, 55–9, 62, 64, 77–87, 91, 104, 111, 118–20, 123, 132, 138, 151
  suicide speech 12, 56–9, 74, 82, 91, 119, 125, 155
  sword 2–3, 11, 16–17, 20–2, 24–5, 31–2, 37, 43, 47, 55–64, 78, 81–2, 94–5, 98, 100, 119, 121–3, 125–6, 132
  tomb 3, 39–40, 84, 93–4
  in underworld 3, 16, 44, 74, 112, 145
Amazons 2
Andromache 25, 34, 47, 61, 80, 94, 105–6
Antigone 6, 102–4, 123, 145
Antilochus 77
Apollo 1, 15–16, 43, 83
Aquila Theatre 151, 158–60
Areopagus 93

Ares 82, 99
Aristotle 5, 10, 67–8, 74, 86, 143,
    148–9
  *Nicomachean Ethics* 87
  *Poetics* 118, 143, 149
  *Politics* 67
  *Rhetoric* 33
armour, contest for, *see* Ajax, contest
    for Achilles' armour
Artemis 99
Asclepius 5, 154
Astyanax 25, 61, 94, 106, 112
*atê* 12, 79, 93
Athena 2–3, 8, 10–11, 16–17, 19, 21–2,
    30, 32–3, 35–7, 44–6, 48, 56, 58,
    61–3, 78–83, 86, 90–1, 98–9,
    101–2, 111, 120, 124, 126,
    132–4, 138, 141, 143–4, 147–8,
    156
Athene *see* Athena
Atreidae 34–5, 46–8, 81, 90, 93, 95,
    97–9, 101–2, 104, 109, 111–13,
    123, 133, 135, 142, 146–7
Atreids *see* Atreidae
Atreus, sons of *see* Atreidae
Attica 6, 9, 93, 136, 138

Briseis 98, 107, 112, 152
Brygos Painter 57, 97, 123
Burian, Peter 160

Calchas 48, 62, 82, 111
Calypso 142
Campbell, Lewis 122
Carson, Anne 68
catharsis 118
Chorus (in *Ajax*) 36–9, 41, 44–6, 56,
    63, 67, 70–1, 73–4, 79–83, 86,
    91–4, 98, 100, 102–3, 108,
    110–11
chorus 5, 9–10, 60, 91–2, 110
Christianity 87
Chrysothemis 102–3, 112
Cimon 5
Combat Stress Injury 151, 153

combat trauma 151–60
Creon 7, 67
Crowley, Jason 152–3
Cyprus 3

Deianeira 77
Delium 7
Demeter 93
Diomedes 16, 21, 34, 44, 133
Dionysia, City (or Great) 5, 9, 153
Dionysus 9
*dithyramb* 9
Dixon, Joe 156–7
Doerries, Bryan 156–7
Douris 19, 21–2
Dugan, Timothy 123
Duris of Samos 6
Durkheim, Emile 85

Easterling, Patricia 126
*ekkuklema* 11, 79, 83, 122, 163
Electra 68, 102–4, 110
Eleusinian Mysteries 92–3
empathy 35, 37, 62, 112, 142–3, 146–9,
    160
Epicaste 77
Epidaurus 154
Erinyes *see* Furies
Eteocles 110
Euripides 6, 77
  *Bacchae* 92
  *Electra* 21
  *Erechtheus* 77
  *Heracleidae* 77, 93
  *Heracles* 158
  *Hippolytus* 10
  *Iphigenia at Aulis* 35, 77
  *Orestes* 110
  *Phoenician Women* 77
  *Suppliants* 77
  *Trojan Women* 94
Eurysaces 3, 4, 10, 25, 34, 40, 49–50,
    61, 70, 73, 80, 82–4, 93–4,
    105–6, 108, 110–13, 121, 127,
    138, 156

Eurysakeion 4
Exekias 17–22, 24, 26–7, 78

Faber, Melvin 84
fame 82, 102, 110
Finglass, Patrick 6, 91, 118, 124
friendship 1, 6–8, 11, 16, 25–6, 32, 35, 37–8, 46, 48, 64, 71, 84, 95, 101, 109, 139, 144, 147
Frost, Robert 11–12
Furies 38, 48, 77, 82, 120

Garvie, Alex 106
Ghanizadeh, Homayun *Ajax and the Report of a Suicide*, ix
gloating 16, 32, 36, 79, 111, 132, 141, 143
grief 7, 37, 41, 67–75, 90, 100, 107, 111–12, 117–18, 121–7, 138
Gurd, Sean 72

Hades 2, 4, 6, 16, 25, 34, 44, 71, 74, 80, 92, 112, 145
Haides *see* Hades
Hector 2–3, 7, 15–16, 22, 24–6, 30–1, 34, 38, 43–4, 47, 49, 56–9, 61–2, 64, 80, 94–5, 105–6, 112, 119, 132, 134, 136
Hector's sword *see* Ajax, sword
Helios 82
Hephaestus 17
Heracles 2, 135, 146
hero-cult 29, 39–41, 50, 62, 89, 93–5
Hesione 2
Hippolytus 10
Homer
 *Iliad* 4, 7, 15–16, 18, 21, 24–7, 29–34, 38, 40–1, 43–4, 47, 49, 56, 59–61, 80, 94, 98–9, 101–2, 105–8, 112, 131, 133–6, 139, 142
 *Odyssey* 3–4, 15–16, 26–7, 29–30, 35, 43–4, 72, 74, 77, 90, 112, 131, 142–3, 145, 158
honour 3–4, 7, 15–17, 25, 29, 32–4, 36–8, 40, 45, 47, 50, 78, 82, 97–100, 102, 104–5, 107–8. 110, 113, 123, 126, 131–2, 134, 136, 138–9, 142, 144–5
hoplite 43, 46, 62–3, 153
Housman, A. E. 12
*hubris* 83, 133–5, 139

Iraq 152, 155–7
Isle of the Sun 142
Ismene 102–3, 112

Kamerbeek, J.C. 101, 104, 123
Kaufman, Phyllis 154
Kleophrades Painter 22, 24–7
*kommos* 117–18, 120, 124, 126
Konstan, David 149, 152

laughter 35–7, 99, 101, 111, 141
Lenaia 9
'Lesser' Ajax 16
Lewis, C.S. 117, 122, 124–5
*Little Iliad* 4, 17, 78
Lloyd, Michael A. 110
Lodewyck, Laura 156, 158–9
Loraux, Nicole 71

McLaughlin, Ellie *Ajax in Iraq*, ix
Megara 50
Meineck, Peter 153, 158–9
*mēkhanē* 11
Melchior, Aislinn 152
Menelaus 7, 10, 25, 33, 48, 62, 81–2, 84, 94, 97, 112, 123–4, 127, 131–6, 138–42, 147
Mercatali, David 156–7
Messenger (character in *Ajax*) 10, 82, 111
Mitchell-Boyask, Robin 154
mockery 8, 35–7, 45, 78–9, 104–5, 111, 123–5, 133, 141, 144
Monoson, Sara 156, 158–9
Morales, Helen 156
Mueller, Melissa 55, 58–9, 62
mystery-cult 26, 89, 93
mystic initiation 91–2

National Endowment for the
    Humanities 158
Nauck, A. 124
Nausicaa 142
Neoptolemus 146
Nestor 101
Nooter, Sarah 72

Odysseus 2–3, 8, 10–11, 15–17, 19, 21, 25–6, 29, 31–8, 41, 44–6, 48–9, 56, 61, 74, 78–9, 83–5, 87, 90, 93, 95, 97–9, 101–2, 104, 107, 111–12, 123–6, 132–3, 136, 138–49, 152
Olyslaeger, Jeroen, *Mount Olympus: to Glorify the Cult of Tragedy* ix
Onesimus 78
*orchestra* 9, 99, 118, 120
Orestes 67, 93, 110, 120
Ormand, Kirk 126

pain 50, 67–75, 82, 90, 105, 111–12, 117, 123, 125, 143, 146
Paris 16, 44, 133
Patroclus 16, 26, 31, 77, 101
Pelasgus 60
Peleus 2, 7
Peloponnesian War 5, 7, 134–5
Penelope 142
Pentagon 155
Periboea 81, 85, 105, 108, 113, 138
Pericles 6, 135
Persephone 92
Persian Wars 131, 134
Persians 132
Philoctetes 146
Phocus 2
Phoenix 2, 15, 32, 107
Phthia 107
Pindar 4, 44, 78
Plato 87, 90
    *Ion* 148
    *Laws* 90
    *Phaedo* 87
    *Republic* 35

Polyneices 7, 145
Poseidon 1, 43
Post-Traumatic Stress Disorder 1, 151–7, 159–60
Priam 7, 26, 38, 133
props 55–64, 95, 158
PTSD *see* Post-Traumatic Stress Disorder
Pylades 110

Rawlings, Louis 152

Salamis (Cyprus) 3
    island of 2–3, 10, 40, 50, 82, 93–4, 99, 107–8, 113, 135–6
    Battle of 4–5, 50, 94
Samos 5–6
satyr play 9
Scarry, Elaine, *The Body in Pain* 67, 69
Segal, Charles 55, 58, 62, 122
Shay, Jonathan 151–3, 159
silence 60–1, 69, 74, 98, 100, 103, 108, 110, 112, 127, 145
Sisyphus 49
*skene* 9–11, 79, 82–3
Solon 86
Sommerstein, Alan 84
Sophocles 1, 4–8, 11–12, 17, 24–7, 29–30, 32, 34–5, 38, 41, 49–50, 55, 59, 61–2, 64, 78, 81–2, 84–7, 91, 97–9, 102, 107, 111–13, 118–20, 122, 125–7, 131, 136–7, 139, 146, 149, 154
    *Antigone* 1, 5–7, 67, 77, 102–4, 136, 145
    *Electra* 40, 68, 102–4
    *Eurysaces* 94
    *Oedipus at Colonus* 84, 93
    *Oedipus Tyrannus* 77
    *Philoctetes* 35, 146, 158
    *Women of Trachis* 77
sorrow *see* grief
Southwark Playhouse 156
Spercheios 40
staging 9–10, 55, 57, 122, 163

Stanford, W.B. 121
Stavros Niarchos Foundation 155

Taplin, Oliver 55, 68, 84, 119, 127
Tecmessa 3, 10–11, 25, 34, 37, 39–41, 44, 47, 56–8, 60–3, 69–71, 73–4, 79–83, 85–7, 90, 92, 94, 97–113, 117–27
Telamon 2–3, 24, 49–50, 83, 85, 94, 104–5, 108, 113, 135–6
Teucer 2–3, 10–11, 24, 30–1, 38–41, 43–5, 48–50, 57, 59–63, 70, 74, 80, 82–4, 86, 90, 94, 97, 108, 111–13, 118, 121–7, 131–2, 134–6, 138–9, 145, 147
Theatre of Dionysus 9
Theater of War project 151, 154–6, 158–60

Thebes 7, 110
Thetis 2–3
*timē see* honour
Timotheus of Zacynthus 55, 59
Traumatic Brain Injury 151–2, 155
Troy 1–4, 7, 10, 15, 20, 25, 31–2, 41, 46–7, 80, 82, 84, 99, 104, 107, 131, 135–6, 139, 141, 146

underworld *see* Hades

Weiss, Naomi 72
Wertenbaker, Timberlake, *Our Ajax* ix, 151, 156–7, 159–60
Wheeler, Everett 152
Williamson, Margaret 156

Zeus 3, 6, 80, 137

www.ingramcontent.com/pod-product-compliance
Lightning Source LLC
Chambersburg PA
CBHW072107010526
44111CB00037B/2020